DISORDER IN THE COUR

RHETORIC, LAW, AND THE HUMANITIES

DISORDER IN THE COURT

MORALITY, MYTH, and the INSANITY DEFENSE

Andrea L. Alden

The University of Alabama Press
Tuscaloosa

The University of Alabama Press
Tuscaloosa, Alabama 35487-0380
uapress.ua.edu

Hardcover edition published 2018.
Paperback edition published 2020.
eBook edition published 2018.

Typeface: Minion and Avenir

Cover image: *The Interior of Bedlam* (Bethlem Royal Hospital); plate 8 from *A Rake's Progress* by William Hogarth, 1763
Cover design: David Nees

Paperback ISBN: 978-0-8173-6003-0

A previous edition of this book has been cataloged by the Library of Congress.
ISBN: 978-0-8173-1972-4 (cloth)
E-ISBN: 978-0-8173-9163-8

To Cheree, who is responsible for my love of the study of rhetoric, and Maureen, who made sure that I didn't give up.

Contents

Acknowledgments

This book represents almost a decade of my life. I have likened it to being in labor for several years, and it is no less difficult and almost as rewarding. I am forever indebted to my mom, Joanne, whose unrelenting support of all my endeavors is the ground on which I stand. I am very grateful for my children, Callie and Evan, for cheerfully surviving my time in graduate school and all the writing days since. And I would like to thank my partner, Josh, for gently refusing to allow me to give up at various phases of this process and also for just being awesome. I am extremely grateful to Clarke Rountree, both because his work had a great influence on me and because he took an interest in making this project part of this series. I must also thank Katie Langford for introducing me to Clarke, because I would never have had the courage to send him the manuscript without her first connecting us. The staff of the University of Alabama Press (especially Dan Waterman) is a delight to work with, and I appreciate that more than they can possibly know. Many brilliant scholars aided in the writing of this book, directly or indirectly. I was fortunate to work with many of them at Arizona State University, including Sharon Crowley, Keith Miller, Elenore Long, James Paul Gee, and Sally Kitch. In addition, I am extremely grateful to Michael Perlin, the legal scholar whose work was foundational for this project, for generously agreeing to read an early draft of this manuscript. A. Cheree Carlson, Maureen Daly Goggin, and Patricia Roberts-Miller at the University of Texas, Austin, were kind enough to help shepherd me through the writing of this book; they were (and continue to be) so generous and helpful, and I could not have asked for a better group of mentors. I am deeply grateful to Jeanne Simpson, whose guidance at the beginning of my career was invaluable and whose friendship I treasure. I have too many amazing friends and colleagues to name, but I will try anyway: Judy Holiday, Kendall Gerdes, and Ryan Skinnell collectively are the best part of graduate school, and their friendship means the world to me. To Lisa Hill, my sister, I am so glad we found each other; ditto for Diane Goodman, who makes being an adult a little more bearable, and also whose willingness to read this manuscript more than once was invaluable.

Introduction

Reasoning with Madness

> "Belief is so often the death of reason."
>
> —Qyburn in *Game of Thrones*

On July 20, 2012, a young man wearing tactical gear entered a movie theater in Aurora, Colorado, in which a midnight screening of *The Dark Knight Rises* was showing. He set off several smoke and gas canisters before opening fire on the audience, killing twelve and wounding seventy. He was arrested behind the theater immediately following the incident and remained in custody through the time of his trial in 2015, during which time his long struggle with mental illness was the subject of much public scrutiny.

His defense team argued that he was not guilty by reason of insanity. That defense was ultimately rejected, and he was found guilty of 24 counts of first degree murder and 140 counts of attempted first degree murder, with a sentence enhancement of a crime of violence. Although the prosecution sought the death penalty, on August 7, 2015, James Holmes was sentenced to life in prison without the possibility of parole. In the study that follows, I explain the failure of the Holmes defense as, in part, a problem of rhetoric that has plagued the insanity defense since its codification in 1843.

The insanity defense is one of the most controversial and discussed subjects in the American legal system, because it is also one of the least straightforward and understood. This book examines the insanity defense in US law and explains the legal standards for the defense as they have evolved since 1843, when they were first codified in England, to 1984, when Congress attempted to revise them through the Insanity Defense Reform Act. Throughout this period, and still today, "insanity" is a legal term rather than a medical one; yet the testimony of psychiatric experts is required in cases in which an insanity defense is raised. Hence, adjudicating such cases by courtroom practice is complicated and caught between two different but overlapping discourses, the legal and the medical, both of which have historically sought to assert and maintain firm disciplinary boundaries. Both expert and lay audiences have struggled to understand and apply the given standards for legal insanity of the time, and the portrayal of the insanity defense in popular culture has only served to further cloud the issue.

As illustrated by the example of James Holmes, recent headlines regarding mass shootings or public violence almost always initially raise the issue of the mental health of the perpetrator,[1] but the debates tend to devolve into political grandstanding about gun rights.[2] Because most of the shooters in widely publicized sprees die during the incidents, we rarely see insanity defense discourse play out in the national news. Following the trial of James Holmes and its ensuing media frenzy—the likes of which we had not seen since the trial of Andrea Yates in 2002—this study takes on greater significance.

In this book, I argue that the problems with understanding the insanity defense are, at their foundation, rhetorical. The legal concept of what constitutes "insanity" and, therefore, an abdication of responsibility for one's actions, does not fit the narrative established by medical research on mental illness in the last two centuries or more. Legal discourse in the United States is dominated by a model of individual responsibility. That legal model presumes, first, that rational individuals are engaged in a cost-benefit analysis of potential punishment. Second, the legal system presumes that "insanity" requires a totalizing loss of rationality, such that any evidence of "normal" functioning precludes the possibility of severe mental illness. And finally, the legal system presumes that all testimony regarding a defendant's mental state is equally valid; in fact, in many cases, the nonexpert testimony is more highly valued than that of experts by both legal professionals and juries.

Additionally, there are multiple layers of persuasion involved in any effort to convince a judge or a jury—or a public, for that matter—that a defendant is or is not responsible for his or her actions at a particular moment in time. At the public level, various special interest groups attempt to influence the laws pertaining to the defense to be narrowed or broadened, and laypeople react with sympathy or outrage at high-profile insanity defense cases. To further complicate the issue, these rhetorical acts invoke conventional (which is to say, hegemonic) narratives about identity, guilt, responsibility, evil, justice, and sanity.

To defend my claims, I examine the court cases that mark the major shifts in the legal definitions of the insanity defense. Despite the fact that all known civilizations have maintained some way to account for mental illness as a mitigating factor in their systems of law, the modern insanity defense has always been fraught with controversy, particularly since its codification in 1843 following the successful insanity plea of Daniel McNaughtan.[3] In the United States, the scope of legal defenses citing mental illness has been widened and narrowed based on public opinion regarding the mental health professions.[4] Because of this strange admixture of popular influence on the medical and legal professions, the insanity defense has continued to be poorly understood and inconsistently applied; each revision of the standards for legal insanity, while motivated by an attempt to "clarify" the standards, has had little to no impact at best, and only resulted in further confusion more often than not.

In keeping with the tradition of Foucauldian critical genealogy, I trace the evolution of insanity defense standards in US law alongside developments in the disciplines of psychiatry and psychology in order to demonstrate points of convergence and divergence in their histories. This endeavor is characteristically *rhetorical* because, in addition to examining the disciplinary discourses of law and mental health medicine, I stress the centrality of public opinion to insanity defense jurisprudence. The rhetoric of public opinion impacts both courtroom practice and legislative decisions but is informed largely by cultural myths about mental illness and mentally ill people that circulate in popular culture. An examination of published news articles and editorials in the popular press (where available) provides a more robust understanding of how the rhetoric of the insanity defense really relies on three mutually influential domains: the legal, the medical, and the popular.

The influence of codes of morality on the law, prisons, mental health practitioners, and popular perceptions of mental illness continue to shape our approach to mentally ill criminal defendants. Even though it was the advent of Enlightenment thinking that shifted cultural understanding of the cause of mental illness from external forces (gods, spirits, demons) to the individual (free will), the perception that ailments of the mind are indicative of moral failure has pervaded thought on mental illness since ancient times. Further complicating this issue are two pervasive binaries that predate Enlightenment ideology: mind/body and nature/nurture. As long as these concepts are understood as entities separate and distinct from one another, a robust understanding of mental illness, particularly in its relation to criminality, is impossible. Current studies in neuroscience as well as the humanities[5] are beginning to deconstruct these long-held binaries, but the law is not structured in such a way that it can account for the endless number of variables, biological or social, that might explain the mental state of a defendant, much less the ways in which that mental state may or may not mitigate culpability.

In sum, the general argument of this book is that the legal practices regarding mentally ill criminal defendants are profoundly rhetorical, and that popular opinion, legal discourse, and medical discourse are shaped by pervasive myths about mental illness. In order to make the case, each chapter will contribute conceptually toward an articulation of what I call the rhetoric of *sanism*. Sanism can be defined generally as an irrational fear of mental illness and people who suffer from it. I wish to demonstrate how the rhetoric of sanism operates in public and institutional discourse on the insanity defense through a number of case studies that are described in the following section.

Conclusion

As we read the history of the insanity defense as it is presented in this study, we can identify the rhetoric of sanism via specific tropes as they are perpetuated by judges, lawyers, the press, and others. The book is primarily structured around the court cases identified as significant historical moments of change in the standards for legal insanity.

Chapter 1 lays the theoretical groundwork for my analysis of the case studies. It begins with a brief outline of the social science approach to research on the insanity defense, after which I try to demonstrate how a rhetorical approach can provide a more effective way to explain why, after many decades of trying to fine-tune the legal definition of insanity, the defense's problems remain intractable.

Chapter 2 provides a brief outline of the history of criminal defenses based on mental illness along with the prevailing medical beliefs about mental illness from ancient times through the mid-1800s. The coverage of each period is necessarily truncated, as we begin with cultures as far back as Babylon and Mesopotamia, but focus mainly on ancient Greece and Rome, the Middle Ages, and the Enlightenment as epochs in which thinking about mental illness developed and retained distinct features.

Chapter 3 focuses on the trial of Daniel McNaughtan, the result of which remains the foundation of contemporary standards for legal insanity. McNaughtan's case established the most basic question of any insanity defense case: Did the defendant, as a result of mental disease or defect, know right from wrong at the time of the crime?

Chapter 4 examines attempts to update the standards for legal insanity based on advancements in the mental health professions. The chapter examines *Parsons v. State* and *Davis v. United States*, which serve as the legal basis for the addition of a volitional prong to insanity defense standards, which has come to be known, albeit erroneously, as the "irresistible impulse" test.

Chapter 5 examines *Durham v. United States*, which expanded the legal standards for insanity further at a time when the mental health professions briefly enjoyed wide public acceptance. This case added what is referred to as the "product" test, so that in addition to the cognitive and volitional prongs of the existing standards, courts could now ask jurors to assess whether the criminal act was a *product* of the mental disease or defect. Additionally, this chapter outlines the attempt by the American Law Institute (ALI) to address what some considered the excessive broadening of the legal standards when they wrote a new definition of legal insanity in the Model Penal Code in 1963, which was indicative of the tensions growing at that time between psychiatric experts and legal experts.

The final chapter examines the trial of John Hinckley Jr., who successfully pleaded not guilty by reason of insanity when he was tried for the attempted assassination of President Reagan; Hinckley was tried under the relatively broad standards outlined by the ALI in 1963. Hinckley's trial is most emblematic of the tropes of sanism, and after significant public backlash and much subsequent political grandstanding, federal legislation was passed that essentially carved the hard-won expansions back down to the parameters they abided by in 1843.

This book is intended as a contribution to long-running debates about the nature of mental illness and what role, if any, it should have in a criminal defense. I am not an expert in psychology or the law. Rather, I approach this problem as a rhetorician attuned to the nuances of language and how it shapes cultural practices. I offer no solution in this book; I simply raise additional questions and suggest ways to untangle the complexities of the rhetoric of sanism in the hope that we might answer them by looking at the issue in a different way. I argue that the unanswered questions are more effectively interrogated if we understand the problem as inherently rhetorical.

The insanity defense has been researched and analyzed extensively by scholars and practitioners of law, as well as experts in the mental health professions; historians and philosophers have also investigated its origins and use. Although it is profoundly rhetorical, rhetoric scholars have yet to investigate the insanity defense in depth; thus, I offer the first book-length rhetorical history and analysis of this legal concept, which is situated precariously at the intersections of popular, medical, and legal discourses.

While the insanity defense is imbricated in multiple complex social issues that cannot be "solved," a rhetorical approach can produce a more coherent understanding of the defense keyed to the nuances of language and its usage as well as the material effects it produces. What counts as legal insanity is radically contextual, negotiated in discrete material moments in time; a rhetorical approach allows us to see how a concept like insanity functions among competing discourses, finding mooring only in consensus facts and established histories. In other words, there is no privileged position from which to make judgments in a rhetorical/historical analysis, which is of particular importance for the insanity defense, as it has been the locus of much struggle for disciplinary dominance over its meaning and use. The stakes of such an analysis are significant for anyone affected by the legal or medical definitions of mental illness, including lawyers, judges, jurors, and especially those suffering from mental illness, whether they are criminal defendants or not.

1

Framing the Issue

What Rhetoric Can Offer to the Conversation

> "Given the influence of social conformity and prejudice, defendants pleading not guilty by reason of insanity face the significant challenges of securing fair and impartial juries. Attitudes and knowledge of the insanity defense are factors that may influence levels of impartiality."
>
> —Tarika Daftary-Kapur et al.

The insanity defense has been extensively debated in the public, as well as in relevant disciplinary spheres, and studied exhaustively through (primarily) social science research. In this chapter, I will first describe the conclusions reached by a recently published study that is representative of common inquiries into the insanity defense that will demonstrate the value of a rhetorical approach due to the limitations of social science methods. I will then elaborate the concept of sanism and describe what its rhetoric achieves. Next, I will outline the concepts that are at the center of my theoretical assumptions, including ideology, hegemony, fantasy, and myth. Finally, I will detail the largest obstacle of undertaking a study of this kind: the moralism attached to both the law and mental illness.

Current Approaches to the Study of the Insanity Defense

There is an extensive body of scholarly research on the insanity defense, primarily in legal studies and also in the mental health professions. Each field approaches its studies in ways characteristic of its discipline: in psychiatric analyses, researchers generally seek to understand how to explain mental illness in a legal setting; in legal analyses, researchers typically seek to understand how different standards for legal insanity affect various aspects of an insanity defense trial, with particular attention to juror decision-making.

Using Google Scholar, which provides a cursory overview of academic articles and books that include the phrase "insanity defense," I was able to determine that, for the period of time this book will address (1843–1984), 17,800 publications discuss the insanity defense. In reviewing scholarship produced during this period, it is difficult to identify the particular decade in which a given publication was written, as the topics of inquiry remain largely consistent, in addition to the venues of their publication: in the nineteenth and early twentieth centuries, the phrase "insanity defense" appears most frequently in the *American Journal of Psychiatry*; articles using the term and discussing the concept began to appear more frequently in law reviews from universities around the country during the mid-to-late twentieth century.

From 1985 to 2017, the same query on Google Scholar yielded 36,300 results, which is significant in that the more recent thirty-two-year period produced more than twice the number of publications on the topic as the preceding 141 years. Again, the titles from decade to decade remain very similar; one primary aspect that distinguishes a study from the 1980s to the present from those in the prior 140-year period is the inclusion of relatively recent diagnostic categories such as Post-Traumatic Stress Disorder[1] and postpartum psychosis,[2] mental illnesses that certainly existed but had simply not been labeled as such until relatively recently, as well as new technologies such as neuroimaging.[3] Otherwise, the issues they take up and the research questions they ask remain consistent with the many decades that precede them. One conclusion that can be drawn from these results is that interest in the topic has increased, and one reason for that is that all of the research on and debate over the defense has yet to produce a satisfactory solution to the problems it presents.

Jennifer Eno Louden and Jennifer L. Skeem's 2007 study sought to examine the effects of "jurors' intuitive prototypes of insanity and case-relevant attitudes" on insanity defense cases. Their article provides a potent justification for a rhetorical approach to insanity defense study.[4] It is very similar to other social science research spanning the last fifty years;[5] this is not to say that it is not interesting or important but rather to highlight that, in spite of both advances in the study of mental illness and two of the major revisions to the standards for legal insanity that occurred during that period of time,[6] it is clear that juror decision-making in insanity defense cases has been largely unaffected by these changes. Furthermore, researchers who study this phenomenon have not made much progress in explaining why. Louden and Skeem begin by saying: "Few psycholegal issues are more controversial than the insanity defense. . . . The public generally has a negative opinion of the insanity defense that varies only in its intensity over time. . . . The legal system assumes that, given several procedural protections, jurors perform [their] duty as 'blank slates,' free of preconceptions and biases. . . .

[However], although . . . standards of insanity change over time and differ across jurisdictions, there is little evidence that jurors actually apply legal definitions in rendering verdicts."[7] Studies, including this one, consistently conclude that, while different legal definitions of insanity *should* provide evidence that jurors will reach different verdicts, it simply is not the case.

The findings of Louden and Skeem's 2007 study, which are consistent with those of similar studies, can be seen as follows:

1. "Jurors' attitudes toward the insanity defense strongly affect their case judgements."[8]
2. "[A] defendant will not obtain a fair trial if some of the jurors impaneled are unwilling to entertain his established legal defense of insanity."[9]
3. "When negative attitudes are identified, simply asking jurors to set them aside will probably insufficiently protect a defendant's right to a fair and impartial jury."[10]
4. "Jurors with strongly held, negative attitudes often overestimate the extent to which they can set their attitudes aside."[11]
5. "Because attitudes bias information processing, merely disseminating accurate information about the insanity defense is unlikely to change public opinion."[12]

The authors cite legal scholar and mental disability law-reform advocate Michael Perlin's major claim: although the many myths about the insanity defense have been proven false, they "persist because they are based on deep-seated, largely socially acceptable prejudices against defendants with mental illness and maintained by faulty reasoning processes."[13] Therefore, they suggest, "it is necessary to target attitudes on a deeper level" in order "to promote jury verdicts that are based on the evidence and legal instructions and less on personal biases about mental illness and criminal responsibility."[14] While this is an admirable goal, it is also one that has been investigated ad nauseam in social science research. These studies are looking for a definitive way to get jurors to make decisions that are not influenced by their existing biases toward mental illness and criminal responsibility. Unlike rhetoric scholars, however, they lack the insight that Aristotle provided over two thousand years ago:[15] decision-making is much more grounded in the way people feel than in their sense of logic; or, more accurately, their sense of logic derives from their emotional attachments, which are largely unconscious.

What Louden and Skeem, and numerous similar researchers, are unable to explain is *how* such attitudes are formed and *why* they remain firmly intact regardless of how much evidence to disprove them exists. It is with Michael Perlin's extensive body of work tackling the many myths that continue to hinder progress in insanity defense jurisprudence that I began this project, and it is his work that provides the justification for a rhetorical approach to understanding this complex phenomenon. I have examined the historical and contemporary trajectories of research on the insanity defense in order to demonstrate a gap which I hope to begin to address with this study. I will now turn to explaining the theoretical basis for a rhetorical approach to a study of the insanity defense.

Understanding Sanism and Its Rhetoric

Sanism[16] is a term used by Michael Perlin, who defines it as prejudice against mentally ill people that causes "individuals with mental illness . . . [to be] frequently marginalized to an even greater extent" than other historically oppressed groups.[17] He contends that sanism maintains the primary characteristic of other "isms" (racism, sexism, ageism, ableism) because it serves as "an ideological rationalization or justification for stigmatizing and marginalizing the other,"[18] and that such stereotypes have resulted in discrimination by legislators, judges, and lawyers.[19] Perlin argues that the way we approach mentally disabled people is governed by "irrational mechanisms" and that the assumptions made by the legal system regarding the nature of mental illness "reflect[s] our fears and apprehensions about mental disability . . . and the possibility that we may become mentally disabled."[20] It is this difficulty understanding mental illness and our discomfort regarding the stability of our own mental health that drive sanist behavior.

Because (as Perlin says) "mental illness has always been inextricably linked to sin, to evil, to God's punishment, to crime, to demons," and the loss of reason (supposedly humanity's defining capacity), the dehumanization of mentally ill people is troubling but not surprising. Highlighting the deeply embedded Enlightenment ideology that undergirds our dualistic cultural constructions of mind/body, reason/emotions, and nature/nurture, cultural historian and professor of psychiatry Sander Gilman says, "The most elementally frightening possibility is the loss of control over the self. . . . The mad are perceived as the antithesis to the control and reason that define the self. . . . What is perceived is in large part a projection; for within everyone's fantasy life there exists . . . an incipient madness that we control with more or less success."[21] Political philosopher Iris Marion Young notes, "Modern philosophy and science established unifying, controlling reason in opposition to . . . the body, and then identified some groups with reason and others with the body."[22] In this binary construction, then, mentally ill people are tied to the inferior body and its unmanageable emotions, which are then positioned in opposition to those who ostensibly maintain bodily control and exist as purely rational beings. In addition, the seeming randomness with which mental illness occurs causes such anxiety that those who do suffer from it are portrayed as having had some hand in their own misfortunes, the rhetorical origins of which will be discussed in the next chapter. This ideological "opposition to affectivity and the body"[23] results in "the devaluation and exclusion of some groups,"[24] people who suffer from mental illness among them.

The moral issues raised by the insanity defense "trigger deep and intense emotional responses"[25] that, while potent, are rarely articulated. These responses are the basis for the rhetoric of sanism, which refers in part to discourse (speech, writing, and other forms of influencing others) that discriminates against mentally ill people, but largely to the unconscious reaction of aversion to mental illness and mentally ill people that lies in the affective domain; we might usefully categorize such aversion as the result of implicit bias. Part of the way in which this rhetoric functions constitutes what Sharon Crowley would call its "ideologic," the ways in which the rhetoric of sanism relies on deeply embedded prejudice in the criminal justice system as well as common cultural perceptions of the insanity defense. The consequences of sanism for the insanity defense are manifested in specific discursive practices that take place both in the courtroom and the public. Perlin has identified multiple widely held cultural myths about the mentally ill and the insanity defense that he believes explain the persistence of sanist behavior in the face of major scientific advances in the understanding of mental illness.

While Perlin's research focuses on jurisprudence, I argue that these cultural myths also function rhetorically. Perlin asks the pivotal questions: "Why do we feel the way we feel about 'these people,' and how do those feelings control our legislative, judicial, and administrative policies?"[26] For Perlin, the answer to these two questions is essential to understanding the incoherence of insanity defense jurisprudence. These myths reveal widespread cultural attitudes toward mental illness and mentally ill people.

Perlin identifies eight distinct myths. For example, one myth is that the insanity defense is overused, and another is that it is typically used in particularly heinous crimes. Another common myth is that the defense is primarily deployed by defendants who are faking mental illness in order to escape punishment. All of these myths hinge on widely held beliefs about the legitimacy of mental illness and those medical professionals who diagnose and treat it. Perlin's work provides us with a number of useful insights for discerning cultural biases and myths, but how do these translate rhetorically?

The discursive practices that represent the rhetoric of sanism are manifested in recurring tropes, all of which can be seen embedded in the myths that Perlin describes. The tropes, in their most basic form, are as follows: 1) the trope of deviancy, or the notion that mental illness is not "real" and is the fault of the afflicted due to weak moral character, poor choices, and so on; 2) the trope of fakery, or the idea that mental illness is easily and frequently faked for the purposes of avoiding consequences; 3) the trope of illegitimacy, or the idea that psychiatry is not a legitimate discipline, and psychiatrists will diagnose based on which side of the court case is paying them; 4) the trope of ordinary common sense, or the idea that anyone of ordinary intelligence can tell if someone is mentally ill or not; 5) the trope of danger, or the belief that if a defendant successfully pleads insanity, s/he will be set free and possibly harm others; and 6) the trope of pandemonium, or the belief that the insanity defense weakens the retributive, deterrent, and incapacitating effects of the criminal justice system.

Having described sanism and elaborated a number of its common rhetorical elements in a series of myths-turned-tropes, it may be helpful to describe their relationship to a number of theoretical assumptions and related concepts undergirding this study. Over the course of the history of the insanity defense, how did these myths and their corresponding tropes become so deeply embedded in the way we think about mental illness? Why do they seem intractable even in the face of a mountain of evidence that disproves them? To answer these and related questions, we must look more closely at the way belief, ideology, and myth shape our culture.

Belief, Ideology, and Hegemony in Sanism

So far I have noted that the concept of *myth* is central to the rhetoric of sanism and the institutional practices concerning the insanity defense, and I have relied on a more or less common understanding of the term as a common cultural story that is misleading or false. The concept of myth does not connote, however, the powerful emotions that they can inspire. Myths become increasingly important to a culture in times of unrest as a means by which ruptures in the narrative can be sutured and scapegoats ("others") identified. While people do engage in reasoning based on evidence, the premises by which they do so are drawn from beliefs, myths, and ideologies that adhere below consciousness; this explains why enduring ways of thinking are difficult, if not impossible, to alter. In this way, the hegemonic status of the law is maintained by myths about the law, and sanism is maintained by the myths about mental illness.

In order to understand how sanism functions, we must address the rhetorical forces that work to support it and other pervasive cultural "isms." According to rhetorical theorist Sharon Crowley, belief and action are primarily motivated not by reason but by "ideology, fantasy, and emotion."[27] She developed the concept of *ideologic* to describe "connections made between and among moments (positions) that occur or are taken up within ideology."[28] Crowley deploys Bourdieu's concept of the *habitus*, which locates belief in the material dimension, since it "includes cultural representations such as history, memory, ideology, fantasy, myth, and lore, and it also includes culturally habituated practices."[29] *Habitus* relates closely to what Young calls "practical consciousness," which "refers to those aspects of action and situation which involve often complex reflexive monitoring of the relation of the subject's body to those of other subjects and the surrounding environment, but which are on the fringe of consciousness, rather than the focus of discursive attention."[30] What is important to understand for the purposes of this study is that belief and ideology are embodied and adhere below consciousness, which is to say they are rarely conscious, even though we constantly act in and through them.

It may be helpful to distinguish the way I understand the difference between belief, which is a moment of ideology, and ideology itself, which is the system within which those beliefs circulate. Beliefs serve the interests of the individual, people, or institutions who harbor them; thus, even when a belief system is shown to be weak or deceptive, it will not necessarily be abandoned.[31] Legal decision-making has illustrated this phenomenon repeatedly in cases in which identities that reinforce social hierarchies are central.[32] Crowley argues that "the more densely beliefs are articulated with one another within a given belief system or across belief systems, the more impervious they are to rhetorical intervention," and because "a densely articulated ideology 'explains everything,' . . . its disarticulation is very costly to a believer."[33] Systems of belief, then, are social, which mark them as commonplaces, defined not by truth but by frequent repetition and widespread acceptance within a community (e.g., the tropes of sanism).[34] Both belief and ideology function rhetorically within a culture and exert persuasive force;[35] thus, it is this rhetorical force that sustains the rhetoric of sanism. Sanism is a densely articulated belief system in this sense, which explains why the law, the lay public, and even mental health disciplines have had difficulty adapting to new ways of thinking about mental illness and how it should be addressed in a legal context.

Hegemony is a concept closely related to beliefs and belief systems. We can think of hegemony as the point at which ideology attains such a strong hold on the beliefs and actions of a given community that it goes without saying; meanings that are constructed appear to be natural once ideology achieves hegemonic status,[36] and the law facilitates the process of naturalizing such ideologies.[37] While ideology can be contested, hegemony is naturalized and relatively closed off to debate. Hegemony and ideology work together to "create identity" and "to disguise or hide the flow of difference."[38] Such identities mark the boundaries of a community.[39] What is outside those boundaries, then, marks what is "other," those who are "not us," but the instability of those boundaries, what Derrida calls "*différance*,"[40] constantly threatens both "us" and "other." The law, I contend, has attained hegemonic status. It is understood to be fixed, stable, monolithic (even though we know it is endlessly interpretable, variable, and evolving). It must be imagined this way in order to serve its social function of maintaining order and imposing appropriate boundaries between us and other.

Antagonisms, including those that occur in a courtroom, expose the limits of hegemony and have the potential to reveal ruptures in dominant narratives. But in Western culture, antagonisms are usually rhetorically buried or "managed discursively by imposition of a logic of equivalence, whereby difference is reduced to sameness,"[41] and the various people who are identified as "other" are cast together as a homogenous group ("gay people," "black people," "crazy people"). This strategy "reduces the multiplicity of difference to a manageable binary," the purpose of which is to minimize the threat such difference poses to the "maintenance of the dominant category itself."[42] For example, the use of stereotypes and labels that maintain our essential discursive categories[43] is a familiar daily rhetorical practice that enables our ability to ignore the ruptures in dominant narratives that antagonisms threaten to expose.

In fact, this kind of rhetorical strategy is implicated in the structure of the law. A defendant can be guilty or not guilty, sane or insane; there is little room for nuance. Commonplaces, then, serve to reinforce the identity of a community and, according to Crowley, are spoken of only to serve an epideictic function: to praise the in-group or blame the "miscreants and outsiders."[44] The criminal justice system has four primary functions: retribution, incapacitation, rehabilitation, and deterrence. All four implicate its rhetorical function, which is to reinforce in-group identity (law-abiding citizens) and limit interactions with the "other" (criminals). Perhaps what is so disconcerting about the insanity defense is that it constructs a liminal category that is neither: a defendant who pleads insanity is not a law-abiding citizen, and therefore, not "us"; but if successful, s/he is also not a criminal because s/he could not be held legally responsible for his or her actions. S/he is still othered, however, by virtue of mental disease or defect, which imposes yet another arbitrary boundary.

The Function of Fantasy and Myth in Group Identity Dynamics

So far I have noted that the concept of myth is central to the rhetoric of sanism and the institutional practices concerning the insanity defense, and I have relied on a more or less common understanding of the term as a common cultural story that is misleading or false. The concept of myth does not connote, however, the powerful emotions that myths can evoke. In the theoretical humanities, one way scholars have tried to understand the powerfully emotional dynamics of cultural myth is through the concept of *fantasy*.[45] We can think of fantasy or the imaginary in the collective sense as a desire for identification with a particular group or community, and, therefore, a particular ideology. Fantasies serve the function of helping groups "cope with their social realities" and "make sense of a common experience."[46] In complex social situations, then, "fantasy simplifies the daunting task of sorting 'us' from 'them.'"[47]

Fantasy and myth are closely related and often used synonymously by rhetorical critics, thus necessitating a little finessing. Crowley helpfully calls myth "a special case of collective fantasy"[48] that reinforces the commonplaces of group identity, and, drawing on the work of Roland Barthes, she suggests that it "generalizes history" to the moral of the story; thus, the "psychosocial meaning" of the myth becomes its most significant feature.[49] In terms of ideology, "once an event becomes mythologized, ideologic trumps narrative. It is the moral—the commonplace—that matters," and thus, "myths can become premises in an ideologic."[50] Admittedly, these are finer points about myth and fantasy that are difficult to untangle. For the remainder of this study, let us specify some working definitions: fantasy refers to the stories or narratives about what defines an individual or a community; fantasies yield specific identities of belonging. Myths are also narratives or stories, but they *belong to no one*, they inhere in culture, and they are put into the service of fantasy.

Myths become increasingly important to a culture in times of unrest as a means by which ruptures in the narrative can be sutured and scapegoats ("others") identified.[51] While people do engage in reasoning based on evidence, the premises by which they do so are drawn from beliefs, myths, and ideologies that adhere subconsciously through fantasy; this explains why enduring ways of thinking are difficult, if not impossible, to alter. In this way, the hegemonic status of the law is maintained by myths about the law, and sanism is maintained by myths about mental illness, as discussed previously.

Since "explicit and discursively focused"[52] "isms" have been formally forbidden by Western capitalist public law, realistically only since mid-twentieth century, they "have receded from . . . discursive consciousness,"[53] which contributes to the "common conviction that ideologies of natural inferiority and group domination no longer exercise significant influence in our society," as evidenced by claims that we live in a postfeminist or postracial society.[54] While not overtly discussed (at least in public discourse), "ismic" ideologies continue to exist in the habitus or practical consciousness, wielding influence on everything from individual behavior to legislation, and they continue "to reproduce relations of privilege and oppression."[55] It is through this mechanism, Perlin argues, that "'ismic' behavior," which operates "on an unconscious level," has served to legitimize ideologies and perpetuate myths that rationalize oppression.[56] Such oppression, rather than appearing "in the form of overt domination," is now enacted through "avoidances, aversions, and separations."[57] According to Perlin, this "separation of others into categorized groups is enough to trigger the psychological processes leading to intergroup prejudice."[58] Such prejudice is intensified when the boundaries between us and others are perceived as more permeable. For example, Young argues that the fragility of the border between gay and straight is the reason that "homophobia is one of the deepest fears of difference."[59] The border between sane and insane is even more fragile; therefore, sanism stems from our deep fear of "going crazy," of losing what makes us human: our capacity to reason.

Kristeva's concept of the abject, which Young takes up, is a useful way to understand aversive reactions to mentally ill people. Kristeva says that the abject's primary quality is that which is opposed to "*I*," that which is other; the abject "disturbs identity, system, order," and "does not respect borders positions, rules."[60] The importance placed on mind and reason and their "abstract[ion] from sensuality" drives an "urge for purity" that "creates some groups as scapegoats, representative of the expelled body standing over and against the purified and abstracted subject."[61] These expelled bodily beings are abject precisely because they expose the fragility of the borders, and the reaction of loathing to the abject is a "means of restoring the border separating self and other."[62] In other words, if I am disgusted or repulsed by that, then I am not that. Much of the discourse on the insanity defense, in both professional and public arenas, is emblematic of this desire to shore up those boundaries by deploying and relying on myth-based tropes, working rhetorically to sew up the ruptures threatened by legal antagonism.

On Morality in the Law and Mental Health Professions

I have introduced the goal of this study as an explanation of the complexities of the insanity defense as the interplay of three agents in tension—public and popular discourse, mental health professionals, and the law—vis-à-vis the rhetoric of sanism. We also have examined a number of theoretical concepts that will help toward this end: ideology, hegemony, myth, fantasy, and so on. We now tackle what I think is the largest obstacle to *any* study of the insanity defense, and something that I believe has heretofore hindered a rhetorical understanding, and that is moralism.

It is important to understand the overtly moralistic origins of both the law and the mental health professions as we know them today, which were, according to Foucault, to discipline the social body and maintain order. Morality is a highly contextual, socially constructed, idealized version of public and private behavior and "conformity to accepted customs of right behavior."[63] Its primary function is to establish firm boundaries between what is acceptable/accepted and what is not and allows, then, for a clear distinction to be drawn between "us" and "other." According to George Lakoff, "moral thinking is imaginative. . . . It depends fundamentally on metaphorical understanding,"[64] which means that the ways in which we think, talk, and act about morality lie in the domain of belief, ideology, and myth. Some pervasive moral metaphors, Lakoff says, are "metamoral," in that they "do not in themselves tell you exactly which actions are moral or immoral," but they "generate moral conclusions about various kinds of behavior,"[65] which helps us "understand concepts like justice, fairness, retribution, and revenge."[66] This way of framing morality is helpful for the purposes of this study in terms of how moral thinking impacts the insanity defense.

Lakoff identifies two familial models that shape very distinct systems of morality extending beyond the family into various social institutions, including the criminal justice system and the mental health system, which are helpful for understanding the rhetorical challenges of putting psychiatry in conversation with law. The first Lakoff terms "Strict Father Morality," which, as the name suggests, is based on a traditional family model in which the paternal figure "teaches children right from wrong by setting strict rules for their behavior and enforcing them through punishment."[67] Parental authority takes priority with the belief that only those who learn self-discipline will ultimately become successful. Lakoff calls the second model "Nurturant Parent Morality," which presupposes that "children become responsible, self-disciplined, and self-reliant through being cared for and respected, and through caring for others,"[68] and that children will be obedient not because they fear punishment but because they love and respect their parents.[69] While Lakoff uses these familial models of morality to explain how liberals and conservatives think differently, a similar challenge is evident in the insanity defense. If we think of the criminal justice system as operating under the Strict Father model, extending the role of the father to the law and the role of the children to those citizens who commit crimes, we can see that in this model, the criminal justice system operates under a moral imperative to appropriately punish those who violate the rules in order to teach them to become self-disciplined. In this model, the system would fail in its role if it did not do so. If we think of the mental health professions as operating under the Nurturant Parent model, extending the role of the parent to psychiatrists and the role of the children to persons suffering from mental illness, psychiatrists have a moral imperative to nurture, care for, and respect their patients and help them become self-reliant through treatment, and would have failed in their role and duty if they did not do so.

The policing of morality takes place both formally and informally, that is, through institutions and social interactions. One of the most prominent formal systems of moral policing is the criminal justice system. The law presumes a social contract between citizen and society, so the criminal becomes paradoxically a person who simultaneously violates that contract by committing a crime and abides by that contract by participating in the punishment it designates. According to Foucault, crime inflicts disorder on the social body;[70] the most significant function of the law, then, is not to punish the individual criminal but to deter other citizens from repeating the crime.[71] We can thus locate anxieties about the insanity defense here, because an insanity defense, by definition, relies upon a claim that a defendant cannot be held responsible for his actions due to mental disease or defect, and if there can be no punishment, so the argument goes, there can be no deterrence.

The myth of fairness that upholds our criminal justice system is based on the notion that the law is not only objective and rational but that the defined crimes and punishments are fairly and equally applied in all circumstances. Although we know that is not the case in practice, without that assumption, the system lacks the necessary credibility on which to maintain its appearance of validity. The image of courts as "impartial decision makers bound down by the law"[72] is one that has been carefully crafted and maintained. The judicial system is based on the assumption that courts apply the law objectively, independent of the personal values of judges or jurors; without this assumption, it would be impossible for people to accept the decisions of courts. The very notion that the law can be "applied" objectively and without bias by judges and jurors is the backbone of our legal system, highlighting the Enlightenment mindset on which our judicial system was founded and continues to operate.

In his analysis of Supreme Court decision-making, Clarke Rountree notes the care with which "the image of objectivity and infallibility that judicial mythology promotes" is maintained.[73] All legal decision-makers take great pains to abide by the mythic narrative: that they are "interpreters rather than creators of law," "that they are chained to judicial logic rather than free to craft arguments from a rich well of rhetorical resources," that they are "above normal human biases," and "that what they assert about the law *is* the law."[74] At the same time, the Judeo-Christian canon and its corresponding belief that all people[75] have the fundamental capacity "to choose between good or evil and the ability to recognize the difference" has undergirded Western law since the sixth century when the Angles and Saxons settled in England.[76] Thus the Law, writ large, constitutes a centuries-old hegemonic belief system, the disarticulation of which would be extremely costly on a societal level; this, at least in part, explains its resistance to change, even in the face of multiple ruptures in this narrative that expose its limits.

While the discipline and practice of psychiatry have evolved significantly over the last century, it is important to recall its fundamentally moral basis. We usually think of medical practice as a "helping" profession, which is generally accurate; however, the societal protocol for dealing with mentally ill people has historically mirrored the development of the prison, and the discipline retains some of the aspects of moral policing on which it was founded. The modern criminal justice system developed along with the treatment of mentally ill people by medical doctors practicing in what were typically called lunatic asylums. Whereas "the mad" had previously been confined in less than hospitable conditions along with poor, indigent, and criminal citizens, the late eighteenth and early nineteenth centuries saw the birth of what was touted as a medical marvel known as the asylum. The "ingenious benevolence" of the asylum imposed a "religious and moral milieu . . . in such a way that madness was controlled, not cured."[77] We will see this narrative operating in the landmark insanity defense trials from the late nineteenth century. The new discourse on madness shifted the locus of insanity from a frightening fate bestowed upon the unfortunate to the morality of the afflicted.[78]

The function of the asylum, then, was no longer to punish but rather to serve as "a therapeutic intervention in the madman's existence."[79] The moral work of the asylum exacted rigorous mental work from its patients; all "exercises of the imagination" were viewed as complicit "with the passions, the desires, or all desirous illusions," which were opposed to reason, underscoring the Enlightenment ideology that upheld these endeavors.[80] The science of mental disease, as it played out in the asylum, centered on observation and classification; these terms are part of the broader concepts of surveillance and judgment[81] that are fundamental tenets of the criminal justice system. The asylum set up a familial model in which the mentally ill were viewed as children, and the "men of reason" who treated them were the patriarchs charged with the maintenance of morality and order through segregating from larger society those whose madness was evidence of their "social failure."[82] The asylum obviated the law, as it became a self-contained juridical institution,[83] the function of which was, according to Foucault, "*to exclude . . . those whose transgressions risk compromising the social order*."[84]

Now consider the collision of these two models when a criminal defendant who is mentally ill raises a defense that suggests that he cannot be held responsible for his or her actions due to that illness. Since the term *insanity* is a legal rather than a psychiatric definition, it "represents a moral conception of insanity and responsibility."[85] Yet in any case in which an insanity defense is raised, at least one psychiatrist must provide testimony as to the defendant's mental health. Recall the law's functions: retribution, deterrence, incapacitation, and rehabilitation. The first three of the four are entirely within the domain of the Strict Father Model, and even the fourth, rehabilitation, is to be achieved through appropriate punishment, so that should not be viewed as an act of nurturing. The ostensible goal of psychiatry is to treat and cure patients through medicalized nurturing, which falls within the domain of Nurturant Parent Morality, with one exception that further complicates the insanity defense: typically (particularly in cases involving violent crimes, which are, of course, the higher profile cases that shape the public perception of the insanity defense, e.g., Hinckley, Yates, Holmes), both the prosecution and defense will employ their own expert psychiatric witnesses; of course the prosecution expert will testify in a manner that is favorable to the prosecution, and the defense expert will testify in a manner that is favorable to the defense, which is accomplished through purposeful interpretation of the legal definition of insanity as well as varying diagnoses of the defendant. This means that we cannot always assume that a psychiatrist is operating as a Nurturant Parent. Similarly, as we will see in the history of the insanity defense, some judges have prioritized compassion for mentally ill people in their attempts to redefine the standards for legal insanity, which means we cannot always assume that the criminal justice system is operating as a Strict Father. If a defendant is successful in an insanity plea, retribution and deterrence cannot be attained, because the criminal cannot be held legally responsible for his or her actions. The goal of the law, then, becomes the incapacitation of the criminal in order to keep the community safe, and since s/he will most likely spend some time (whatever the duration of his criminal sentence would have been, but typically even longer) confined in a mental health facility, rehabilitation is possible but not the primary goal. Both the legal and mental health systems, however, constantly operate in and through ideologies of morality with the competing goals of punishment and treatment.

In the chapters that follow, then, we will review the history of the insanity defense in Western law. I hope that using the previously outlined concepts will allow readers to see more clearly why this issue is so complex. We will see that the problems endemic to insanity defense jurisprudence have remained relatively unchanged, certainly from its codification in 1843, but even before that, as the tropes that plague it are much older. The next chapter will take us from ancient times to 1843 in a brief exploration of the concept of mental illness and its relation to the law.

2

A Brief History of Western Thought on Mental Illness and Its Relevance to the Law

> "Men differ in education, wealth, background, and values, and even in the strength of their emotions, their sense of compassion, their susceptibility to reason, and their capacity to feel duty or guilt. If the law is to operate at all, and to maintain any pretense of egalitarianism, it must disregard these differences, but some are too great to ignore."
>
> —Thomas Maeder

Beliefs about mental illness have always run along a spectrum between the supernatural and the biological. Rather than developing in a linear fashion as we might expect, with older cultures attributing mental disturbance to spirits, gradually evolving with medical knowledge to assign causes to neurobiological imbalance, the trajectory has been more of a swinging pendulum. From the time of Western civilization as we in the humanities know it, each distinct epoch has maintained some tension between spiritual and biological explanations for mental illness, and in each period, this tension has been complicated by the differing goals of medicine, law, philosophy, and popular belief.

The earliest known civilizations, such as the Babylonians and Mesopotamians, attributed madness to supernatural forces: "spirit invasion, sorcery, demonic malice, the evil eye, or the breaking of taboos"[1] might all be considered the source of the disorder. This perception of mental illness as having some connection to the supernatural has never entirely left the cultural mythology surrounding mental illness, but in those times, the belief was more explicitly articulated, and those afflicted were treated accordingly. For example, human skulls dating back to 5000 BC have been found with evidence of trephining, the boring of small holes, which suggests a primitive "surgery" designed to allow the possessing spirits to escape.[2] Other rudimentary treatments like shock or starvation were also common, which makes sense because these ancient civilizations were rooted in their belief in animistic spirits.[3] Such barbaric methods, however, have continued in many forms well into our relatively recent history.

Through extant myths and epics, we know that the preclassical Greeks understood mental illness as exculpatory, even before the existence of written laws.[4] In Homeric epics (written sometime between the eleventh and eighth centuries BC), terminology for the individual agent did not yet exist, nor did concepts like will and reason. At this time, rather, all beings and their actions were seen as subject to the whims of supernatural forces external to themselves.[5] It was not until the fifth and fourth centuries BC that thinking on the psyche took a form that would be somewhat familiar to us today; indeed, this period "set the mould for mainstream reasoning about minds and madness in the West."[6]

Greek philosophy and medicine challenged earlier superstitious thinking about madness, as the origin of mental disturbance was located in the body, specifically the brain. Pythagoras was actually the first philosopher to locate the intellect and mental disturbances in the brain as well as adopt a concept of bodily humors that influenced temperament.[7] Hippocrates and his followers wrote texts denouncing those who attributed mental disorders to divine sources, stating that their causes were as natural as any other disease.[8] Basic concepts of health were explained in terms of bodily humors: blood, choler, bile, and phlegm, the imbalance of which might cause illnesses[9] that could be physical or mental; in this holistic way of thinking, however, the two were not polarized.[10] At the same time, philosophical thought taught that the development of such diseases in which reason was thwarted were brought on by "bad rearing, bad habits, and ignorance," and that by cultivating a virtuous life, man could attain the good life,[11] which suggests that notions of individual responsibility for mental health were firmly in place by this period.

As medical knowledge developed, so did a formal legal system. The implicit logic of most legal systems is that the rule of law only applies to those who have the capacity "to comprehend its terms and abide by its prescriptions."[12] The foundations of ancient law demonstrate very similar principles as those outlined by Foucault in his genealogy of Western law in the eighteenth and nineteenth centuries in which the nature of law is a social contract, the very condition of citizenship. In classical Greece, there is clearly an understanding of the relationship between psychology and law, "between principles that are binding because of the psychological capacity of rational beings to be *bound by principle*."[13] Thus, the distinction between wild beasts and humans is precisely that capacity, because it is the very condition of humanity. As Aristotle writes, "For man, when perfected, is the best of animals, but, when separated from law and justice, he is the worst of all."[14]

Greek philosophy also developed the paradigm of the ideal man. Socrates and Plato assessed the contents of the psyche as being made up of "reason, spirits, the passions, and the soul,"[15] and Aristotle believed that man was potentially the best of animals; thus, the rational human (who was also an educated, propertied male) became the pinnacle of humanness. Defining rationality necessitated the presence of its counterpart, irrationality, and the dangers of the passions were believed to be kept at bay only by the pursuit of virtue and reason.[16] Thus, the philosophical binary was enshrined: rational/irrational, mind/body, reason/emotions, and although scientific developments from this period to today suggest the error of this polarization, our thinking has not shifted significantly.

Philosophers also began to think through the relationship between reason, or the deprivation thereof, and the law. In *Laws*, Plato provides explicit recommendations for the care of the mentally ill as well as cases involving a mentally ill criminal defendant. Madmen are not to be free, "at large in the city,"[17] but rather cared for by their families, and if the family is unable to provide such care, a class-based penalty schedule is provided. Upon commission of a crime, Plato suggests that madmen should be exempt from most penalties except for having to pay the victim for the damages, but if the crime was murder, then the perpetrator should be banished from the country for one year.[18] Plato's recommendations illustrate the still pervasive view that whatever level of sanity must be present in order to carry out a homicide is sufficient to hold the murderer responsible for the act.[19] In the *Nichomachean Ethics*, Aristotle allows for certain conditions of ignorance that might mitigate criminal responsibility, including ignorance of "the person, the instrument, or the motive,"[20] which indicate that "the doers are not yet on this account unjust or wicked; for the hurt did not arise from depravity."[21] For Aristotle, then, the madman lacks the capacity for evil, which is the primary requirement of fitness for punishment.

In Rome, medical knowledge and treatment of mentally ill people remained relatively the same as it had been in Greece. While some physicians opposed common methods of dealing with madmen at the time, which included bloodletting, restraints, and confinement in dungeons,[22] most maintained that these methods, in addition to starvation and intimidation, were the most effective means of treatment. Others claimed, as they had in Greece, that the excesses of the elite class's lifestyle contributed to their susceptibility to illness.[23] Galen is seen as the last significant contributor to medicine and psychology in Rome, and his theories remained dominant through the seventeenth century.[24] He emphasized the importance of empirical observation and evaluation and argued "against untested primitive and philosophical hypotheses" of disease.[25] His concept of the *spiritus anima* asserted that "humans possessed an extra-physical life-giving force" in order to explain the difference between organic and inorganic matter.[26] He viewed pathologies of the mind as neurological in origin but believed that animal spirits were responsible for mental activity and both voluntary and involuntary instigated actions. In this way, his theories were accommodating to the notions of the influence of evil spirits on the bodily humors that would develop in the Middle Ages.[27] His taxonomy, however, encompassed many of the psychiatric disorders we recognize today, including mania, depression, and psychosis.[28]

As medical theories of mental disturbance evolved, so did legal theories regarding the relationship of mentally ill people to society. In the Roman Empire, like in classical Greece, the basis of the law was the duty of individual citizens to the state, the "enrichment and perpetuation" of the collective being the primary duty.[29] A life cut off from the collective was no life at all; it was, in fact, "unnatural and defective,"[30] or, we might say, abject, to use Kristeva's term. The elite were held to higher standards than the lower classes, as the same belief existed that "the inferior side of one's nature," a trait that all citizens bore within them, could be suppressed by "good upbringing" and "developed character."[31] There existed a tendency to equate insanity with childlikeness or infancy; both the infant and the madman were unfit for citizenship, nor would either benefit from punishment.[32] The freedoms bestowed upon citizens could be revoked by the rule of law, but the mad were seen as unable to participate in the social contract and thus excluded from citizenship and all its benefits.[33] Roman law was only concerned with the madman to the extent of his practical affairs: estates, property, and any damage or injury he might cause to others.[34] The nature of his inner mental state was of little importance, and the existence of mentally ill persons was accepted as a matter of fact.

Whereas the nature of the madman's inner mental state was not the concern of classical jurisprudence, it was the domain in which the Church was intensely interested. Roman law's concerns were limited to the "outward and public manifestations" of mental illness insofar as the actions of madmen infringed upon "the interests of the collective," while emerging Christianity sought to "penetrate the innermost precincts of conscience" in its judgments.[35] The collapse of the Roman Empire brought with it many hybrid versions of medicine and law that fused ancient thought with Christian dogma, including ideas about madness and how it should be addressed in a legal context.[36]

The influence of Greek culture is evident in the various exorcisms described in the New Testament; *daimona*, or demons, were part of ancient Greek life, though they were not necessarily evil. Within the Christian paradigm, *daimon* referred exclusively to evil spirits. During this time, much of the behavior that was attributed to demonic possession can now be easily recognized as symptoms of neurological disorders, primarily epilepsy, or many common mental illnesses, such as depression, bipolar disorder, and schizophrenia.[37]

The medical theories developed in the Middle Ages reflect the influence of Christianity on the medical approach to psychopathology. This period marked a regression from the humanistic approach that had developed during the Roman Empire and a return to "a moralistic and judgmental" view of mental illness.[38] Physicians believed that mental disturbances arose from an imbalance of bodily humors or animal spirits and recommended some of the older, more unpleasant treatment methods such as bloodletting, force-feedings, and "the inhalation of vile substances."[39] Some discouraged engagement with philosophy and suggested that madness might actually be caused by too much thinking; other suspected causes included trauma to the head or "too much love for philosophy, glory, or money."[40] Millon's comprehensive history of psychiatry notes this turn away from philosophy and back toward the supernatural as a means of understanding the world is the hallmark of the Patristic period.[41]

Augustine, or as we better know him, St. Augustine, was one of the most influential philosophers of his time. While he attempted to synthesize Greek perspectives on mental illness with emerging Christian doctrine, his view of science was charitable only when it reinforced his theological beliefs, and he was otherwise skeptical when it did not. For Augustine, knowing God was the only goal of life, and to seek anything else "would not only be in vain, but would assuredly lead to error and corruption."[42] Truth could be understood in two ways: spiritual sources provided revelations, while self-reflection provided personal insight, and freedom of the will was paramount to the enrichment of one's existence. It is this concept—freedom of the will—that causes the most difficulty in understanding mental illness. Augustine's influence was far-reaching; his teachings dominated religious doctrine for the next eight centuries, ushering in a climate of increasing fear as the political power of the church grew and the eventual barbarism of the medieval period became inevitable.

Ultimately, Roman jurisprudence weighed heavily in the development of Christian canon law, and it was the belief common to Roman and Christian cultures—that all things originated with some rational principle—that sealed this bond,[43] although the issue of mental illness was far more complex in the Christian world. What distinguished a legal offense from a genuinely sinful one? If madness was visited upon people as punishment for sins, then mental illness was not exculpatory but instead, further proof of guilt.[44] The Western empire of the early Middle Ages was characterized by a conversion of existing "discourse on crime and punishment into the idiom of sin and retribution"[45] and a notable absence of the medical and scientific understandings of disease, including diseases of the mind, that had enriched classical legal thought.[46]

This climate produced hardships on mentally ill or mentally retarded people accused of crimes. Some men of God, including St. Ambrose, St. John Chrysostom, and St. Augustine, spoke out on the position that punishing mentally ill people for their actions was unjust.[47] More serious offenses, however, continued to require some form of penance. Whether this was an effort to maintain the social order or to punish the sinner whose deeds resulted in his own mental affliction is difficult to say. What we do know is that mental illness, rather than being accepted as a matter of fact, now came with "heavy burdens of shame and concealment."[48] Within the fusion of classical teachings and Christian doctrine, there existed a theory of human nature that included Satanic and demonic elements. Whereas previously, the existence of mentally ill people was an accepted part of life, witches and witchcraft were now understood as matters of fact by both Christianity and folk medicine.[49]

The first Angles and Saxons to settle in England in the fifth century adopted the legal principle that the presence of both a wrongful act (*actus reus*) and the intent to commit that wrongful act (*mens rea*; literally "guilty mind") were constitutive of a crime, allowing special consideration for those defendants who might experience a loss or lapse of their senses or wits.[50] In contrast to Greek thought in which "reason was the essence of man," Christian doctrine emphasized faith, divine will, and sin.[51] It was the canon law of Christianity that articulated and institutionalized mental illness as a personal moral failure, as it taught that people have free will and the ability to choose good or evil and also to be able to distinguish the difference.[52] In fact, any suggestion that a person could be robbed of his free will, by any source, demonic or not, was rejected wholesale, and by the thirteenth century, magic was not just demonic, it was heresy.[53]

The *Edictum Rothari* was the first written collection of Lombard laws codified by King Rothari (Rothair) in 643, and it specifically addressed mental illness and revealed the prevailing attitudes toward it and its sufferers. Edict 180 outlines proper procedure for a betrothed girl who "becomes leprous or mad or blind in both eyes."[54] In such a case, the husband-to-be is to be refunded any investment he has made into the marriage and not be required to go through with the arrangement; furthermore, "he shall not be guilty in this event because it did not occur on account of his neglect but on account of her weighty sins and resulting illness."[55] Edict 323 likewise states, "If a man, because of his weighty sins, goes mad or becomes possessed and does damage to man or beast, nothing shall be required from his heirs."[56] This new emphasis on the sins of the sufferer as the root of disease is the logical result of the influence of Christianity on Germanic law. Rome's culture of civic virtues and duty to the state was fundamentally incompatible with such notions as sin, redemption, life after death, and a personal God in which "all misfortune is somehow earned and thus deserved."[57]

As the authority of canon law expanded, the theological importance of witchcraft grew. By the ninth century, Gratian's *Episcopi Eorumque*, which condemned wicked women who entertained beliefs in witchcraft, concocted potions, and cavorted in the night hours riding beasts, took on greater importance,[58] although the great witch panic was not yet underway. The end of the High Middle Ages into the Late Middle Ages were dismal times for those whom we would now recognize as mentally ill, as they were believed to be either possessed by or willingly in league with the Devil, and texts like the *Malleus Maleficarum* dominated theory and practice regarding the proper treatment of such people. Long-term confinement, torture, and violent executions were not uncommon. Some two hundred thousand people, most of them women, were executed during this period.[59] Well into the seventeenth century, certain ailments were readily attributed to demonic possession, and at the time, medical doctors were believed to be "the ones best qualified to distinguish between maleficium and natural disease."[60] It was not until the 1700s that most of Europe's literate classes abandoned belief in demonic possession.[61]

This transformation coincided with the Enlightenment. Reason and individualism are the hallmarks of this intellectual movement, and it remains deeply embedded in current ways of thinking, particularly in relation to the law as well as mental illness. Descartes is, in many ways, the founder of Western philosophy who sought with intellectual rigor a philosophical system that could withstand the skepticism of his peers. For Descartes, the mind was composed of innate ideas such as God, time and space, and the self along with derived ideas that came from our experiences. The codification of mind-body dualism can be attributed to Descartes; the mind thinks but lacks substance, while the body, a complex machine, is limited by mechanical functions.[62] The ideals perpetuated by Cartesian thought, that the basis for all of nature was reason and logic and that humankind, God's crowning achievement, exemplified these traits, continued to contribute to the mistreatment of mentally ill people who, seen as devoid of reason and logic, were regarded as more animal than human.[63]

In his 1690 *Essay on Human Understanding*, John Locke (1632–1704) wrote "that madness was due to faulty associations in the processes" in which "sense data were transformed into 'ideas.'"[64] The concept of "(mis)-association of ideas"[65] was co-opted into developing ways of thinking about madness. The metaphysician and philosopher Immanuel Kant (1724–1804) was concerned primarily with the validity of knowledge. He considered psychology "an empirical search for the laws of mental functioning," and his work sought to expose the limitations of empiricism.[66] Enlightenment thought had a profound influence on the development of psychiatry, as we will see in the next chapter.

Enlightenment thinkers, as had their Greek predecessors, elevated reason as man's defining trait; thus, those without reason "were seen as having descended to a brutish state."[67] Thomas Willis was among the first English physicians to write extensively on the nature and treatment of madness; his 1685 text, *The Practice of Physick: Two Discourses Concerning the Souls of Brutes*, reflected the notion that mentally ill people were closer to animals than humans.[68] The guidelines for the care of such brutes, therefore, reads similarly to instructions for breaking wild animals, with a focus on intimidation, domination, and treatments that resulted in physical weakness: bloodletting, purging, emetics, chemical agents to induce nausea, starvation, caustic agents to cause blistering of the skin, along with regular beatings and the use of restraints.[69] The belief was that inducing intense suffering would divert the patient's attention away from his raving thoughts. Such treatments also undoubtedly instilled a great deal of fear in these patients, which provided their "caregivers" with some level of control over them.[70]

At Edinburgh University's medical school, established in 1726, William Cullen medicalized Locke's ideas in producing a paradigm of madness that was more psychologically oriented. Attributing madness to "excessive irritation of the nerves," he believed that "acute cerebral activity" was the precipitating cause of insanity.[71] The term "neurosis" actually originates with Cullen, although its meaning for him referred specifically to a disorder of the nervous system. Cullen, however, integrated concepts like "unusual and commonly hurried association of ideas," "false judgment," and "disproportionate emotions" into his somatic model; in other words, madness was a mental disorder grounded in neurophysiology.[72]

Insanity remained a domestic responsibility in some countries, such as Japan, until the twentieth century. Care for the mentally ill in Christian Europe typically fell to the family, often in deplorable conditions; or they might be set free to wander and beg. Due to the implications of demonic possession or simply bad breeding, "insanity was deeply shameful to a family."[73] Toward the end of the Middle Ages, "the Christian duty of charity" brought about a more formal system of segregation for lunatics. What would eventually become known as London's infamous Bethlem ("Bedlam") Hospital was originally founded in 1247 as the religious house of St. Mary of Bethlehem, which "was catering to lunatics by the late fourteenth century."[74] Prior to 1800, no country required any form of professional medical supervision of asylums, "nor did medical overlordship . . . ensure good care."[75] The long-held belief that the mad were akin to wild beasts was borne out in the barbaric methods they were subjected to in the name of "treatment."[76]

By the eighteenth century, Bedlam was devoted mostly to caring for the poor insane, as families of means sent their disturbed relatives to private madhouses, a business that developed in the first part of the century.[77] These private facilities became a convenient way to get rid of bothersome family members; if a physician would attest—for a fee, of course, paid to both the doctor and the madhouse owner—that a man's wife had developed some form of madness, he could have her sent to a boarding house to be "treated."[78] The private madhouses that served primarily those from families of means still treated their "patients" harshly. A 1774 law, the Act for Regulating Madhouses, Licensings, and Inspections, formally prevented commitment without the certification of a physician,[79] which meant that "physicians were now the sole arbiters of insanity, a legal authority that made the mad-doctoring trade more profitable than ever."[80]

The 1788 onset of madness in King George III followed by his successful "recovery" gave credence to the public that mad doctors possessed curative powers. Prominent physician Francis Willis "treated" the King with the known methods of the time: restraint, blistering, bloodletting, purging, sedation, and a variety of other tortures. What appeared to be a miraculous recovery some months later is now widely attributed to the remission of a rare blood disorder called porphyria; in fact, historians suggest that Willis's treatments probably aggravated the King's condition and prolonged his illness. At the time, however, this very public triumph of the treatment of madness gave the field (and the trade) a significant boost.[81]

Over the next thirty years, the number of private madhouses doubled, and mad doctors all over Europe devised new treatments, including dunking patients in water, pouring water on patients from great heights, various devices that could blast water at patients with great force, and the "Bath of Surprise," which involved the blindfolded patient being "dropped through a trapdoor into a tub of cold water" in the hopes that the sudden terror would somehow restore the senses,[82] and near-drowning. A "therapeutic" invention by Joseph Mason Cox, a mechanical swinging chair, which we might imagine as a carnival ride featured in a horror film, became very popular and spawned a number of imitations, such as spinning beds, stools, and boards. Such "twirling devices" were eventually banned, much to the dismay of madhouse owners.[83]

The eighteenth and nineteenth centuries were a time of rapid development, both medical and entrepreneurial. A number of high profile trials in England involving a plea of insanity shocked the nation and led to significant changes to the law. These and the most influential insanity defense trial in history are the subject of the next chapter.

3
Knowing Right from Wrong
The Trial of Daniel McNaughtan

> "Because the mind has a firm hold upon the body, it is quite often through the mind that illness arises, and my habit has always been to heal the mind before proceeding to the body."
>
> —Dr. Clitandre in *L'amour Médecin* by Molière

On January 20, 1843, Daniel McNaughtan shot Edward Drummond in the back "in the open street, and in the broad face of day."[1] Five days later, Drummond succumbed to his injuries and died. Drummond was not McNaughtan's intended target; rather, it was his employer, Prime Minister Sir Robert Peel, whom Drummond served as a private secretary. McNaughtan's desire to assassinate the Prime Minister stemmed from his belief, now more easily recognizable as a paranoid delusion, that the Tories had been persecuting him. McNaughtan's trial is widely considered the most significant insanity defense case in history, primarily because its outcome is still, almost two centuries later, the primary basis of the legal standards for insanity in the United States.[2]

The State of Psychiatry: Moral Management

Prior to 1800, there was no medical discipline known as psychiatry; however, by the time of McNaughtan's trial, the emerging field had benefited somewhat from the gradual shift over the previous three centuries to move explanations of mental illness away from the supernatural, which led to cruel and harsh methods of "treatment" for the afflicted, and more toward medical, psychological, and even social explanations for these puzzling afflictions. What we might call the "humanitarian turn" in the treatment of the mentally ill was accelerated by Enlightenment thought in the eighteenth and nineteenth centuries. The medical understanding of mental illness remained rudimentary; the major medical texts of the time indicated that "excessive irritation of the nerves" was the primary cause of madness.[3] The endeavor of psychiatric treatment was fundamentally a religious and moral one,[4] and the "lunatic asylum" continued to dominate the confinement of mentally ill people. Reformers of the time were focused on the conditions to which those confined were subjected. It was in the asylums that psychiatry developed as a means of managing (in other words, controlling) those in confinement.[5]

William Battie (1703–1776), the supervising physician at London's St. Luke's Asylum as well as an owner of private asylums, was an early proponent of the therapeutic potential of the institution.[6] British historians of psychiatry refer to Battie as the forerunner of his time. In his 1758 *Treatise on Madness*, he emphasized that mental disorder could be cured.[7] Denouncing the abominable treatments common at the time, Battie argued that *management* rather than *medicine* would yield greater success; he pushed for close individual contact to address each patient's particular needs,[8] foreshadowing the psychoanalytic theories that were still over a century away. According to Edward Shorter, Battie's work marked the birth of modern psychiatry, although his name has been largely erased.[9]

Following Battie, two major figures in reform efforts in England pioneered groundbreaking ideas on the function of asylums. First, William Hack Tuke (1732–1822) established the York Retreat in 1797. As a lay-led institution, York was somewhat of "a thorn in the side of the medical profession's call for a medical monopoly" over the jurisdiction of asylums.[10] Tuke, a Quaker, had a humanistic ideological orientation; he had also experienced the death of a close friend due to mistreatment in an asylum. He objected strongly to the use of harsh restraints as well as other common practices such as bloodletting, promoting instead supportive treatment by well-trained staff.[11] The model at York was to reflect "ideal bourgeois family life where patients and staff lived, dined, and worked together in settings where praise and blame as well as rewards and punishment enhanced recovery, all with the goal of restoring a healthy outlook and increased self-control."[12] Tuke's grandson, Samuel, first adopted the term "moral treatment" to describe the methodology of The Retreat, a term he borrowed from Pinel (described later in this chapter).[13] Second, John Conolly (1784–1860), superintendent at Hanwell Hospital, espoused the elimination of all restraints as well as other harsh treatments. Like William Hack Tuke, he placed great importance on having well-trained, compassionate staff who could "find constructive means of exerting a favorable influence on [patients'] lives,"[14] attempting to engage them in daily activities while living in comfortable accommodations and being treated with sympathy and kindness.

Another major figure in psychiatry, Phillippe Pinel[15] (1745–1826), a contemporary of the Tukes and Conolly, was at the same time pioneering significant reforms in France. According to Shorter, "in most conventional histories, . . . modern psychiatry begins with Pinel."[16] Prior to the French Revolution, the standard brutality of the asylum held true in Paris's Bicêtre and Salpêtriêre,[17] where "more than half of men admitted to the asylums died within a year from starvation, cold and disease."[18] Pinel's philosophy of treating mentally ill patients was inspired by the success of Bicêtre's superintendents, Jean Baptiste Pussin and his wife, in treating patients with sympathy rather than brutality. Such treatment was a novel concept at the time, but it was driven by the sentiments behind the Revolution, after which Pinel concluded that gaining the confidence of the patients (rather than dominating them into submission) was the key to successful treatment.[19] Pinel began the practice of taking patient histories and recording their responses to various treatments; his attitude toward prevailing methodologies was skeptical at best, and he traded in physical remedies for what came to be called "management of the mind."[20] The success of his nurturing approach led him to conclude that organic or biological explanations for madness were wrong, and his 1801 book, *Traité Médico-Philosophique sur l'Aliénation Mentale: Ou la Manie* (translated into English in 1806 as *Treatise on Insanity*), catapulted moral therapy to the fore of treatment protocols.[21] For Pinel, "moral treatment" (*traitment moral*) was likely ideologically quite different from Samuel Tuke's use of the concept, as *moral* in French refers more to "morale" or esteem,[22] or simply "mental,"[23] than to the moralistic connotation of its translation to English. Influenced by "Enlightenment psychology and a progressive social philosophy acquired in the salons during the [1780s], Pinel's head was filled with reformist ideals of both a humanitarian and therapeutic nature."[24] Pinel believed that "the experience of incarceration itself" could be used "in a healing manner."[25] Pinel's student Jean-Etienne Esquirol, who became the administrator of the psychiatric ward at Salpêtriêre in 1811, made his mark with a doctoral thesis in 1802 on "the role of the 'passions' in mental illness,"[26] again highlighting the Enlightenment dualism that characterized this period's thought on the function of the mind. Esquirol's ideas represented a departure, however, from the emphasis on a neurobiological explanation for madness at the time.[27] Even the centuries-old practices at Bedlam were influenced by the shift toward moral treatment, as John Haslam, its medical officer, agreed that taking some time to talk to the patients might actually aid in their treatment.[28]

The more colloquially termed "mad doctors" were formally referred to as "alienists" during the profession's early years and through the twentieth century, as in those who treated "mental alienation."[29] The dominant belief was that madness was the result of a disturbance "of internal, rational discipline on the part of the sufferer,"[30] reinforcing the dualistic ideology that undergirded the practice. Although Pinel was the first to suggest in 1801 that "madness need not signify a deficit in reasoning powers,"[31] in other words, that mental illness was not synonymous with totalizing incapacitation of all normal functioning, the rhetorical structure of legal insanity only permitted such an articulation of madness in McNaughtan's trial, and the sane/insane binary has continued to plague insanity defense cases ever since.

Psychology and the Law

By now, men of law had been working for some time to establish correct procedures for dealing with mentally ill criminal defendants. As early as the thirteenth century, Judge Henry de Bracton wrote about criminal insanity. In his treatise on the common law, he suggested that a crime requires "the will to harm," and that children, animals, and madmen lacked the capacity to possess such will.[32] The comparison of "madmen" to children and animals dominated legal thought for centuries, as will be seen in several of the examples in the next section. While less explicitly articulated, this trope is very much evident in discourse on mental illness even today. Eventually, the legal criteria were narrowed to "the wild beast test," which defines insanity for legal purposes as "stark raving mania" or "florid melancholia."[33] There was no consideration for varying degrees of insanity or temporary insanity. In Bracton's time, a verdict of not guilty by reason of insanity did not exist; thus, the more common practice was to treat mentally ill criminal defendants as children in the eyes of the court.

Sir Matthew Hale was the first chief justice in England to attempt to apply theories of medicine to criminal law. His 1736 publication *The History of the Pleas of the Crown* influenced judicial practice for more than two centuries. Hale attempted to distinguish between people of low intelligence and those with mental illness. For Hale, mental illness could be permanent, or it could be lunacy, which was madness with lucid intervals (these were assumed to be influenced by lunar phases, as indicated by the word "lunacy"). Hale acknowledged the possibility of partial insanity as a defense, suggesting that the defendant must possess less understanding than a child in order for it to be exculpatory and insisted that the burden of proof must be on the defendant in such cases.[34]

Prior to McNaughtan

In the eighteenth century, criminal insanity cases were rare, but a few garnered a great deal of attention due to the social status of either the defendant or the victim. Since these cases were reported thoroughly in the popular presses, they became the precedents on which evolving standards for legal insanity were determined. More significantly, they introduced the use of skillful defense attorneys and expert witnesses in cases involving a plea of insanity, both of which have continued to influence the practices of insanity defense trials.[35]

The first fully reported insanity defense trial was that of "Mad Ned" Arnold who unsuccessfully attempted to assassinate Lord Onslow in 1723. Onslow, according to Arnold, had been persecuting him. The judge's instructions to the jury in this case were based explicitly on the "wild beast" test. The judge posed two questions to the jury: first, whether the defendant completely lacked understanding and memory, knowing no more what he was doing "than an infant, a brute, or a wild beast," and second, whether the defendant was able to distinguish between good and evil at the time of the crime.[36] The jury found Arnold guilty, but he was later granted a royal pardon at the behest of his victim, Lord Onslow. While the "wild beast" test dominated Arnold's trial, the emerging "right from wrong" determination was beginning to make headway as the dominant paradigm for determining legal insanity.

In 1760, Earl Ferrers, an aristocrat, was charged with the murder of his former employee. Not permitted defense counsel, Ferrers protested the injustice of "requiring a lunatic to prove himself insane without the assistance of counsel."[37] The prosecution emphasized evidence of premeditation as proof that Ferrers was sane enough to be held responsible, while Ferrers argued that he suffered from occasional insanity and was prone to be driven to a poor mental condition.[38] The significance of Ferrers's trial is the emergence of consideration of temporary insanity and "irresistible impulse," which would be further developed in the nineteenth century. Of additional importance, Ferrers's trial marked the beginning of expert testimony in insanity defense trials; in his case, superintendent of Bethlem Hospital, Dr. Monro, testified and attempted to provide a definition of "lunacy." Dr. Monro offered three common symptoms of lunacy: "'uncommon fury' not caused by liquor but raised by it; violence against others or the self; and . . . jealousy or suspicion without reasonable cause."[39] While Dr. Monro's explanation adequately encompassed Ferrers's alleged condition, he was unable to state conclusively that lunatics did not understand their actions. Ferrers was convicted and subsequently hanged in front of a large crowd who "seemed to regard the execution of a lord for the murder of a commoner as a noteworthy triumph of . . . justice."[40]

James Hadfield, a veteran of the Napoleonic Wars who had suffered head injuries during his service, had been known to behave irrationally on occasion since returning to civilian life. In 1800, he developed the delusion that the world was coming to an end and that "like Jesus Christ he was to sacrifice his life for the salvation of others."[41] He believed that if he attempted to assassinate the King, the crowd would intervene and kill him. At Drury Lane Theatre, he attempted to carry out his plan but was captured instead and brought to trial for high treason. The nature of his crime afforded him more privileges as a defendant, so he was allowed to have defense counsel, call witnesses, and address the court. Thomas Erskine, son of a Lord, Member of Parliament, and also the most sought-after defense attorney of the time, agreed to represent Hadfield. Erskine conceded that Hadfield did not meet the requirements for either the wild beast or right from wrong test, as he had clearly premeditated and understood the consequences of his actions. He skillfully argued, however, that both of those tests, if strictly applied, would exclude almost anyone. Erskine vastly expanded the use of expert medical testimony, producing several doctors who examined Hadfield after the shooting, and all of them testified that the defendant's actions were the direct result of his brain injury.[42] With twenty witnesses yet to testify for the defense, the judge stopped the trial and invited the jury "to consider a special verdict of not guilty 'being under the influence of insanity at the time.'"[43] This special acquittal was designed to provide for the continued detention of Hadfield, as a standard not guilty verdict might have allowed him to go free. Parliament then quickly rushed through a provision for the "safe custody" of mentally ill criminal defendants, the Criminal Lunatics Act 1800, which retroactively applied to Hadfield.[44] This ad hoc statute allowed legislators to avoid the task of crafting a precise definition of legal insanity as well as official court procedures to accompany such cases, which criminologist Richard Moran suggests was "designed to limit the rights of defendants charged with criminal offences . . . [and] deter the mentally ill through the fear or dread of punishment."[45] Hadfield spent the remainder of his life institutionalized where he went on to kill another patient in the hospital. According to Bartee and Bartee, the primary significance of *Hadfield* was that it "showed how a persuasive defense attorney, utilizing expert witnesses, could sway judges and jury to accept a new test . . . for criminal insanity."[46]

In 1812, John Bellingham, convinced that the British government owed him some form of compensation for his failed business ventures, shot and killed Prime Minister Spencer Percival in the lobby of the House of Commons. The trial took place only four days following the incident. Bellingham was provided defense counsel only one day prior to the trial, leaving no time to adequately prepare a defense or secure expert witnesses. The prosecution relied on the precedents set in *Arnold* and *Ferrers*. Lord Chief Justice Mansfield, openly distraught over the death of Percival, determined that the defendant's state of mind was irrelevant. Bellingham was found guilty and executed a mere eight days after the crime.[47]

Another assassination attempt, this time against Queen Victoria in 1840, raised important issues for mentally ill criminal defendants. The trial of her would-be assassin, eighteen-year-old Edward Oxford, demonstrated both an increasing acceptance of mental illness as exculpatory and the need for more clear standards and procedures for cases involving mentally ill defendants. Oxford fired two pistols at the Queen, though she was not hit. No ammunition was discovered at the scene of the crime; however, some documents were found at Oxford's residence that led to some suspicion of his involvement with a conspiracy.[48] Oxford's defense counsel first argued that since the pistols were not loaded, he was guilty of a misdemeanor at most, and secondly, that madness ran in his family, securing the testimony of several medical experts who claimed that he was mentally ill. The jury found Oxford "not guilty, he being insane at the time."[49] He was ordered to be detained "at Her Majesty's Pleasure," after which he spent twenty-seven years in Bethlem Hospital before being released. The doctors at Bethlem regarded him as sane, and Oxford maintained that the whole thing was a childish prank motivated by "a foolish love of notoriety."[50] The proximity of Oxford's trial to McNaughtan's would ultimately lead to a radical reformulation of the insanity defense that has remained the predominant standard for the nearly two centuries since.

McNaughtan's Trial

Immediately after shooting Drummond, McNaughtan was taken into custody where he refused to give any information about himself, although he reportedly maintained a polite demeanor. The day following the shooting, McNaughtan was brought before Chief Magistrate Hall for an examination. After the evidence had been presented, McNaughtan declined to make a statement; however, he quickly changed his mind after being escorted to the waiting area, at which time he asked to be returned to the court in order to make what would be his first and only public statement regarding his motives. He said: "The Tories in my native city have compelled me to do this. They follow, persecute me wherever I go, and have entirely destroyed my peace of mind. They followed me to France, into Scotland, and all over England. In fact, they follow me wherever I go. I cannot sleep nor get rest from them in consequence of the course they pursue towards me. I believe they have driven me into a consumption. I am sure I shall never be the man I was. I used to have good health and good strength but I have not now. They have accused me of crimes of which I am not guilty, they do everything in their power to harass and persecute me; in fact, they wish to murder me. It can be proved by evidence. That's all I have to say."[51] Following his speech, the statement was read aloud and signed by McNaughtan who was then returned to confinement awaiting trial.

After Drummond died, McNaughtan was brought before a grand jury. The recorder delivered the charge of murder and advised the jurors that the question of the defendant's sanity should not be addressed, because such a determination could only be made during the course of a proper trial, while "the grand jury's job [was] to determine whether the act committed, if it were done by a person of sound mind, would have amounted to murder."[52] Assurances were given to the jury that if the defendant was in fact insane, that no undue hardship would befall him as the law already provided for such cases. The recorder then read the legal definition of murder to the grand jury: "When a person of sound memory, and age of discretion, unlawfully killeth any reasonable creature in being, and under King's peace, with malice aforethought, either express or implied, so as the party die of the wound within a year and a day after the same, it is murder; but the offence cannot be committed by an *idiot, lunatic, or infant*."[53] Although his prior instructions suggested that the question of insanity not be addressed, he added that the defense would have to prove that, at the time of the crime, the defendant was incapable of distinguishing right from wrong in order to prove legal insanity; in other words, the defense must show he lacked the ability to engage in reason. The recorder further noted that the fact that McNaughtan mistakenly killed Drummond when he instead intended to kill Peel in no way mitigated his guilt because the law still "presumed malice aforethought."[54] Finally, in a radical departure from his duties, the recorder offered the following commentary on the concept of mental illness as exculpatory: "If the fact of the commission of any great crime was in itself to be held or considered a proof of insanity, there would be no safety or security for the public."[55] This statement highlights one of the primary tropes of sanism: the trope of pandemonium, which holds that the insanity defense diminishes the deterrent effect of the law. The following day, the grand jury returned with a charge of murder. While there were no codified standards in place yet to specifically address the issue of mental illness as a mitigating factor, the existing legal definition of murder contained the language within it as a sort of safety valve: "the offence cannot be committed by an idiot, lunatic, or infant," which accurately reflects this period's understanding of mentally ill persons as either stupid, stark raving mad, or childlike in nature, which was shared across the disciplinary boundaries of medicine and law.

At his arraignment two days after the grand jury's decision, McNaughtan refused to answer when asked how he wished to plead. After some encouragement, he replied that he "was driven to desperation by persecution," and when pressed further to state whether he was guilty or not guilty, he stated, "I am guilty of firing."[56] Lord Chief Abinger decided that this amounted to a plea of not guilty, and Mr. Clarkson, attorney for the defense, was granted a postponement in order that a proper defense might be prepared. The trial began six weeks later.

McNaughtan's trial was widely publicized and drew a large crowd of spectators including "persons of high status who had obtained tickets,"[57] Charles Dickens among them. In his opening statement for the prosecution, solicitor general Sir William Follett attempted to preempt the strategy of the defense, telling the jury that their decision would depend on the defendant's state of mind at the time of the crime: "If you believe that when he fired the pistol, he was incapable of distinguishing between right and wrong . . . that he did not know he was violating the law both of God and man: then, undoubtedly, he is entitled to your acquittal."[58] He emphasized, however, that the absence of a complete lack of understanding of the nature of the act would require a guilty verdict, reinforcing the "all-or-nothing" approach to mental illness, which holds that legal insanity must mean totalizing loss of reason such that no evidence of "normal" functioning be present. Follett delivered a legal history of insanity pleas, as was the convention for such a trial; he quoted Hale, discussed Erskine's defense in *Hadfield*, the decision in *Bellingham*. He then provided a brief history of McNaughtan's life, primarily for the purpose of establishing his sanity: McNaughtan had run a business and resided in lodging houses with what was described as rational and responsible conduct, all of which surely proved that he could not possibly be of diseased mind. The prosecution's evidence reinforced Follett's opening statement: McNaughtan's landlady, one of his friends, and a former teacher were called as witnesses to attest to his mental health, and all three confirmed that, in their interactions with the defendant, "he had never exhibited any evidence of mental aberration."[59] Here we see evidence of the trope of common sense, that any reasonable person can tell if someone is mentally ill, along with the value placed on such testimony in a trial in which an insanity defense has been raised. This evidence concluded the prosecution's case, at which time Chief Justice Tindal granted defense counsel, Mr. Cockburn, a continuance until the following morning.

The defense of McNaughtan was heavily influenced by the work of Sir Isaac Ray.[60] Cockburn opened the next day by insinuating that the widely publicized case and the ensuing public outrage over the assassination of a high-ranking official might impede his client's right to a fair trial; however, he then went on to flatter the jury, telling them that he was confident in their abilities to be fair and impartial, as good British subjects must,[61] appealing to their senses of patriotism and duty. Cockburn conceded that his client did indeed shoot Mr. Drummond as well as the prosecution's claim that the decision would rest on the defendant's state of mind at the time of the crime. He then supplied them with an alternate definition of insanity that reinforced the rhetoric of the prevailing Enlightenment ideology: "Madness is a disease of the body operating upon the mind,"[62] highlighting mind/body dualism, while suggesting that a bodily ailment could affect the functioning of the faculties of reason. Cockburn went on to describe the mind as divided into two separate and distinct compartments, one housing intellect (perception, judgment, reasoning), and the other moral faculties (sentiments, affections, passions). He claimed that modern science had determined that either compartment might be diseased while the other remained perfectly intact, the diseased compartment still having the capacity to cause "fearful delusions."[63] In doing so, he attempted to rebut the assumption that a total lack of rationality was necessary to achieve legal insanity, and instead, that it was possible to observe some "normal" functioning in a person who was otherwise mentally ill. Cockburn chided the prosecution for its reliance on legal authorities to define what was clearly in the domain of medical science, reminding the jury of *Bowler* and *Bellinger* in which both defendants were executed in the wake of public outrage; he argued that each of these men would likely be considered legally insane by the current standards and urged the jury to avoid making the same barbaric mistake with McNaughtan. Cockburn's version of McNaughtan's life portrayed a long history of precursors to mental illness; he closed his speech by reminding the jury that were they to find the defendant not guilty by reason of insanity, he would be safely confined to an asylum where he could do no further harm[64] in an attempt to subvert the trope of danger that so often lurks in the minds of jurors and publics. Witnesses for the defense portrayed McNaughtan as a man who had long been afflicted by delusions of persecution, and the testimony of several medical experts sealed the case. Dr. Thomas Monro, who had examined McNaughtan four weeks after his arrest, claimed "that he did not entertain 'the slightest doubt' that the defendant's *moral faculties were impaired* by extraordinary delusion."[65] Six additional medical examiners supported Monro's testimony. Mr. Forbes Winslow, author of *Plea of Insanity in Medical Cases*, claimed that McNaughtan's delusions caused him to commit the crime, after which Chief Justice Tindal asked the prosecutor if he had any medical experts who would testify contrary to the expert witnesses of the defense. When Follett replied, "No, my Lord," Tindal, in an unprecedented move, stopped the trial.[66]

In his closing argument, Follett made an attempt to recover the case for the prosecution by reminding the jury that "the 'attainment of public justice'" was the ultimate goal of the trial.[67] In his instructions, however, the judge "practically told [the jury] to find the defendant not guilty by reason of insanity": "The whole of medical evidence is on one side. . . . It seems almost unnecessary that I should go through the [other] evidence. If he was not sensible at the time he committed that act, that it was the violation of the law of God or man, undoubtedly he was not responsible for that act or liable for any punishment whatever flowing from that act. . . . If . . . you think the prisoner capable of distinguishing between right and wrong, then he was a responsible agent and liable to take all the penalties the law imposes."[68] The jury simply huddled in the jury box rather than retiring to chambers for deliberation and returned their verdict in under two minutes: They found McNaughtan not guilty on the grounds of insanity.

The Public Response

The local press had been reporting on McNaughtan's case since his arrest. Even before the question of insanity was raised in the courtroom, reporters immediately began speculating on the issue in print. A reporter from the *Times* who was present at McNaughtan's first court appearance noted that the prisoner appeared "cool and collected" and offered the opinion that McNaughtan showed no apparent evidence of insanity.[69] Another reporter commented that while McNaughtan's first and only statement as to the motive for his actions made him seem mentally unsound, his appearance was "extremely healthful."[70] Both of these statements exemplify the trope of common sense. Some observers expressed concern that McNaughtan was feigning insanity and "that his statement had been designed to lay the foundation for a plea of not guilty by reason of insanity,"[71] illustrating the trope of fakery. After McNaughtan was indicted for murder by the grand jury, the London newspapers were abuzz with expressions of public sentiment regarding the case, which frequently offered another of the well-worn tropes: pandemonium. The primary response was a desire for retribution, along with fear that exempting anyone from punishment for any reason weakened the deterrent effect of the law. An editorial in the *Times* expressed hope that minor incidents of odd behavior in McNaughtan's past would not be seen by the "soft headed" as evidence that he was insane, concluding that "those laws are most merciful which deter men from the most atrocious crimes."[72] Articles in the *Morning Herald* cautioned that it would be a mistake to think that insane persons could not be deterred from crime, drawing on *Bellingham* and *Oxford* as proof that failure to properly punish mentally ill criminals had lead to similar crimes; since Bellingham was executed and Oxford was not, according to the author, "the former remained without imitators, while the latter had no fewer than four."[73] Reporters for the *Manchester Courier* took the position that the political violence of the time was to blame, arguing that it was "the festering anti-Tory rhetoric in an unsound mind that led to the murder of Edward Drummond."[74] McNaughtan was of Scottish heritage, thus, Scottish reporters were slightly more sympathetic to his plight; they claimed that there was substantial evidence as to the defendant's insanity, so he could not be held accountable for his crime. One reporter took the most progressive stance, writing, "The 'deprivation of reason' is one of the worst curses that can befall an individual, and to punish a person for being ill is 'to inflict death because of disease.'"[75]

Following the verdict, an article in the *Times* lamented the result, claiming that even if McNaughtan had actually been persecuted in the way his delusions led him to believe he had, he should still be held legally accountable for his crime. An article in the *Standard* claimed that "monomaniacs" (the term at the time for persons suffering from insanity in only one aspect) could ethically be punished because their mental defects were the result of their own indulgence and depraved habits. An article in the *Illustrated London News* suggested that those who willingly intoxicate themselves with "doctrines of socialism and infidelity" cannot claim to be entirely without legal or moral responsibility.[76] These responses reinforce the moralism attached to mental illness in their emphasis on the sufferer's own responsibility for his condition.

Finally, the press also raised the issue of the role of medical experts in legal issues, expressing the trope of illegitimacy that has always loomed over the medical study of mental health. An article in the *Times* expressed concern "that the physicians had invaded the traditional province of the judiciary," saying that "'the judge in his treatment of the madman yields to the decision of the physician, and the physician in his treatment becomes the judge,'"[77] which also highlights the disciplinary territoriality that marks insanity defense trials. Another article in the *Standard* decried the way that "mad doctors" were dictating the law, and, worse, that the court gave credence to their "absurd" dictums. The *Examiner* questioned the reliability of the diagnoses provided by these experts since none of them had examined McNaughtan until after he committed the crime, at which time his life literally depended on his being found insane.[78] Only the *Weekly Chronicle* exhibited some sympathy in an article that argued the insane could not be deterred by punishment because they were "not subject to the ordinary constraints on human behavior." The proposed solution, however, was less charitable; the writer suggested that all monomaniacs be immediately restrained in order to protect the public.[79]

Following the verdict, the public was outraged. Several newspapers published the following satirical poem by Thomas Campbell that highlights three of the tropes of sanism:

CONGRATULATIONS ON A LATE ACQUITTAL

Ye people of England: exult and be glad,
For ye're now at the will of the merciless mad.
Why say ye that but three authorities reign—
Crown, Commons, and Lords!—You omit the insane!
They're a privileg'd class, whom no statute controls,
And their murderous charter exists in their souls.
Do they wish to spill blood—they have only to play
A few pranks—get asylum'd a month and a day—
Then heigh! to escape from the mad doctor's keys,
And to pistol or stab whomever they please.
No the dog has the human-like wit in creation
He resembles most nearly our own generation:
Then if madmen for murder escape with impunity,
Why deny a poor dog the same noble immunity?
So if dog or man bit you, beware being nettled,
For crime is no crime—when the mind is unsettled.[80]

Line two illustrates the trope of danger in suggesting that the good citizens of England are "at the will of the merciless mad." In lines five and six, Campbell refers to the insane as a "privileg'd class" with hearts full of malice who cannot be controlled, again relying on the trope of danger. In lines seven through nine, the trope of fakery emerges when Campbell suggests that people can get away with murder by feigning insanity and spending just a short time in an asylum, after which they can escape to do further harm, returning, in line ten, to the trope of danger. In the closing lines the trope of pandemonium emerges, when Campbell uses the phrase "escape with impunity" to emphasize the failure to achieve retribution in an insanity defense, and he suggests that crimes are not crimes for the mentally ill.

The Effects on the Insanity Defense

Following the McNaughtan verdict, Queen Victoria, having recently been the target of a failed assassination by a defendant who claimed insanity as a defense, urged the Prime Minister to take action. The House of Lords met for the purpose of addressing what some saw as a defect in the law that allowed "persons laboring under partial insanity to be relieved of all criminal responsibility."[81] Lord Brougham openly expressed his great displeasure with

McNaughtan's trial, suggesting that the published accounts must be inaccurate "since they revealed so many improprieties," including inadmissible evidence and witness statements, the abrupt termination of the trial by Tindal before the prosecution had the chance to call any medical experts, and the fact that the prosecution was not given the chance to rebut the arguments put forth by the defense. The chancellor decided on March 13, 1843, that all Supreme Court judges would be summoned to assist with amending the law where it concerned defenses of insanity. Lord Lyndhurst was asked to formulate a series of questions raised by McNaughtan's trial to be addressed when all of the judges convened.[82]

This event took place on June 19, 1843, and the following questions were posed to all in attendance:

> 1st What is the law respecting alleged crimes committed by persons afflicted with insane delusions, in respect of one or more particular subjects or persons: as, for instance, where at the time of the commission of the alleged crime, the accused knew he was acting contrary to the law, but did the act complained of with a view, under the influence of insane delusion, of redressing or revenging some supposed grievance or injury, or of producing some supposed public benefit?
>
> 2nd What are the proper questions to be submitted by the jury, when a person alleged to be afflicted with insane delusion respecting one or more particular subjects or persons, is charged with the commission of a crime (murder, for example), and insanity is set up as a defence?
>
> 3rd In what terms ought the question to be left to the jury, as to the prisoner's state of mind at the time when the act was committed?
>
> 4th If a person under an insane delusion as to existing facts, commits an offence in consequence thereof, is he hereby excused?
>
> 5th Can a medical man conversant with the disease of insanity, who never saw the prisoner previously to the trial, but who was present during the whole trial and the examination of all of the witnesses, be asked his opinion as to the state of the prisoner's mind at the time of the commission of the alleged crime, or his opinion whether the prisoner was conscious at the time of doing the act, that he was acting contrary to the law, or whether he was labouring under any and what delusion at the time?[83]

The judges drafted answers to these five questions. Chief Justice Tindal delivered their response with the caveat that it is difficult to apply general principles to any particular case without having heard the evidence in court. A summary of the judges' responses is as follows:

> (1) If a person commits a criminal act "under the influence of an insane delusion, with a view of redressing or revenging some supposed grievance or injury or of producing some public benefit, he is nevertheless punishable if he knew at the time he was acting contrary to the law."
>
> (2) and (3) A person is presumed sane unless it can be "clearly proven that, at the time of the committing of the act, the party accused was labouring under such a defect of reason, from disease of the mind, as not to know the nature and quality of the act he was doing; or, if he did know it, then he did not know he was doing what was wrong. . . . The mode of putting the latter part of the question to the jury. . . . has generally been, *whether the accused at the time of doing the act knew the difference between right and wrong*."
>
> (4) A person labouring under "partial delusion only, and [who] is not in other respects insane, . . . must be considered in the same situation, as to responsibility, as if the facts, in respect to which the delusion exists, were real."
>
> (5) A medical doctor, who never examined the accused, cannot be asked his opinion of the defendant's state of mind at the time he committed the offense. Such a question involves a judgment of the truth of the facts, which is the province of the jury.[84]

These responses became known as the McNaughtan Rules (commonly referred to as the M'Naghten Rules due to the many versions of the spelling of McNaughtan that were published).[85] The combined answer to the second and third questions, that the standard for legal insanity is that, as a result of mental disease or defect, the defendant did not know "the nature and quality of the act," or, if he did know, that he did not know it was wrong, has remained the most significant and widely used test of legal insanity still today in both England and the United States.

In their analysis of the insanity defense of John Hinckley Jr., Bonnie, Jeffries, and Low note three significant features of the McNaughtan Rules' formulation: "First, it is predicated on proof that the defendant was suffering some form of mental disease or defect"; second, "once such a 'disease' is shown . . . the interest of the law under this test is in the ability of the defendant to 'know' certain things," which is why this standard is sometimes referred to as the "cognitive" test; and finally, the McNaughtan Rules define two things the defendant must know in order to be guilty: One "is the 'nature and quality of the act,' . . . the other is that the act 'was wrong' . . . the question is whether the defendant was 'capable' of knowing these things, that is whether the mental illness had deprived the defendant of the capacity to know what 'normal' people are able to know about their behavior."[86] The central ambiguity of the McNaughtan Rules, specifically with regard to the meaning of the words "know" and "wrong," became a major point of criticism over the next few decades. Critics argued that these standards were too narrow in scope and did not account for those criminals who may have the cognitive capacity to know right from wrong but lack the volitional capacity to control their actions. This issue was taken up in the late nineteenth century, which is the subject of the next chapter.

4

Late Nineteenth-Century Insanity Defense Jurisprudence

Parsons, Davis, *and the "Irresistible Impulse" Test*

> "Madness was no longer to strike fear into people's hearts, nor would it be able to—it was itself to be afraid, helplessly, irrevocably afraid, entirely in thrall to the pedagogy of good sense, truth and morality."
>
> —Michel Foucault

Psychology in America

The development of the asylum system in America drew its inspiration from Europe and followed a similar course in its humanitarian reforms, while the understanding of the causes and treatments of mental illness, still rudimentary at best, also continued to develop. Beginning in the 1840s, the government wanted to gather data on idiocy and lunacy, terms that actually appeared on the census that year. By 1880, the census contained seven categories of mental illness: "mania, melancholia, monomania, paresis, dementia, dipsomania and epilepsy."[1]

A ward for the insane at Philadelphia's Pennsylvania Hospital, cofounded by the Society of Friends in 1752, was among America's earliest hospital-based settings for patients suffering from mental illness. It was here that Benjamin Rush (1746–1813) practiced. Rush, widely considered the father of American psychiatry, embraced many of the European methods, citing Dr. Booerhave, the Leyden physician who had initiated near-drowning as a cure for madness, as his own inspiration.[2] Rush was firmly in the biomedical camp in terms of explaining madness, attributing it to abnormal circulation of the blood to the brain, which he believed could be caused by any number of events or habits, including extreme weather, hard labor, masturbation, or excessive imagination. Rush's primary methods involved the usual treatments of the time: bloodletting (many of his contemporaries saw his as excessive; one of his patients was reportedly bled of four gallons of blood over the course of forty-seven treatments), the use of blistering agents (to either draw blood away from or allow prolonged discharge from the overheated head and brain), spinning while strapped horizontally to a mechanically operated board (to restore proper circulation to the brain), along with the standard tactics of restraints, fear, and intimidation.[3] Rush's "Tranquilizer Chair" was the first American psychiatric treatment to be exported to asylums in Europe: Patients were strapped into the chair from head to toe, immobilizing them completely, their sight blocked. A bucket beneath served as a toilet, as confinement could go from hours to, in some reported cases, months. The powers of this chair to make even the most irascible inmates gentle and submissive were lauded on both sides of the Atlantic.[4] As the beacon of American medicine of his time, Rush was not without many imitators, and his 1812 book, *Medical Inquiries and Observations Upon the Diseases of the Mind*, was the first American text on psychiatry. His treatment protocols, however, very soon fell out of favor due to the rise of moral treatment.

Eventually finding the facility at Pennsylvania Hospital too small and its procedures too archaic based on European reforms, the Society of Friends established the Frankford Retreat, modeled after England's York Retreat, on land purchased outside the city. At Frankford, "chains were never to be used to confine patients and the 'law of kindness' was to prevail."[5] The Hartford Retreat was founded in 1824 by the state medical society of Connecticut under the supervision of physicians Samuel Woodward (1787–1850) and Ely Todd. Woodward was another of America's early proponents of "the change from manacles, chains, by-locks, and confining chairs, to the present system of kindness, confidence, social intercourse, labor, religious teaching, and freedom from restraint."[6] Woodward claimed that he was able to discharge 80 to 90 percent of his patients, and his claims of curability garnered national attention, spurring the founding of additional state-funded hospitals throughout the United States.[7] Another physician, Pliny Earle (1809–1892), would eventually call into question such claims of curability, and his major contribution to the development of the mental health system in the United States was an emphasis on "the importance of accurate hospital records."[8]

One of the nineteenth century's most notable names where the treatment of mental illness is concerned was not a psychiatrist or even a physician: Dorothea Dix (1802–1887) was a schoolteacher in Massachusetts whose investigations into the abominable conditions of privately funded treatment institutions lead to significant reforms. Dix argued that "insanity was a product of inhumane conditions in society; hence, society should assume full responsibility for the care of its victims,"[9] and her efforts established the "modern principle of public responsibility for the mentally ill."[10] Her work over four decades played a significant role in the building of thirty state hospitals for people with mental illness.

One of Samuel Woodward's followers, John S. Butler (1803–1890), author of *The Curability of Insanity* (1887), was selected by Dix as Boston Lunatic Hospital's superintendent in 1839, and four years later, he took on the same role at "the Hartford Retreat, where his vigorous leadership brought it to the vanguard of mental hospitals for the next 40 years."[11] Butler, along with his contemporaries in the United States and Europe, espoused humane treatment, though one controversial feature of his treatment was to separate patients with acute illnesses from those with chronic illnesses, as he believed exposure to the chronically ill might impede the progress of those experiencing acute symptoms. Furthermore, Butler wrote this about prevention: "We can also more efficiently apply the means of insanity's prevention and remedy, when we can better measure its varied and pernicious causes, such as erroneous educational and social influences, neglect of family training to reverence and obedience, sensational reading, evil habits of body and mind, and idle, aimless, or sensual lives, and learn more exactly as we shall surely learn, how very early in life the predisposing causes of insanity are planted in the child."[12] Here we can see an understanding that material conditions can influence the mental health of individuals; however, the emphasis on morality still looms large.

Perhaps the best-known American psychiatrist of the time was Isaac Ray (1807–1881). His text on what is now commonly referred to as forensic psychiatry, *A Treatise on the Medical Jurisprudence of Insanity*, "became the standard for the mental health profession for the better part of the nineteenth century."[13] Ray was very interested in the intersection of mental illness and the law and was concerned that "'the law of insanity, especially that relative to criminal cases, [was] still loose, vacillating, and greatly behind the present state of knowledge of that disease.'"[14] However, by the time *A Treatise on the Medical Jurisprudence of Insanity* was in its fifth edition in 1871, Ray seems to have felt that much progress had been made, writing: "The bench and the bar have yielded more or less to the progress of ideas, and, in spite of some attempts to maintain the old landmarks, they have, on the whole, liberally responded to the requirements of science. Society, too, has become more tolerant of innovations upon the time-honored philosophy of crime, and more willing to accept the conclusions of science."[15] The views of Ray and his contemporaries had a significant impact on the way the insanity defense evolved in the latter part of the nineteenth century, as we will see in the discussion of *Parsons v. State*.

Parsons v. State

On January 31, 1885, Nancy Parsons's daughter Joe shot Bennett Parsons (Nancy's husband and Joe's father) at Nancy's urging. At the time of the murder, Nancy Parsons believed her husband to be in possession of supernatural power "to inflict her with disease, and power by means of a supernatural trick to take her life . . . [which] had caused [her] to be sick and in bad health for a long time."[16]

At this time, the American legal system had adopted, without modification, the insanity defense standards outlined by the McNaughtan Rules from England, so the decision[17] was to be made on the basis of the defendants' abilities to "know right from wrong." The defense asserted a plea of insanity on behalf of both Mrs. Parsons and her daughter. The record from the appellate court reads, "The evidence on behalf of [the] defendants tended to show that . . . Joe Parsons was, at the time of said killing, and had always been, an idiot; and that . . . Nancy Parsons was, at the time of said killing, insane."[18] Furthermore, due to Mrs. Parsons's belief that her husband's supernatural powers were adversely affecting her health, she "was under the insane delusion that she was in great danger of the loss of her life from [her husband], to be effected by a supernatural trick."[19] Evidence of generational insanity in the families of the defendants was introduced, including testimony by a Mrs. James Nail, a longtime acquaintance of the family, who testified "that 'she had known Joe Parsons from her infancy, that she has been idiotic all her life, and she is idiotic now.'"[20] An objection was raised by the state to this evidence, however, and it was sustained. The jury was instructed as follows: "When insanity is relied on as a defense to crime, and such insanity consists of a delusion merely, and the defendant is not shown to be otherwise insane, then such delusion is no justification or excuse for homicide, unless the perpetrator was insanely deluded into the belief of the existence of a fact or state of facts which, if true, would justify or excuse the homicide under law applicable to sane persons."[21] At the request of the state, further instructions were provided that stated "only insanity of a chronic or permanent nature which, on being proved, is presumed to continue," and that "[if] the jury believe, from all the testimony, that the defendants at the time of the killing were in such a state of mind as to know that the act they were committing was unlawful and morally wrong, they are responsible as a sane person, if the jury believe they committed the act with which they are charged."[22] Further instructions, which were requested by the jury in writing and refused by the court, stated:

> In order to constitute a crime, the accused must have memory and intelligence sufficient to know that the act she is about to commit is wrong, to remember and understand that if she commits the act she will be punished, and, besides this, reason and will to enable her to comprehend and choose between the supposed advantage at the gratification to be obtained by the criminal act and the immunity from

> punishment which she will secure from abstaining from it. . . . If the jury [believes] from the evidence that the prisoners or either of them was moved to action by an insane impulse controlling their will or their judgment, then they are, or the one so affected is, not guilty of the crime charged. . . . If the jury believe from the evidence that the prisoners committed the act in a manner which would be criminal and unlawful, if they were sane, the verdict should be 'not guilty,' if the killing was an offspring or product of the mental disease in the prisoner.[23]

The jury for the City Court of Birmingham returned a verdict of guilty of murder in the second degree. The defendants appealed the verdict, which was heard by the Supreme Court of Alabama. The conviction was reversed on July 28, 1887, at which time the "control" test came to define the next rhetorical shift in the standards for legal insanity. While the McNaughtan Rules used the "knowledge" or "cognitive" test (did the defendant know right from wrong at the time of the crime?), Parsons created an additional dimension: "freedom of will" (that is, the question of whether mental disease or defect could destroy a person's capacity to *choose* between right and wrong even if she were able to *know* the difference).[24]

Alabama Supreme Court Justice Somerville authored the opinion in which the lower court's decision was reversed. He writes of an "imperious sense of duty" in reopening the subject of insanity as it relates to issues of law, writing of the court's "conviction that the law of insanity as declared by the courts on many points, and especially the rule of criminal accountability, and the assumed tests of disease, to that extent which wafers [*sic*] legal irresponsibility, have not kept pace with the progress of thought and discovery in the present advanced stages of medical science."[25] Here we see an exceedingly rare moment in which the inadequacies of the law pertaining to insanity in relation to the "advanced" medical knowledge of the time are acknowledged by a judicial authority. Somerville might be thought of as quite progressive for his time and, frankly, for contemporary thinking on mental illness and the law.

Somerville goes on to lament the unwillingness of the English House of Lords to follow the progress of science in their treatment of mentally ill criminal defendants, making a point to distinguish between "moral or emotional insanity" and "mental disease," reflecting the broader understanding of mental illness at the time, and praising "the progress of Christian civilization" for "the establishment of the most beneficent of modern civilized charities,—the hospital and asylum for the insane."[26] Citing "medical authorities" who find the "right and wrong" test to be "founded on an ignorant and imperfect view of the disease," Somerville puts forth the question presented to the court as deciding whether to adhere to an outdated "rule of legal responsibility" of which he writes that medical professionals "who have made insanity a special subject of investigation" argue "is wrong, and tout there is no single test by which the existence of the disease, to that degree which exempts from punishment, can in every case be infallibly detected."[27] Somerville asserts that "it is everywhere admitted . . . that an Idiot, lunatic, or other person of diseased mind, who is afflicted to such an extent as to not know whether he is doing right or wrong, is not punishable for any act which he may do while in that state,"[28] but asks whether this is or should be "the only test or rule of responsibility."[29] Citing "a writer on psychological medicine" who described a state of mind "in which the reason has lost its empire over the passions, and the actions by which they are manifested, to such a degree that the individual can neither repress the former, nor abstain from the latter," Somerville suggests that an insane person may be capable of understanding right from wrong but be "so far under *the duress of such disease* as to destroy *the power to choose* between right and wrong."[30]

In explaining the court's decision, Somerville addresses the ongoing confusion about the role of the jury and the court in a trial concerning "a case of this nature," writing that it is the duty of the jury to determine the facts and the duty of the court to state the law.[31] Touching on the ever-present tension regarding the role of expert testimony and the issue of courts declaring matters of fact as law, he cites *State v. Pike*: "If . . . the tests of insanity are matters of law, the practice of allowing experts to testify what they are should be discontinued; if they are matters of fact, the judge should no longer testify without being sworn as witness, and showing himself to be qualified as an expert.[32] The first consideration in any criminal trial, Somerville explains, is "the proper legal rule of responsibility," which must have two elements: "(1) Capacity of intellectual discrimination; and (2) freedom of will."[33] In other words, in the absence of either, no criminal responsibility can be said to exist. The next consideration Somerville addresses is "the probable existence of such a diseases [*sic*], and the test of its presence."[34] Here, he compares the skepticism with which "the existence of such a cerebral disease"[35] tended to be met with similar reactions to historical scientific breakthroughs such as: "the Copernican system of the universe, the efficacy of steam and electricity as a motive power, or the possibility of communication in a few moments . . . by magnetic telegraph, or that of the instantaneous transmission of the human voice . . . by use of telephone."[36] Somerville suggests that in years prior, the courts might have denied the existence of all of these things and, as with all scientific discoveries, such facts must first be "discovered by experts before becoming matters of common knowledge."[37] Therefore, he argues, the kind of mental disease in question, that which destroys the volitional capacity of the afflicted, "is earnestly alleged" by those "who constantly have experimental dealings with the insane," such as "superintendents of insane hospitals, and other experts," and that "the truth of their testimony . . . in each particular case is necessarily a matter for the determination of the jury from the evidence."[38]

Proceeding with the assumption that "such a cerebral disease" exists, Somerville addresses the question of a proper test for it. Citing experts in medical jurisprudence, such as Bishop and Ray, he argues that no such "invariable or infallible" test exists because "the symptoms and causes of insanity are so variable, and its pathology so complex, that no two cases may be just alike."[39] Again, Justice Somerville expresses a quite progressive legal understanding of mental illness, even by current standards; he was truly ahead of his time. He continues to praise the marvels of modern "asylums for the custody and treatment of the insane, which Christian benevolence and statesmanship have substituted for jails and gibbets" as "peculiar opportunities, never before enjoyed in the history of our race" as a means of ascertaining the origins and effects of mental disease; medical experts, he writes, could now examine the "moral, psychical, and physical" causes of mental disease, as well as "what effect may be exerted on the patient by age, sex, occupation, the seasons, personal surroundings, hereditary transmission, and other causes."[40] What Somerville demonstrates here is a rare expression of respect for the work of doctors specializing in mental disease, a stark departure from the typical competition between legal and medical experts for authority in the courtroom, a battle that reemerges in subsequent cases.

The inadequacies of the current insanity test, the McNaughtan Rules, are the next issue taken up by Somerville. He writes, "The courts, in effect, charge juries, as a matter of law, that no such mental disease exists . . . which destroys the patient's power of self control provided only he maintains a mental consciousness of right and wrong."[41] Again, Somerville defers to experts in the field of psychiatry and cites numerous statements reflecting the inaccuracy of the McNaughtan Rules in explaining mental disease. He writes, "Nowhere do we find the rule more emphatically condemned than by those who have the practical care and treatment of the insane in the various lunatic asylums of every civilized country."[42] In London in 1864, a resolution was passed at the annual meeting of the British Association of Medical Officers of Asylums and Hospitals for the Insane, which Somerville cites: "Resolved, that so much of the legal test of the mental condition of an alleged criminal lunatic as renders him a responsible agent, because he knows the difference between right and wrong, is inconsistent with the fact, well known to every member of this meeting, that the power of distinguishing between right and wrong exists very frequently in those who are undoubtedly insane, and is often associated with dangerous and uncontrollable delusions."[43] The appropriate conclusion, according to Somerville, is that the courts could no longer ignore these scientific facts, and he expanded his support for this argument to include the "modern law writers" who also disapproved of the outdated test; this move seems to suggest that if the credibility of medical experts was not enough to persuade men of the law, then perhaps they might find the arguments of experts within their field more convincing.

Citing no fewer than ten cases from both England and the United States that supported the consideration of a volitional component of mental disease that could prevent a person who knew the difference between right and wrong from controlling his actions, Somerville proceeds in literary fashion to describe the challenges faced by courts in overseeing insanity defense cases: "The practical trouble is for the courts to determine in what particular cases the party on trial is to be transferred from the category of sane to that of insane criminals; where, in other words, the border line of punishability is adjudged to be passed. But, as has been said, in reference to an every day fact of nature, no one can say where twilight ends or begins, but there is ample distinction between day and night. We think we can safely rely in this matter upon the intelligence of our Juries, guided by the testimony of men who have practically made a study of the disease of insanity; and enlightened by a conscientious desire, on the one hand, to enforce the criminal laws of the land, and, on the other, not to deal harshly with any unfortunate victim of a diseased mind, acting without the power of volition."[44]

In this statement, Somerville expresses three novel assumptions for his time: First, that psychiatry is a legitimate discipline; second, that there exists a kind of mental disease that is a real illness and not a moral failure; and, finally, that people suffering from such a disease are deserving of compassion.

The court's recommendations for jury instructions in all future criminal trials in which an insanity defense is raised are as follows:

> *First*. Was the defendant at the time of the commission of the alleged crime, as a matter of fact, afflicted with a *disease of the mind*, so as to be idiotic or otherwise insane? *Second*, If such be the case, did he know right from wrong, as applied to the act in question? If he did not have such knowledge, he is not legally responsible. *Third*, If he did have such knowledge, he may nevertheless not be legally responsible if the two following conditions occur: (1) If, by reason of the duress of such mental disease, he had so far lost the *power to choose* between right and wrong, and to avoid doing the act in question; as that his

> free agency was at the time destroyed; (2) and if, at the same time, the alleged crime was so connected with such mental disease, in the retaliation of cause and effect, as to have been the product of it solely.[45]

Thus, the lower court's judgment in *Parsons* was reversed, and a rhetorical shift in the insanity defense was written into the record.

The dissenting opinion in this decision is worthy of analysis, as it expresses many of the common tropes that have been discussed thus far. Justice Stone authored the dissent, writing that the McNaughtan Rules are quite sufficient for determining insanity as it pertains to criminal responsibility, further arguing that "moral" insanity is not an acceptable "defense against a criminal accusation."[46] Stone expresses concern regarding the authorities cited in Somerville's opinion, specifically the medical experts, whom he claims "deal too much in the abstruse or metaphysical," arguing that legal principles must be presented to juries "so simply and clearly as to be easily understood by the class of men who generally perform that service."[47] The trope of distrust toward psychiatry is evident from the start of Stone's dissent.

In his own review of existing cases, Stone notes what he perceives to be too many courts accepting "moral insanity as a defense to criminal prosecution," which he finds indicated in such phrases as "sudden impulse" and "overpowering or subverting the will."[48] This, Stone argues, is incorrect because "impulse is emotional rather than intellectual," reflecting the mind/body or reason/emotion binary in his explanation of how the mind's executive faculty, "the will," cannot be subverted or it would cease to have purpose.[49] He belabors his explanation of the distinction between perversion of the will "by a disease of the brain or intellectual faculties," which he notes *is* exculpatory, and perverted will that is "the offspring of moral depravity, debauched appetite, blunted sense of right, or other kindred prompting of a wicked heart," which he argues is not sufficient for a defense of insanity. Here, Stone falls back on the longstanding trope that explains mental illness as the result of the afflicted's moral failure. In his own analysis of the concept of "delusion" and how it is not, in his opinion, within the purview of the law, Stone writes: "I hold we should take our steps cautiously, in adopting these theories of psychological enthusiasts, lest we disarm retributive justice of all its restraining energy . . . I . . . still fear, that the effect of [this] ruling will be to let in many of the evils which result from allowing the defense of emotional insanity . . . I think the line cannot be too clearly and sharply drawn which separates the pitiable, unfortunate victims of diseased mental faculties from the recklessly depraved, whose chief evidence of insanity is found in the causeless atrocity of their crimes . . . the lawless should be made to feel that the way of the transgressor is hard. The terror of the law may thus become a minister of peace."[50] Here, Stone concludes with the trope reflecting the ongoing public anxieties about the use of insanity as a defense eroding the functions of the law, both its retributive and deterrent effects. He also foreshadows criticisms that would soon be directed at the volitional component of insanity defense standards, namely that they too greatly expand access to the defense.

Davis v. United States

At the Creek Nation of Western Arkansas in August 1894, Dennis Davis shot and killed Sol Blackwell from "within 15 or 20 yards" away "while he was picking cotton, and immediately ran away."[51] Both Davis and Blackwell were African American; at the time of the crime, Davis was renting land from Blackwell to grow a sugar cane crop, and the murder followed a dispute between the two men. Davis immediately surrendered himself to police in the nearest town and detailed the circumstances of his actions.[52] Davis's own description of the incident, according to a witness named A. H. Brown, was: "that he killed the deceased; that he had cleared up a little patch of cane, and there was no understanding, and he (defendant) made up his part, and Blackwell told him that if he did not make up his (Blackwell's) part he would kill him; that he (defendant) stayed in his house all day and night afraid to go out, and the next day he saw Blackwell picking cotton in the field and he slipped out and got a gun and shot him."[53] In a second appeal to the United States Supreme Court,[54] the record states that the time between the dispute and the murder was more than a week.[55] Whatever the actual time frame was, we know that some dispute between landowner and tenant farmer occurred; Davis claimed to fear for his safety, and he shot and killed Blackwell.

In his first trial in the circuit court for the Western District of Arkansas, a defense of insanity was raised based on testimony from physicians, neighbors, and other witnesses who had been acquainted with the defendant that he was "weak minded" and regarded as "half crazy" and "not of sound mind."[56] According to a medical expert for the defense, one Dr. Amis, the defendant "would sit down on his spittoon, and gaze down on the floor as if looking at some object, when none was there, manifesting no interest in anything that was going on; that although violently ill, he was indifferent and unconcerned during his illness, was never worried about his condition; never saw any change in his expression, but he would sit and gaze in a dreamy, melancholy way, with his mouth open and under jaw hanging down, having a vacant, meaningless stare, his face expressionless,—just a blank."[57] Dr. Wright, another defense expert, was asked by the district attorney whether, in his opinion, Davis killed Blackwell because "he threatened his life," to which he responded, "Well, in part; and because he thought his own life was in danger, and because he thought he had the right to destroy this menace to his own life."[58] Davis, however, was found guilty and sentenced to death by hanging. When a motion for a new trial was overturned, an appeal was brought before the Supreme Court of the United States on October 30, 1895. Although the higher court's decision centered on issues of burden of proof, many of the charges of error listed in the appeal illustrate revealing moments worthy of note from the original trial for the purposes of understanding the pervasive rhetoric of sanism.

The appeal centered on the instructions given to the jury, which were against the requests for instructions submitted by the defense. The following reflects the trial court's instructions regarding the meaning of insanity as it pertains to the law. The judge states: "The term 'insanity,' as used in this defense, means such a perverted and deranged condition of the mental and moral faculties as to render a person incapable of distinguishing between right and wrong or unconscious at the time of the nature of the act he is committing; or where, though conscious of the nature of the act and able to distinguish between right and wrong, and know that the act is wrong, yet his will, by which I mean the governing power of his mind, has been, otherwise than voluntarily, so completely destroyed that his actions are not subject to it, but are beyond his control."[59] Here, we continue to see language that includes morality and the judge intent on making a distinction on just how one's "will" can come to be destroyed, namely that such an affliction can be brought on voluntarily by the afflicted. The judge continues: "For a person to be excused from criminal responsibility it is not necessary that he be a raving maniac, but ordinarily it requires something more than mere eccentricity of a natural character. Such insanity does not excuse."[60] Here we see some acknowledgement that the "stark raving lunatic" archetype need not be observed, but just being odd is still not sufficiently exculpatory. And finally, to reiterate the standards by which he expected the jury to assess the criminal responsibility of the defendant, he states: "The law assumes the existence of the power of consciousness for persons of ordinary intelligence or capacity to distinguish between right and wrong with reference to the particular act charged against him, or unconscious at the time of the nature of the act, or if he was deprived of his will power to such an extent as to render him at the time unable to control his passions, he would be excusable. And when I say 'deprived of his will power' I mean not that he has voluntarily thrown it off and abandoned himself to his passions or his whims."[61] Again, the distinction made between will and passions in the judge's instructions upholds the reason/emotions binary, and he repeats the caveat that "voluntary" abandonment of one's reason does not constitute a legal excuse. The very notion that a person could choose to abandon his reason in favor of his passions shows just how embedded in Enlightenment ideology the legal understanding of mental illness was at this time.

The other interesting portion of the trial judge's instructions concerns the role of expert witnesses in insanity defense cases, which was encompassed in the appeal. The judge made the following statements in reference to psychiatric expert testimony:

> It has been discovered that no expert, no matter how learned or incorrupt he might be, speaks for his science as a whole. . . . Peculiarly is this case in matters psychological, in which there is no hypothesis so monstrous that an expert can not be found to swear to it on the stand and to defend it with vehemence when off the stand. . . . Hence it is that apart from the partisan temper, more or less common to experts, their utterances, now that they have as a class become the retained agents of parties, have lost all judicial authority. . . . [A] large allowance must be made for the bias necessarily belonging to men retained to advocate a cause who speak not as to fact, but as to opinion, and who are selected on all moot questions either from their prior advocacy or from their readiness to adopt the opinion to be proved."[62]

This portion of the trial judge's instructions speaks volumes on the trope that holds psychiatric experts lack any and all credibility in a legal setting, because they are hired by either the prosecution or the defense to state the opinion that is needed to make the case for guilt or innocence, in addition to the trope that questions the legitimacy of the discipline of psychiatry as a whole.

The appeal was decided by the United States Supreme Court on December 16, 1895. In the opinion delivered by Justice Harlan, it is clear that the primary issues at stake were questions of what constitutes reasonable doubt in insanity defense cases and on whom the burden of proof rests when evidence of insanity is presented: "If it appears that the deceased was killed by the accused under circumstances which—nothing else appearing—made a case of murder, can the jury properly return a verdict of guilty of the offense charged if, upon the whole of the evidence, from whatever side it comes, they have a reasonable doubt whether, at the time of the killing, the accused was mentally competent to distinguish between right and wrong, or to understand the nature of the act he was committing? . . . If the evidence was in equilibrio as to the accused being sane,—that is, capable of comprehending the nature and effects of his acts,—he was to be treated just as he would be if there were no defense of insanity, or if there was an entire absence of proof that he was insane."[63]

Citing existing case law extensively, Harlan weighs the presumption of innocence against the presumption of sanity. While the bedrock principle of the legal system is that all defendants are presumed innocent until proven guilty and that the burden of proof beyond a reasonable doubt lies with the prosecution, the procedure at this time began with a presumption of sanity, with the burden of proof on the defendant who raised the defense. The prosecution was supposed to have no duty to prove the defendant's sanity beyond a reasonable doubt. Yet, Harlan writes: "Giving to the prosecution, where the defense is insanity, the benefit in the way of proof of the presumption in favor of sanity, the vital question, from the time a plea of not guilty is entered until the return of the verdict, is whether, upon all the evidence, by whatever side adduced, guilt is established beyond a reasonable doubt. If the whole evidence, including that supplied by the presumption of sanity, does not exclude beyond reasonable doubt the hypothesis of insanity, of which some proof is adduced, the accused is entitled to an acquittal of the specific offense charged. His guilt cannot be said to have been proved beyond a reasonable doubt . . . if the jury . . . have reasonable doubt whether he was legally capable of committing crime."[64] In other words, according to Justice Harlan, if credible evidence is presented that raises reasonable doubt as to the defendant's mental capacity, the jury must acquit, and the decisions of numerous justices cited in the opinion provide him ample support.[65] The court reversed the defendant's conviction and ordered a new trial.

Unfortunately, the outcome of Davis's second trial was the same, and on his second appeal to the Supreme Court in 1897, his conviction was upheld. Justice Brewer wrote the following opinion in which he states: "The court charged the law in accordance with the rule laid down by this court [in the previous appeal],—quoting the very language of our opinion,—and also defined what was meant by insanity, in language which, under the circumstances of this case, was in no degree prejudicial to the rights of the defendant."[66] Thus, although this decision retained both the cognitive and volitional components of the insanity defense in its ruling, Davis was unable to avoid the death sentence that awaited him in Arkansas.

The Public Response

Neither *Parsons* nor *Davis* received a great deal of public attention, likely because the victims and perpetrators were average citizens in rural jurisdictions. Research in the state historical archives in both Alabama and Arkansas yielded only one mention of each in a local newspaper.[67] Neither the crimes, the trials, nor the decisions made national headlines.

A February 4, 1885, issue of a Birmingham, Alabama, newspaper, *Weekly*

Iron Age, provides one extensive article about the Parsons murder. A brief mention in the section entitled "In the County Jail" is headlined "The Wife and Daughter of Bennett Parsons brought to Birmingham." Here the reporter primarily describes the women's appearance, stating: "The mother is tall and slender, and has the general appearance of a country woman; the daughter, who is only eighteen years of age, is prepossessing of appearance, and has such an air of sweet innocence about her that no one would look at her and say she was a murderess—a patricide. Neither of the women seem to be aware of the enormity of the crime with which they are charged."[68] A lengthier section, a full article written by a reporter who visited with the Parsonses while they were in jail, provides a more detailed description of the victim, the crime, and the perpetrators in an article titled "A Foul Murder: A Horrible Crime Committed Near Jonesboro." The report on the Parsonses' crime is notably gendered, with much attention devoted to the women's appearance and demeanor, particularly that of Josephine (Joe), and the reporter hints at what seems to be an evident mental defect in the young woman.

Calling the crime "one of the most horrible murders that has ever been committed in Jefferson County," the reporter describes the victim, Bennett Parsons, as a "respected citizen" and "an old man" who was murdered by his second wife, Nancy Parsons, thirty-five years his junior. Bennett Parsons had previously told his son-in-law that "his wife had said she would kill him if ever he came to the house again," but "for reasons unknown," he went to the house, and the next morning, she and her daughters reported to neighbors that he had been murdered. When neighbors went to the home, they found Parsons's body shot and partially burned. The initial story told by the wife and daughters was that Parsons went into one of the rooms of the double log cabin home, and they went out to the yard, after which they heard gunfire but did not pay attention to it, finding the body "dead and . . . burning on the hearth" the next morning.[69]

The article details the first marriage and children of Bennett Parsons, referring primarily to the husbands of the two surviving daughters from that marriage, calling them "good citizens of this county, both of whom have large families." Parsons's nineteen-year marriage to Nancy Jane Cochrane produced five children, the eldest being Josephine (who was eighteen at the time of the murder). The reporter describes with shock and dismay that "a daughter could possibly be so heartless as to murder her own father, and he an old man and a cripple! This done, too, with the knowledge and perhaps at the instigation of the girl's mother—the poor harmless old man's wife."[70]

In describing his encounter with Nancy and Joe Parsons, the reporter says, "On two stools the prisoners sat and leaned over a smoldering fire, their chins resting upon their hands. They did not seem aware of the reporter's entrance into the room." When the reporter greeted the women, "the old woman looked sharply up, and the young girl arose and offered him a seat," after which Nancy said to her daughter, "Don't tell him anything, Josephine. There's time enough for that, and the time ain't come yet." The reporter said he only wanted "to know who killed old man Parsons," to which Joe replied she did, and "she looked at the reporter as calmly as if she was speaking of the killing of an animal." The reporter asked what part her mother played in the murder, and she said, "She wanted him killed and I did it for her." The reporter began to question Nancy who remained evasive and said, "Nobody knows what I have suffered, and there ain't no use talking about it now."[71]

While Nancy began to weep, Joe, who "was unmoved," got up and "chatted and laughed with someone outside [the cell] for several minutes." When Joe returned, the reporter asked her what her father was doing when she shot him, to which she said, "He was standing near the fire with something in his hands. I don't know what he was doing. I fired the gun and left the room without going near him." Silenced by her mother before she could provide any more details, Nancy stated, "We were just tired of leading a dog's life. That man was just too mean for anybody to live with, and we got tired of him." The reporter then asked Joe if she believed in "a God," and she replied, "I suppose I do." He then asked if she knew she had a soul or believed in "a hereafter," but she "walked slowly to the window and gazed through the bars as if she had not heard . . . the last questions." The reporter told the women that they "might be hanged for killing old man Parsons," and Joe looked at Nancy, "her brown eyes a trifle wider, showing for the first time any interest," as Nancy "shook her head slowly from side to side and half muttered, 'Let 'em hang, let 'em hang.'"[72]

The article then returns to the women's physical appearance, describing Nancy as "tall, very slender and [with] the appearance of a person to whom trouble has been a constant visitor." Joe is described as "of medium height and very stout. Her hair and eyes are brown, her complexion a little pale, and if well dressed, she would be called an exceedingly pretty girl." The reporter suggests that "no one could say that the light of reason does not shine" through her brown eyes, yet "something wrong" is evident, which he describes as "the absence of a soul—a moral turpitude. That girl would show her hands to you red with her father's blood, with no more horror than if they were stained with the blood of a slaughtered animal; and yet, under a strict construction of the moral law, she would not be a murderess." As the reporter went to leave, he found the door barred and had to call for a jailer to open it; Joe "laughed and said: 'You see what you have got yourself into now, don't you? You are locked up with the murderers!'" When the door was opened, "the reporter hastened away with the young woman's unpleasant, almost horrifying remark ringing in his ears."[73]

A September 28, 1894, page in *The Weekly Elevator*, an Arkansas newspaper, devotes one paragraph in "The Indian Territory" section to the murder of Sol Blackwell by Dennis Davis. The report contains very little detail about the men involved and mentions nothing about the mental state of the defendant. It mentions the quarrel between Blackwell and Davis three days prior to the crime "which ended in Blackwell chasing Davis into his house with a gun," after which Davis "remained about the home for three days when seeing Blackwell in a field picking cotton he crept up near him and killed him with a Winchester."[74]

The Effects on Insanity Defense Standards

Since *Davis*, there have been many iterations of the control test. As a concept that addressed the capacity of the accused to control his conduct in addition to his capacity to know the difference between right and wrong, the control test would seem to solve the problem noted by those critics who found the McNaughtan Rules too reductive and not adequate for taking into account the complexity of mental illness. Some cases have addressed the issue of mental disease having taken the actions of a defendant beyond his own control; others added the term "impulse," asking whether the defendant's mental disease rendered him incapable of resisting an impulse (hence the misnomer, "irresistible impulse" as a blanket term for the volitional component of the insanity defense). It should be clear that there is no universal legal statute called "The Irresistible Impulse Test," nor is the word "impulse" even a requirement for the use of a volitionally based insanity defense. The word, however, was the point on which subsequent debate hinged, the focus of most of its critics, and the primary explanation for the inadequacies of the new insanity defense standards.[75] Some criticisms argued that if the McNaughtan Rules are properly construed, then the addition of control tests were unnecessary: "Starting from the premise that the human personality is integrated, [legal scholar Professor Jerome] Hall concludes that any case of impaired volition which can satisfy the 'control' rule will also be marked by the failure of knowledge demanded by McNaughtan, provided the word 'know' is given a broad construction."[76] Others suggested that the control test was actually still too narrow. Legal scholar and professor Henry Weihofen states: "Both tests fail to give due emphasis to the fundamental concept that the mental processes are interdependent and interrelated. Both fail particularly to provide adequate bases for judging severe psychoneurotics and others whose criminal acts seem to stem from unconscious motivation. Both fail to take account of the now-recognized fact that all persons—even the normal—are usually more influenced by their emotions than by reasoning."[77] And naturally, some critics worried that the addition of the control test made the test too broad and accessible to any criminal: "This is said to follow from the impossibility of determining which acts were uncontrollable, rather than merely uncontrolled, and the attendant suspicion that the former category does not really exist; from the fact that weaknesses in self-control are to be found in most men; and from the consequent ease of asserting an inability to control one's conduct. The result prophesied under a 'control' test is a dramatic rise in successful insanity pleas and a marked reduction in the deterrent impact of the criminal law."[78] This final concern echoes the dissenting opinion in *Parsons* and would become the driving force behind the next rhetorical shift in insanity defense standards in *Durham v. United States*, which is the subject of the next chapter.

5

Mid-Twentieth-Century Insanity Defense Jurisprudence

Durham v. United States *and the "Product" Test

> "Everyone concedes that the present [legal] definition of insanity has little relation to the truths of mental life."
>
> —Justice Cardozo to the New York Academy of Medicine in 1928

Psychiatry in America in the Early to Mid-Twentieth Century

In the late nineteenth century, amid Darwin's revelations, the push to establish psychiatry as a truly scientific discipline again became the focus of many notable practitioners. Influential but little-known German doctor Emil Kraepelin's work is truly the basis for the *Diagnostic and Statistical Manual of Mental Disorders* (*DSM*) as we know it today,[1] as he emphasized the symptoms and the course of the illness, which led to significant progress in the classification of mental disorders; most significantly, Kraepelin described a degenerative condition he called "dementia praecox," which is what we now call schizophrenia.[2] According to historian Roy Porter, "Pinelian optimism" had run dry by 1900, as "the psychiatrist seemed to have been reduced to acting as society's policeman or gatekeeper, protecting it from the insane."[3] Eugenicists' and degenerationists' theories primed later policies that deemed the lives of some, including the severely mentally ill, not worth living; in fact, over 70,000 mental patients were murdered by Nazis in gas chambers between 1940 and 1942, their names chosen "by nine leading professors of psychiatry and thirty-nine top physicians."[4] Lest we think this was a distinctly Nazi endeavor, by 1900, various lobbies were working toward "compulsory confinement, sterilization, [and] . . . the use of psychiatry in immigration control" in the United States.[5]

Against the pessimism of the asylum psychiatrists emerged new styles of dynamic psychiatry, which, based on the work of Franz Mesmer, among others, included the use of hypnotism.[6] The famous neurologist Jean-Martin Charcot, while teaching at Salpêtrière, used hypnosis to diagnose hysteria; he believed that only hysterics could be hypnotized. He failed, however, to connect the "supercharged theatrical atmosphere" of the asylum with the performances of his "'star' hysterics."[7] Freud studied with Charcot in 1885. Those months of study had a significant impact on Freud's own development, and Porter argues that this is one of the main reasons psychoanalysis has failed to shake the accusations that the cures it offers are simply the result of suggestion from the analyst. Sigmund Freud began to publish his work on the origins of some mental disorders at the turn of the century, the twin pillars of his work being the Oedipal complex and the unconscious mind.[8] Subsequently, psychoanalysis emerged as the dominant paradigm of psychiatry for the first half of the twentieth century,[9] both in Europe and the States; as more Jewish practitioners were forced to leave Europe, "the United States became the world headquarters of psychoanalysis, and by the mid-twentieth century American psychiatry . . . was heavily psychoanalytically oriented."[10] Freud's theories on neurosis, however, bore little relevance to the treatment of severe mental illness; such patients at the time were still subject to confinement in state-run mental institutions.

At the time of Monty Durham's trial, the *Diagnostic and Statistical Manual of Mental Disorders* was one year away from its first edition's publication. A publication titled the *Statistical Manual for the Use of Institutions for the Insane*, however, which was created by the Committee on Statistics of the American Medico-Psychological Association (the precursor to the American Psychiatric Association), along with the Commission on Mental Hygiene, went through ten revisions between 1917 and 1942. This manual separated mental illness into twenty-two distinct groups, expanding the seven classifications determined in 1880.[11]

The Crimes of Monty Durham

The crime at the center of *Durham v. United States*[12] was a "housebreaking" conviction in Washington DC (what we would now call "breaking and entering"). However, Monty Durham had a history of mental illness and petty crimes that began when he was discharged by the navy at the age of seventeen; a "psychiatric examination had shown that he suffered 'from a profound personality disorder,'"[13] after which his interactions with both the criminal justice system and the state asylum system were quite frequent. In 1947, Durham was given probation for violating the National Motor Theft Act, soon after which he attempted suicide and was institutionalized. In

1948, his probation was revoked when he was caught passing bad checks, and he was then ordered to serve the remainder of his 1947 sentence in jail. A few days into his incarceration, Durham's conduct led to a lunacy inquiry in which "a jury found him to be of unsound mind," so he was recommitted to the hospital (St. Elizabeths), where "he was diagnosed as suffering from 'psychosis with psychopathic personality.'"[14] This time, his hospitalization lasted fifteen months, and Durham was discharged in July 1949 as "recovered." He was then sent back to jail to serve the remainder of his sentence. Though he was conditionally released in June 1950, Durham violated his parole by leaving the District of Columbia area. When he found out there was a warrant for his arrest, he fled to the South and Midwest, writing fraudulent checks to obtain funds. When he was eventually found and returned to DC, "the Parole Board referred him to the District Court for a lunacy inquisition" where a jury again found him to be of unsound mind. Durham was readmitted to the hospital in February 1951 where he was diagnosed as "without mental disorder, psychopathic personality."[15] He was discharged in May 1951, and on July 13, 1951, he committed the housebreaking offense on which his trial and subsequent appeal centered, and another version of the insanity defense was born.

The Trial

The District Court convicted Durham without a jury. His defense was that he "was of unsound mind at the time of the offense."[16] According to Durham's mother and the psychiatrist who examined him in September 1951, after his last stay at St. Elizabeths ended, he immediately began to experience hallucinations. In October, two psychiatrists determined that Durham "suffered from 'psychosis with psychopathic personality.'"[17] He was recommitted and "given subshock insulin therapy."[18] After six months, Dr. Silk, the acting superintendent of St. Elizabeths, declared Durham mentally competent to stand trial for the housebreaking offense in an ex parte[19] statement. The prosecutor in the trial court noted that he was aware of Durham's history of mental illness; his main concern with not pursuing the charges was any future crime Durham might commit: "If that man committed a murder next week then it is my responsibility. So we decided to go to trial on one case . . . and let him bring the defense, if he wants to, of unsound mind at the time the crime was committed, and then Your Honor will find him on that, and in your decision send him back to Saint Elizabeths Hospital, and then if they let him out on the street it is their responsibility."[20] Here we see the game of "pass the buck" that was Durham's life in the hands of the criminal justice system and the state asylum system. Nobody knew what to do with him, and nobody wanted to be responsible for him or his actions, so they just shuffled him back and forth between jail and the hospital.

When Dr. Silk's statement was brought into question, the trial judge suggested to the defense that when a defendant has previously been judged to be of unsound mind, that an ex parte certificate "is not sufficient to set aside that finding," and that another lunacy hearing could be ordered; "However, if you want to waive that you may do it, if you admit that he is now of sound mind."[21] The judge has just suggested to Durham's defense attorney that it would be a good idea to request another lunacy hearing, which is his client's right, and then offers him, an attorney and not a psychiatrist or mental health expert, the option to waive that right on behalf of his client if he, an attorney and not a psychiatrist or mental health expert, judges his client to currently be of sound mind. The record reflects that Durham's attorney did in fact opt to waive his client's right to an additional lunacy hearing even though both counsel for the prosecution and defense had informed the judge that Durham continued to assert, even on the very day on which this conversation took place, that he was in need of further hospitalization. The trial judge, acknowledging what amounted to a revolving door of jail and hospitalization, responded, "Of course, if I hold he is not mentally competent to stand trial, I send him back to Saint Elizabeths Hospital and they will send him back again in two or three months."[22]

The only expert witness to appear at the trial, Dr. Gilbert, who examined Durham on September 3, 1951, emphasized the progressive nature of Durham's condition, stating that it "did not 'arrive overnight.'"[23] Following his testimony, the judge questioned Dr. Gilbert regarding his ability to know based on his examination in September how ill Durham would have been two months earlier when he committed the crime, asking, "Then it is reasonable to assume that it is not possible to determine how far this state of unsound mind had progressed by July 13th? Isn't that so?" Dr. Gilbert responded, "As to the seriousness of the symptoms as compared with them and the time I observed him, that's true, except that his travels were based, according to his statement to me, on certain of the symptoms and his leaving Washington, his giving up his job and work and leaving the work he had tried to do."[24] The judge then reiterated his claim as a question: "'But you can't tell, can you, how far those symptoms had progressed and become worse by the 13th of July?'" to which Gilbert replied, "No, not how far they were, that is correct."[25] On recross, Dr. Gilbert was asked by the prosecutor if knowing that Durham had been "released from St. Elizabeths just two months before as being sound of mind" would change his opinion as to the defendant's mental state on the date of the commission of the crime.[26] The judge interrupted to say that based on Dr. Gilbert's previous answers to his questions, he had already stated "that he doesn't know and he can't express a definite opinion as to his mental condition on the 13th of July."[27] On redirect, defense counsel asked Dr. Gilbert to say whether Durham was able to know the difference between right and wrong on the date of the crime. He replied, "If the question of the right and wrong were propounded to him he could give you the right answer."[28] The judge interrupted, and the following exchange took place:

> The Court: "No, I don't think that is the question, Doctor—not whether he could give the right answer to a question, but whether he, himself, knew the difference between right and wrong in connection with governing his own actions. If you are unable to answer, why, you can say so; I mean, if you are unable to form an opinion."
>
> The Witness: "I can only answer this way: That I can't tell how much the abnormal thinking and the abnormal experiences in the form of hallucinations and delusions—delusions of persecution—had to do with his anti-social behavior. I don't know how anyone can answer that question categorically, except as one's experience leads him to know that most mental cases can give you a categorical answer of right and wrong, but what influence these symptoms have on abnormal or anti-social behavior."
>
> The Court: "Well, your answer is that you are unable to form an opinion, is that it?"
>
> The Witness: "I would say that it is essentially true, for the reasons I have given."[29]

At some point, defense counsel asked Dr. Gilbert to further explain his answers regarding the "right and wrong" test but was cut off by the judge who warned that these questions had already been answered.

These exchanges clearly illustrate how the imprecise nature of psychiatric assessment is a problem in Durham's trial, as it is in most cases in which a defense based on mental illness is raised. Even before the era of television crime drama, which has convinced the viewing public that conclusive physical evidence is always possible to obtain and, in fact, necessary to prove a case, the law wanted more than could ever be made available regarding evidence of the defendant's mental state at the moment during which he committed the crime. The questions by the prosecution and the judge tend toward requiring the expert to know what the defendant was thinking or able to know during a particular moment, and any suggestion that it is not possible to know such things is typically viewed as evidence of psychiatry's limited utility in determining criminal responsibility.

What is perhaps most significant about Durham's case is the way in which the cycle of incarceration and institutionalization plays out. Durham, a nonviolent repeat offender with a well-documented history of mental illness, was in perpetual limbo between jail and mental hospitals for his entire adult life; any brief period of freedom without any support structures in place to help him cope with his illness ultimately led to his committing additional petty crimes, which brought him back into the criminal justice system and often the asylum. The asylum did not "cure" him, and jail did not "rehabilitate" him. What is clear from the trial excerpts quoted in the appellate court's opinion is that no party in the trial—not the judge, not the prosecutor, not his own defense counsel—had any modicum of sympathy for Monty Durham or his pitiable life of endless encounters with ineffectual disciplinary systems. This lack of compassion is evidenced by the disdain with which the judge and the prosecutor describe this very cycle, along with his own counsel's seeming disinterest in advocating for his client. Ultimately, Durham was convicted based on the trial judge's rejection of his defense of insanity.

The Effects on Insanity Defense Standards

The appeal was brought to the United States Court of Appeals District of Columbia Circuit in March 1954, and the case was decided on July 1, 1954. The *Durham v. United States* opinion was authored by Circuit Judge Bazelon, and the conviction was reversed "(1) because the trial court did not correctly apply existing rules governing burden of proof on the defense of insanity, and (2) *because existing tests of criminal responsibility are obsolete and should be superseded*."[30] The way in which the judge stated his decision provided the grounds for the appeal and the ultimate reversal of the conviction. Noting both the cognitive and volitional aspects of an insanity defense, the trial judge stated:

> I don't think it has been established that the defendant was of unsound mind as of July 13, 1951, in the sense that he didn't know the difference between right or wrong or that even if he did, he was subject to an irresistible impulse by reason of the derangement of mind. While, of course, the burden of proof on the issue of mental capacity to commit a crime is upon the Government, just as it is on every other issue, nevertheless, the Court finds . . . there is no testimony concerning the mental state of the defendant as of July 13, 1951, and therefore the usual presumption of sanity governs. While if there was some testimony as to his mental state as of that date to the effect that he was incompetent

> on that date, the burden of proof would be on the Government to overcome it. There has been no such testimony, and the usual presumption of sanity prevails. . . . Mr. Ahern,[31] I think you have done very well by your client and defended him very ably, but I think under the circumstances there is nothing anybody could have done.[32]

This, Bazelon writes, "reflects error requiring reversal" because "the requirement of 'some evidence,'" as set forth in *Tatum v. United States*,[33] "was satisfied."[34] Bazelon argues that the requirement of "some evidence" of mental disorder has previously been met by "considerably less than is present here [in Durham's trial]," and that "the psychiatric testimony was unequivocal that Durham was of unsound mind at the time of the crime."[35] The only expert witness at the trial, Dr. Gilbert, asserted this fact in spite of efforts by the prosecution "to establish that Durham was a malingerer who feigned insanity whenever he was trapped for his misdeeds."[36] Bazelon argues that the prosecution "failed to present any expert testimony to support this theory."[37] In addition, he writes that the testimony of Durham's mother supported Dr. Gilbert's assessment as to the defendant's mental condition during the period of time between his release from the hospital and the date of the crime.

Bazelon reasons that "the trial judge regarded this psychiatric testimony as 'no testimony' on two grounds": first, that it did not sufficiently cover Durham's condition on the date of the offense, and second, that it did not answer the question of Durham's ability to know right from wrong. He argues, however, that neither of these reasons adequately explains the trial judge's assessment of the psychiatric testimony in question as "no testimony," that the "testimony was adequate to prevent the presumption of sanity from becoming conclusive," that the burden of proof was on the Government as a result, and that the court failed to consider "the whole evidence" in rendering its judgment.[38] Bazelon writes that Durham's defense counsel "ably argued . . . that the existing tests . . . for determining criminal responsibility, i.e. the so-called right-wrong test supplemented by the irresistible impulse test, are not satisfactory criteria for determining criminal responsibility," and that based on "nearly a century of agitation for reform," a new test was needed for the retrial of this case.[39]

In his review of the history of insanity defense standards in the District of Columbia, Bazelon notes that the right-wrong, or cognitive, test, based on the McNaughtan Rules, was approved in 1882 and used exclusively until 1929 when the irresistible impulse supplement from *Parsons* and *Davis* was approved in *Smith v. United States*. Citing Isaac Ray, who in 1838 noted the inadequacies of the cognitive test, Bazelon writes that Ray's claim "has long been substantiated by enormous developments in knowledge of mental life."[40] In 1953, the British Royal Commission on Capital Punishment issued a report, which Bazelon cites, based on agreement among medical experts "that the mind functions as an integrated whole and that it is impossible to isolate the separate functions of cognition and control."[41]

During the process of writing that report, many participants argued for the retention of the McNaughtan Rules, either because they felt no better rule could be formulated or they felt that the cognitive test was already being interpreted in a manner that was sufficiently broad. The Commission ultimately decided that it was unwise to rely on "interpretation" to address the problem, a moment which illustrates the unwillingness to admit the rhetoricity of the law; they did, however, issue two recommendations: "to abrogate the [McNaughtan] Rules and to leave the jury to determine whether at the time of the act the accused was suffering from disease of the mind (or mental deficiency to such a degree that he ought not be held responsible," or, alternatively, that "the jury must be satisfied that, at the time of committing the act, the accused, as a result of disease of the mind (or mental deficiency) (a) did not know the nature and quality of the act or (b) did not know that it was wrong or was incapable of preventing himself from committing it."[42] The justices in *Durham* "insisted that a standard of responsibility was necessary to limit arbitrariness on the part of the jury, to promote uniformity of decision, and to aid the jury in deciding between the conflicting testimony of the experts. . . . If the law provides no standard, members of the jury are placed in the difficult decision of having to find a man responsible for no other reason than their personal feelings about him."[43] This process reveals the decades-long struggle to establish clearer, more concrete standards for defining legal insanity, but also the common legal myth that "the personal" can somehow be bracketed for the purposes of fair and objective legal decision-making.

In England, neither of the Royal Commission's recommendations were adopted, but they proved to be profoundly influential on the development of the next iteration of insanity defense tests in the United States. When Bazelon cites the Royal Commission report along with The Preliminary Report by the Committee on Forensic Psychiatry of the Group for Advancement of Psychiatry, he states that both groups "present convincing evidence that the right-wrong test is 'based on an entirely obsolete and misleading conception of the nature of insanity.'"[44] Thus, Bazelon concludes, a test that considers only knowledge or reason is insufficient in matters so complex as "mental responsibility for criminal behaviors."[45] Here he begins to outline the errors in dualistic thinking about mental illness: "Nine years ago we said: 'The modern science of psychology does not conceive that there is a separate little man in the top of one's head called reason whose function it is to guide another unruly little man called instinct, emotion, or impulse in the way he should go.'"[46] The cognitive test, therefore, leaves the judge and jury with what is scientifically demonstrated to be "inadequate, and most often, invalid and irrelevant testimony,"[47] as was evidenced during Dr. Gilbert's testimony at Durham's trial.

Bazelon next addresses the volitional (control, irresistible impulse) supplement to the cognitive test, arguing that, while useful, it "carries the misleading implication that 'diseased mental condition(s)' produce only sudden, momentary, or spontaneous inclinations to commit unlawful acts," citing the Royal Commission's report that found that in certain varieties of mental disease, such as melancholia, schizophrenia, or paranoid psychosis, the changes of mood alter the entire existence of the afflicted and that his criminal act may in fact be the opposite of impulsive—thought out and planned over a long period of time—but still "the act of a madman."[48] Thus, a new test was needed as both existing tests were insufficient: the cognitive test because it was based solely upon one criterion that medical science had already proven erroneous, and the volitional test because it failed to recognize "mental illnesses characterized by brooding and reflection."[49] The new rule would be simply that "an accused is not criminally responsible if his unlawful act was the product of mental disease or defect."[50] This test came to be known as the product test.

Bazelon first attempts to outline the distinction between a mental disease and a mental defect, writing that a disease is "a condition . . . capable of either improving or deteriorating," while a defect is "a condition which is not . . . capable of either improving or deteriorating and which may be either congenital, or the result of injury, or the residual effect of a physical or mental disease."[51] While he admits that "an instruction which would be either appropriate or binding in all cases" is not possible, Bazelon outlines proper jury instructions using the new test: "If you the jury believe beyond a reasonable doubt that the accused was not suffering from a diseased or defective mental condition at the time he committed the criminal act charged, you may find him guilty. If you believe he was suffering from a diseased or defective mental condition when he committed the act, but believe beyond a reasonable doubt that the act was not the product of such mental abnormality, you may find him guilty. Unless you believe beyond a reasonable doubt either that he was suffering from a diseased or defective mental condition, or that the act was not the product of such abnormality, you must find the accused not guilty by reason of insanity."[52] In his efforts to clarify the standards for future jurors, Bazelon's revisions leave as much room for interpretation and personal bias as previous versions. While nothing in previous standards for legal insanity necessarily inhibited the use of expert testimony, it had unquestionably been a contentious issue,[53] due largely to skepticism regarding the disciplinary legitimacy of the mental health professions. In the opinion, Bazelon goes on to address the role of expert testimony, saying:

> Whatever the state of psychiatry, the psychiatrist will be permitted to carry out his primary court function which . . . "is to inform the jury of the character of the accused's mental disease (or defect)." The jury's range of inquiry will not be limited to, but may include, for example, whether an accused, who suffered from a mental disease or defect did not know the difference between right and wrong, acted under the compulsion of an irresistible impulse, or "had been deprived of or lost the power of his will" . . . Finally, in leaving the determination of the ultimate fact to the jury, we permit it to perform its traditional function which . . . is to apply "our inherited ideas of moral responsibility to individuals prosecuted for crime." Juries will continue to make moral judgments, still operating under the fundamental precept that "Our collective conscience does not allow punishment where it cannot impose blame." But in making such judgments, they will be guided by wider horizons of knowledge concerning mental life. The question will simply be whether the accused acted because of a mental disorder, and not whether he displayed particular symptoms which medical science has long recognized do not necessarily, or even typically, accompany even the most serious mental disorder.[54]

The problems of such a collective and universal morality are clearly not addressed here in Bazelon's construction of how psychiatrists and juries will work together, but he assumes that jurors operate under the same precepts of neutrality and objectivity, emphasizing the prevalence of judicial mythology along with moral ideology.

Criticisms of *Durham* and the product test soon followed. The primary criticism was that it was too similar to the Royal Commission's first proposal that some argued was really a nonrule that provided no standard by which the jury could effectively assess the evidence, avoided the factors with which the law was concerned such as impairment of reason and control, and left the jury wholly dependent upon the testimony of experts who would claim that the defendant's behavior was a "product" of mental disease.[55] While *Durham* attempted to shift the focus of the debates away from the particular language of the test and toward the evidence presented as to how the actions of an individual defendant were affected by mental disease, the cultural climate was in the process of becoming more hostile toward psychiatry. Indeed, the very concept of mental illness was coming under attack: "It was becoming apparent that 'mental disease' is as much a social concept as a psychiatric one, that its content is affected by the ends for which the diagnosis is being made,"[56] which highlights the conflicting purposes of the law, to punish and deter (Strict Father), and psychiatry, to treat and cure (Nurturant Parent).

Following the ruling in *Durham*, only Maine and the Virgin Islands formally adopted the new test, but it continued to impact the conversation about the insanity defense in the United States. The District of Columbia became somewhat of a laboratory for both the substantive and procedural ramifications of the new test.[57] There was, as predicted by those who were concerned that the new test made the standards too broad, a significant increase in not guilty by reason of insanity verdicts; however, this is most likely attributable to the redirection of those who would previously have been deemed incompetent to stand trial into trials using a defense of insanity.[58] In fact, the reverse of this has proven to hold true: In states in which the insanity defense was abolished in the 1980s, the number of defendants declared incompetent to stand trial has risen sharply.[59]

Ultimately, it was decided that juries need guidance, that allowing terms like "mental disease" and "product" to speak for themselves was insufficient, and that any standards for legal insanity would need to describe the effects of mental disease that impacted a defendant's capacity to comply with the law.[60]

The Public Response

Like the *Parsons* and *Davis* cases, *Durham* did not garner much attention; neither he, his crimes, nor his victims were high profile enough to do so. A mention of Monty Wayne Durham and "the Durham Rule" came when US Circuit Court Judge David Bazelon announced he would be assuming semi-retired status after almost thirty years as an appellate judge, fifteen of those as chief judge of the US Court of Appeals. Bazelon said he hoped with that ruling that "psychiatrists would be able, in the context of a criminal trial, to give juries some insight into what motivated a criminal," as he felt that the law had been closed off to new information on this issue.[61] Bazelon was known throughout his career as a "liberal, activist judge,"[62] namely because he was concerned with social justice and a consistent advocate for the rights of defendants.

The ALI Model Penal Code

In 1962, the American Law Institute (ALI) attempted to "solve" the problems with the insanity defense by drafting the Model Penal Code. In doing so, they rejected the advice of their psychiatric advisory committee, which actually endorsed the product test, and instead adopted language very similar to the Royal Commission's second proposal. The ALI standard read as follows:

> (1) A person is not responsible for criminal conduct if at the time of such conduct as a result of mental disease or defect he lacks substantial capacity either to appreciate the criminality of his conduct or to conform his conduct to the requirements of the law.
> (2) As used in this Article, the terms "mental disease or defect" do not include an abnormality manifested only by repeated criminal behavior or otherwise antisocial conduct.[63]

In substituting the word "appreciate" for the word "know," this version indicated a recognition that emotional awareness is an important aspect of cognitive capacity. By substituting the word "conform" for the word "control," this version attempted to avoid the problematic concept of the "irresistible impulse." Finally, by referring to "substantial capacity," this version worked to distance itself from previous iterations that insisted on a totalizing loss of reason or will.[64] Still, we might ask, are the words "appreciate," "conform," and "substantial" any less vague than their predecessors, "know," "control," and "total"?

The ALI standard was not without its critics. Some felt that it was an effort to prevent "psychopaths" from using the insanity defense, while others argued that such an effort was necessary in preventing "the defense from swallowing up the whole of criminal liability, as it might if all recidivists could qualify for the defense merely by being labeled psychopaths."[65] This particular criticism reflects the trope about the insanity defense weakening the law's deterrent effect, in this case by making it available to all repeat offenders.

Again, the debate about the language of the standards for legal insanity can be traced to one simple truth that explains the most basic ideological rift in the issue: "The insanity defense is not really intended to raise medical questions,"[66] and it is certainly not equipped to answer them. Bazelon writes presciently in the *Durham* opinion, "We do not, and indeed could not, formulate an instruction which would be either appropriate or binding in all cases,"[67] and Goldstein writes shortly after the ALI Model Penal Code was published, "A precise definition of insanity is impossible."[68] Thus, the entire enterprise of the insanity defense exists within the hegemonic structure of the law that is impervious to intervention by psychiatry. All of the previous attempts to define legal insanity came to a head two decades later when the very high-profile trial of John Hinckley Jr. dominated the headlines. This trial is the subject of the next chapter.

6

Late Twentieth-Century Insanity Defense Jurisprudence

The Trial of John Hinckley Jr. and the Insanity Defense Reform Act

> "It only takes a split second to shoot a US president and three of his men but the news of what transpires in that split second ripples through the public communities, institutions, mass media, and subcultures that constitute society and thereby provides a litmus test of where individuals stand on matters affecting the habitability of life in their own society."
>
> —C. David Mortensen

On March 30, 1981, John Hinckley Jr. attempted to assassinate President Ronald Reagan. As Reagan walked to his limousine after an appearance at the Hilton Hotel in Washington, DC, Hinckley opened fire, wounding Reagan along with three others. The events were televised and took place in the presence of a large crowd. Hinckley was apprehended and taken into custody immediately following the attack.[1] This incident initiated the single most famous American insanity defense trial of the twentieth century.

The State of Psychology

Between *Durham* and the Hinckley trial, the mental health professions underwent a major transformation. The biomedical turn in psychiatry, a period identified by the discipline's historians as emerging between 1950 and 1990,[2] refers to the move away from psychoanalytic psychiatry and toward a biological explanation for mental illness based on diagnosable symptoms. The core tenets of the biomedical model of mental disorders suggest that they "are caused by biological abnormalities . . . located in the brain," that "there is no meaningful distinction between mental . . . and physical diseases," and that biological (meaning psychopharmacological) treatment is needed to treat mental diseases,[3] shifting the emphasis away from psychoanalytic "talk" therapy. The hope of advocates of this model was that informing the public about the biological basis for mental illness would reduce the stigma toward mentally ill people.

The first version of the *Diagnostic and Statistical Manual* (DSM) was published in 1952,[4] and DSM-II was published in 1972. Due to the efforts of the American Psychiatric Association (APA) to root the discipline firmly in the realm of medicine and science, however, the DSM-III, published in 1980, "marked a major turning point for American psychiatry" and was referred to as the "triumph of science over clinical ideology."[5] While DSM-III did not establish the existence of any new disorders, devise any new methods of treatment, or offer any new explanation for mental illness, many psychiatrists hailed the "ascendance of scientific psychiatry," making such sweeping claims as "the old psychiatry derives from theory, the new psychiatry from *fact*."[6] DSM-III ushered in 265 diagnostic categories over the course of 494 pages, along with "an official definition of mental disorder, . . . a philosophy of empiricism to the nosology that had heretofore been absent, . . . and it self-consciously asserted that the new classification manual represented the best that psychiatric research had to offer."[7] The narrative of the new, field-tested, "scientifically proven" manual would experience a major rupture in the trial of John Hinckley Jr., as the psychiatrists for the prosecution and the defense would deploy their interpretations of Hinckley's disorder using DSM-III categories.

The Crime: Backstory

The story of Hinckley's life, specifically the years preceding the crime, are important to understand, particularly for his defense. From adolescence, Hinckley was described as troubled and socially withdrawn, as evidenced by his difficulties in establishing peer relationships. He dropped out of Texas Tech in 1976 to pursue a songwriting career in Hollywood. It was at this time that Hinckley developed an obsession with Martin Scorsese's film *Taxi Driver*, specifically its central character Travis Bickle (played by Robert DeNiro); Hinckley's obsession manifested in his imitation of Bickle's attributes, such as wearing army fatigues, keeping a diary, and developing a keen interest in firearms.[8]

How a fixation on a fictional character led Hinckley to stalk one of the film's real-life actors and, ultimately, to attempt to assassinate a US president may seem unclear; indeed, it was a process that took some time, a point on which Hinckley's defense team placed a great deal of emphasis.[9] To understand the link, we must understand the plot of the film. In *Taxi Driver*, Cybill Shepherd plays Betsy, the first object of Travis Bickle's affection; Betsy works for a presidential candidate. After Bickle is rebuffed by Betsy, he decides to assassinate the candidate. He also redirects his attention toward a young prostitute named Iris;[10] the role of Iris is played by Jodie Foster, who was twelve years old at the time of filming (but a college freshman by the time of the attempt on Reagan's life). Hinckley stalked Foster during his preparation for the assassination attempt; why Hinckley chose the fictional character Bickle and the real-life actor Foster remains unclear, but, for the defense, these delusions were indicative of serious mental illness.

Between 1976 and 1980, Hinckley lived in and moved between a number of different locations: Hollywood, trying to establish his songwriting career; Colorado, trying to either live on his own or at his parents' home; and Lubbock, trying to continue his education at Texas Tech. During this period, he experienced severe depression, along with other symptoms. In 1979, Hinckley purchased his first handgun; a self-taken photograph from early 1980 shows Hinckley holding a gun to his head. Hinckley's parents, continually frustrated by their son's inability to get his life together, sent him to a psychiatrist (this psychiatrist was employed by one of Hinckley's father's businesses). What emerged from this treatment was Hinckley's renewed commitment to a career as a writer.[11]

In 1980, after Hinckley signed a formal contract with his parents outlining the terms of their support for his endeavor, they funded his move to Connecticut to take a writing course at Yale. He never had any intention of enrolling in the course; instead, he planned to make contact with Jodie Foster, who was by then attending the university. In pursuit of this goal, Hinckley wrote letters and poems that he placed in Foster's mailbox; he also called her twice and recorded the conversations. Foster reported these incidents to the dean of her college, but no action was taken.[12] With his goals for a relationship with Foster unfulfilled, Hinckley returned to Lubbock, not to reenroll in college but to add to his weapons arsenal; he would soon possess three handguns and two rifles.[13]

Returning to the other part of the *Taxi Driver* plot, Hinckley decided that he was going to assassinate the president (at that time, Jimmy Carter) in order to get Foster's attention. Over a period of three days, Hinckley traveled to Washington, DC, Columbus, Ohio, and Dayton, Ohio, following Carter on his campaign trail, even attending an October 2 event at which Carter was present; Hinckley reported to the psychiatrists who interviewed him after his arrest, however, that he left his guns in his hotel room because he was unable to get in the proper frame of mind to carry out his plans. Throughout the month of October, Hinckley continued to stalk both Foster, leaving her notes, and Carter, traveling around the country to follow him.[14]

Eventually, Hinckley ran out of money and was forced to return to his parents' home in Colorado. It was during this period that Hinckley was put under the care of psychiatrist Dr. John Hopper after telling his parents that he had taken an overdose of medication (whether he actually did or not has never been established). Over the four months that Hopper treated Hinckley, no mention was made of his stalking activities, his arsenal of weapons, or his plans to assassinate a president. Dr. Hopper requested that Hinckley prepare an autobiographical sketch in which Hinckley reported that "all he cared about were a writing career and Jodie Foster,"[15] but Dr. Hopper did not notice any cause for alarm.

In a drunken monologue he recorded on New Year's Eve, Hinckley discussed his fears that he was "on the road to insanity" and his frustrations with his failure to win Foster's affections (he said that if he were unable to establish his desired connection with her, "it would be 'suicide city'").[16] During the period between February 9–19, 1981, Hinckley traveled between Washington, DC, to stalk newly elected President Reagan; New Haven, to leave more notes and poems for Foster; and New York, after the death of John Lennon, which apparently had a profound impact on him. Hinckley spent some time at the site of Lennon's murder, where he later told the court-appointed psychiatrists that he contemplated committing suicide but was unable to act on his thoughts.

Hinckley's final appointment with Dr. Hopper took place on February 19; he returned home to Colorado while his parents were away on vacation, but since he had failed to uphold his promise to get a job by the end of the month (per the contract with his parents), he left, going again to New York and New Haven. He left more notes for Foster, one of which read, "Jodie, after tonight, John Lennon and I will have a lot more in common. It's all for you."[17] When he ran out of money again, his parents paid for him to come back to Colorado but refused to let him stay in their home on the advice of Dr. Hopper "as part of a plan to make John less dependent on his parents."[18] His mother provided him with some money, hiding this fact from his father. He stayed in two Denver hotels between March 7 and 25, made one trip back to Hollywood to try to sell one of his songs, and then took a bus to Washington, DC, arriving on March 29. He checked into the Park Central Hotel; the next day, he wrote a letter[19] to Foster detailing his plan to assassinate President Reagan before heading to the Hilton where the infamous shooting took place.[20]

The Trial

Hinckley's trial began on May 4, 1982, and lasted seven weeks; he was charged with thirteen separate offenses. His primary defense was that he was not guilty by reason of insanity, and the ALI Model Penal Code was the standard by which the jurors were to decide his fate. The test asked whether or not, due to mental disease or defect, the defendant lacked substantial capacity to appreciate the wrongfulness of his act or to conform his conduct to the requirements of the law. Attorney Vincent Fuller from the DC-based firm Williams and Connolly, hired by Hinckley's parents, was senior defense counsel. The defense's lead psychiatric expert was Dr. William Carpenter, who was a noted expert on severe mental illness and, at the time, a professor at the University of Maryland Medical School and the director of the Maryland Psychiatric Research Center. The senior prosecutor was Roger Adelman, and his star expert witness was Dr. Park Dietz. Dietz was, at the time, only thirty-three years old and already a member of the faculty at Harvard Medical School; he had served as a forensic psychiatrist for prosecutors in over a hundred cases at the time of Hinckley's trial.

The high profile nature of the crime, the people involved, and the trial itself made Hinckley the kind of insanity defense case that Perlin argues skews public perception of the use of the defense in general. It did involve a heinous crime; Hinckley did come from an affluent family, so accusations of his manipulation of the justice system seemed more plausible to the general public. It did involve a "battle of experts," which will become evident in the portions of their testimony that I will present. Additionally, the centuries-long turf war over whose authority counts in the courtroom became a central issue, particularly in the prosecution's argument.

Before the trial was underway, the language of the standards for legal insanity were being debated in a pretrial hearing. Specifically, the way in which the word "appreciate" would be interpreted was the subject of controversy. The prosecution argued that what the drafters of the Model Penal Code *really* meant was similar to the McNaughtan test and that "appreciate" should be taken to mean essentially "knowing" right from wrong, without consideration of the defendant's emotional or volitional capacities. The defense, of course, argued that "appreciate" must encompass both cognitive and emotional factors. This motion was decided in favor of the prosecution; Judge Parker ruled that he would "approach the word appreciation within the context of a cognitive definition."[21]

The Prosecution

On the Issue of Mental Disease

Dr. Dietz asserted that Hinckley did not meet the diagnostic criteria for any psychotic disorder, suggesting, based on the opinions of a team of four experts, that Hinckley suffered from "dysthymic disorder," which he described as "sad mood disorder"; "narcissistic personality disorder," which he described as "self-centered or self-absorbed personality disorder"; and "schizoid personality disorder," which he explained was characterized by a lack of friends and emotional coldness or aloofness.[22] Dietz emphasized the relative commonness and less serious nature of these disorders, as compared to psychotic disorders.

In order to undermine any claim made by the defense that Hinckley was suffering from a psychotic disorder, Dr. Dietz focused on all the ways in which Hinckley appeared able to function normally: his enrollment in college, his many cross-country travels, and his interactions with others, including Jodie Foster. That he rarely attended class and performed poorly in college, that his travels were primarily for the purpose of stalking either Foster or the presidents he planned to assassinate, or that he spent most of his time alone and his interactions with others were few and brief, were not of consequence for Dr. Dietz. Highlighting the trope of common sense, witnesses for the prosecution included two hotel maids who worked at hotels at which Hinckley had stayed, including the one in which he stayed the night before he shot Reagan; the Secret Service agent who apprehended Hinckley immediately after the shooting; an FBI agent who spent several hours with Hinckley following his arrest; and the surgeon who examined Hinckley that night. These witnesses described Hinckley as "calm," "unemotional," "not out of touch with reality," and "just a normal all-American boy."[23] That Hinckley did not conform to popular notions of a stark raving lunatic and was able to perform "normal" functions became the crux of the prosecution's argument against the insanity defense.

Regarding Hinckley's delusions, Dr. Dietz testified that the obsession with Foster could not be characterized as delusional, because Hinckley recognized that his affections were not reciprocated. The judge interjected, asking, "Are you saying that in the absence of a return of interest that there was no delusional pattern?" Dr. Dietz answered that in order to be a delusion, "there has to be a view that the other person somehow shares the relationship,"[24] and that Hinckley's "interest" in Foster "took a perfectly normal course," from seeing her in a film to becoming attracted to her, and that when his efforts to establish a relationship with her failed, his acknowledgement that she was unattainable demonstrated that he was not suffering from delusions. Dr. Dietz said that Hinckley did not have a fixed false belief; rather he had "unrealistic hopes." Dr. Dietz said that Hinckley was not delusional; rather, he was "a dreamer."[25] In terms of the recorded phone conversations between Hinckley and Foster, along with the poems and letters he wrote to her and left in her mailbox, Dr. Dietz argued that these demonstrated that Hinckley understood the "social nuances" of the situation. As far as Hinckley's claims that his plans to assassinate the president were to "impress [Foster], almost to traumatize her . . . to link myself with her for . . . the rest of history," Dr. Dietz claimed that, at most, this was indicative of narcissistic personality disorder based on a preoccupation with fame and infamy.[26]

The issue of "the wave" that became so hotly debated was brought up,[27] and Dr. Dietz did not believe Hinckley's experience of this incident constituted an idea of reference (the interpretation of a commonplace and random event as if it has highly personal meaning). According to Dr. Dietz, in his interview with the defendant, Hinckley said, "[Reagan] was looking right at me, and I waved back. I was kind of startled but maybe it was just my imagination,"[28] and upon further inquiry, Hinckley eventually said that it was nothing more than a "hello" and that he was probably the only one Reagan could see. To further bolster this part of his argument, Dr. Dietz pointed to the notes of Dr. Johnson, the psychiatrist who examined Hinckley within days of the shooting; Dr. Johnson's notes stated, "President got out and waved. John waved back." Based on this assessment, Dr. Dietz suggested that Hinckley had only begun to attach any significance to the event some two months later when he was examined by the trial experts. Adelman suggested that "manipulation" was one inference that could, and should, be made, and Dietz agreed. Here we see the trope of fakery emerging in the suggestion that feigning or exaggerating symptoms of mental illness is a common tactic in insanity defense cases; by invoking this trope, the prosecution and its expert witness attempted to manufacture reasonable doubt as to Hinckley's defense.

On cross-examination, Fuller attempted to get Dr. Dietz to admit that what he characterized as narcissistic personality disorder in his earlier testimony could also be interpreted as grandiose delusions, which are often the hallmark of schizophrenia. Dr. Dietz conceded that grandiose delusions are found in schizophrenia, citing examples of people believing they are Christ or Napoleon, to which Fuller asked, "Well, there are other grandiose delusions short of thinking you are Napoleon, are there not?" Dr. Dietz admitted that, yes, there is a vast array of delusions that would be categorized as grandiose. Fuller returned to "the wave," presenting People's Exhibit 22, which was the only photograph taken near the time of Reagan's arrival at the Hilton in which Hinckley was fully visible in the crowd. When asked if Hinckley was "the only person that could be seen by one moving from the limousine to the entrance of the Hilton," Dr. Dietz answered that because the image was captured prior to the president's arrival, the cameramen did not yet have their cameras up to their faces, so many faces were visible, adhering to his previous testimony that by the time Reagan arrived, Hinckley would have been one of the only visible faces in the crowd.[29]

On Capacity to Appreciate the Wrongfulness of the Act

On direct examination, Dr. Dietz asserted that each and every decision Hinckley made, both in the months leading up to the crime and on the day of the shooting, showed that he did, in fact, appreciate the wrongfulness of his act(s). Any conscious choice, argued Dietz, clearly demonstrated that Hinckley could not possibly have been insane by legal standards: Hinckley studied famous assassinations, which indicated that he was "studying up" on how to go about the one he was planning; he replaced his larger weapons with small, concealable handguns, which showed that he had some awareness of the situation; he staked out potential assassination sites in advance, which was evidence of planning—Dietz clearly equated planning with rationality; Hinckley did not share his plans with his family or his psychiatrist, which means he knew what he was doing was wrong; he wrote a letter to Foster before leaving his hotel in which he states that he may die committing this act, again, showing he knew it was wrong; and finally, he loaded the gun, put it in his right pocket (he was right-handed), waited until he had a clear shot at Reagan, drew the gun, and fired it, this last sequence of events for Dr. Dietz being evidence of rational behavior, ergo sanity. Again, we see that the prosecution's expert was determined to rely on the widespread myth of the stark raving lunatic as the only acceptable version of legal insanity. On cross-examination, Fuller attempted to introduce some of the DSM-III criteria into the testimony, asking if "qualities of emotional coldness" would have any bearing on one's ability to appreciate the wrongfulness of an act. Adelman, of course, objected to express his concern over issues pertaining "to emotional appreciation of conduct" being allowed in; he was overruled, and Dr. Dietz responded definitively that no, emotional characteristics could "not be translated into a legal concern with the appreciation of wrongfulness."[30]

On Capacity to Conform Conduct to the Requirements of the Law

On direct examination, Dr. Dietz argued that Hinckley did not lack substantial capacity to conform his conduct to the requirements of the law. Every instance of restraint, both on the day of the shooting and in the months leading up to it, indicated that Hinckley was "conforming his conduct to his own wishes, that he had the ability to control, to think, to decide," therefore that the innate capacity to conform to the law was present and that not to do so was a conscious choice. On cross-examination, Fuller directed his questions toward eliciting testimony that would confirm the presence of Hinckley's mental disease or defect based on the notes of Dr. Dietz and his team of experts. Dr. Dietz conceded that yes, Hinckley had some sort of mental illness but that none of the evidence suggested that he "was so impaired that he could not appreciate the wrongfulness of his act or conform his conduct to the requirements of the law."[31]

The Defense

On the Issue of Mental Disease

On direct examination, Dr. Carpenter testified that Hinckley met the DSM-III criteria for schizophrenia, characterized by delusions, which he described as "the development of a false belief that is not shared by others and is not readily shaken by evidence to the contrary," and ideas of reference, which he explained as when "a person's mental state is such that they will interpret in a highly personal and idiosyncratic way . . . what may be commonplace events."[32] According to Dr. Carpenter, Hinckley's delusional state was evidenced by his "withdrawal from reality and the development of the relationship . . . with Jodie Foster," and his ideas of reference were evidenced most poignantly by one specific event on the day of the shooting that became a major point of contention: Hinckley reported to Dr. Carpenter that while waiting outside the Hilton, he observed Reagan's arrival at the hotel; according to Hinckley, as Reagan walked into the hotel, he looked at him and smiled and waved. Dr. Carpenter claimed that Hinckley's interpretation of that moment was highly personal, as he believed that the president was smiling and waving directly at him.[33] Dr. Carpenter's assessment of Hinckley's mental state at the time of the shooting, which is technically the only relevant information in determining legal insanity, was that he was experiencing "despair, depression, and a sense of the end of things," and that "his primary purpose . . . [was] to terminate his own . . . existence."[34]

On cross-examination, Adelman attempted to discredit Dr. Carpenter's diagnosis. He asked, "What you are saying is that nobody, including you, has ever found any observable delusions in . . . Mr. Hinckley, right?" and, "You are telling us in that long response that nobody observed active delusions in Mr. Hinckley, right? Or manifestations?"[35] Dr. Carpenter attempted to explain that delusions are mental processes that are impossible to observe, saying, "You can no more see a delusion than you can see whether someone believes in God."[36] Regarding the ideas of reference, Adelman quoted Hinckley's statements in his interviews with the prosecution's experts in which he apparently said, regarding the waving incident, that "I was probably the only one he could see, so that is probably why he picked me out."[37] Dr. Carpenter defended his prior testimony saying that it was still clear that Hinckley believed he was being singled out when no clear evidence to support that version of events existed, saying that it was "unlikely, that of all the people there the only person [Reagan] could see was . . . Hinckley, and in his description of the events to me, it was my inference that it was a highly personalized experience."[38]

On Capacity to Appreciate the Wrongfulness of the Act

Dr. Carpenter testified on direct examination that Hinckley, on the day of the shootings, "did have a lack, a substantial lack of capacity to appreciate the wrongfulness of his conduct."[39] As Dr. Carpenter attempted to explain his understanding of the word "appreciate," he was interrupted when the judge called the attorneys to the Bench and asked Fuller what Dr. Carpenter's answer was going to be; this, of course, is in reference to the pretrial hearing regarding the proper definition and use of "appreciate" in this trial. This entire exchange is highly illustrative of the tension that emerges when mental health experts are engaged in a legal setting, particularly in a case as high-profile as Hinckley's. Adelman's statements to the judge, and later to the jury, demonstrate the trope of illegitimacy by disparaging the defense expert as well as his profession. They are furthermore quite illustrative of the territoriality endemic to trials that hinge on the testimony of experts, particularly when those experts are psychiatrists.

Fuller replied that the doctor was going to use the definition of "appreciate" from *Brawner*[40] in order to explain Hinckley's reasoning abilities, at which point Adelman interjected, primarily to discredit Dr. Carpenter by making such remarks as, "Your Honor, our concern is that this man [Carpenter] is typically confused," and that the "only concern here is that the doctor . . . obviously doesn't know the law like we do," saying that the judge should instruct Dr. Carpenter to testify solely in terms of cognition, not volition or emotion.[41] Fuller rebutted, saying that Dr. Carpenter would testify that the mind could not be divided neatly into compartments, each of which houses cognition, will, and emotion separate from one another, and that cognition is more complex than the ability to state whether something is right or wrong. Adelman responded that Dr. Carpenter was intelligent enough to follow a simple instruction by the court to limit his answer to discussing cognition, "otherwise he is going to slip back into that area that Your Honor ruled out,"[42] "that area" being any mention of volition or emotion.

The judge expressed concern over "shackling" Dr. Carpenter's testimony, saying that what an expert witness says and what the jury would ultimately be bound by were two different things; Fuller concurred, citing *Washington*,[43] while Adelman continued to object, arguing that "the problem is we now have experts defining a legal standard."[44] The judge explained that the jury would be instructed that they would have heard a wide variety of testimony from the psychiatric experts and that they were to disregard such testimony that exceeded the boundaries of the law, which, on one hand, arguably mitigates the impact of any expert testimony, but, on another, suggests that jurors can somehow "unhear" certain information once instructed to do so. Next came a brief debate regarding whether such instructions should be given before or after Dr. Carpenter's testimony; it was decided that these instructions would be delivered after, and he was then allowed to return to the stand.

Dr. Carpenter explained that "the ability to reason that is implied in appreciation"[45] involves both intellectual and emotional processes, describing how Hinckley's reasoning processes in preparing for and carrying out his plans were focused not on whether or not these actions violated the law but solely on achieving this union with Foster and ultimately terminating his own existence. Dr. Carpenter described Hinckley's emotional impairment in appreciating the wrongfulness of his acts, saying that "the emotional consequences of the acts . . . were in his experience solely in terms of the inner world he had constructed."[46] On cross-examination, Adelman again turned toward the facts, which he hoped the jury would see were not open to interpretation. He went over the months leading up to the shooting: when in Ohio stalking President Carter, Hinckley once left his gun in his hotel room, which showed he knew it was wrong to carry a gun, especially in the presence of the president; Hinckley traveled to Nashville and into the airport complex so he could be closer to the president, which showed that he could behave in an organized manner; Hinckley hid his weapons in his suitcase, which showed that he appreciated the wrongfulness of carrying around an arsenal of firearms; Hinckley destroyed one of his diaries after he was detained in Nashville, which showed that he knew the plans it detailed were wrong in the eyes of the law.[47] Adelman wanted the jury to understand mental illness as a totalizing loss of normal function; his argument was that *any* evidence that Hinckley planned or made logical choices meant he was sane. Dr. Carpenter asserted that all of Hinckley's decisions were based on his delusions and that intellectual knowledge of the law should not be conflated with an appreciation of the wrongfulness of his acts.

On Capacity to Conform Conduct to the Requirements of the Law

On direct examination, Dr. Carpenter argued that by the day of the shooting, Hinckley's psychosis had progressed to the point that he could not conform his conduct to the requirements of the law, saying that he was entirely dominated by his inner state. On cross-examination, Adelman relied on specific facts regarding Hinckley's conduct in the time leading up to and on the day of the shooting that showed he had conformed his conduct to the requirements of the law on numerous occasions. Adelman asked if Hinckley was under the same compulsions when he did not go through with his plans to assassinate both Presidents Carter and Reagan or to commit suicide; Dr. Carpenter responded that on a number of occasions, Hinckley was under these compulsions but found himself unable to go through with his plans. Adelman used these incidents as evidence that Hinckley was conforming his conduct to the requirements of the law, while Dr. Carpenter continued to assert that this had nothing to do with consideration of the law or even with having control over his own actions, but rather that Hinckley simply could not, at those times, "get himself to do it."[48]

Adelman continued with this line of questioning for some time, which culminated in a detailed recounting of every step of Hinckley's day leading up to the shooting: Was Hinckley "under the compulsions of these inner forces" when he woke up that day? If so, then the fact that he "didn't load his gun and go outside and shoot" immediately showed that he was able to conform his conduct to the requirements of the law.[49] Dr. Carpenter explained that was not necessarily how such a compulsion would affect Hinckley; Judge Parker offered him the opportunity to elaborate on this point. Dr. Carpenter described Hinckley's mental illness as a process, one that had been developing over a substantial period of time; it was this process that brought Hinckley to DC in the first place, although over the course of such a process, major catastrophes would not be expected to occur constantly.

Closing Arguments

The Prosecution

Adelman focused on Hinckley's apparent ability to think, deliberate, and plan, arguing that this meant he was not "out of control or in a frenzy," and, therefore, able to both appreciate the wrongfulness of his act and conform his conduct to the requirements of the law. He pointed out that rather than addressing the events on the day of the shooting, the defense centered on establishing Hinckley's mental disorder; he said, "The defense never bothered to deal with that question. Why? Because they can't. Because they can't. All these doctors' CAT scans, delusions, fantasies and everything else. Miles away from that question."[50]

Adelman relied on the trope of illegitimacy throughout the trial but particularly in his closing argument; by discrediting the discipline of psychiatry, he sought to discredit the testimony of the defense experts, an endeavor in which his own expert witness had been complicit. Dr. Dietz had, at one point in the trial, remarked that "narcissistic personality even applies to some doctors," which Adelman recalled in closing argument, saying, "We didn't count noses on that one, but I think we could all put it on some of the psychiatrists." Perhaps sensing that his tone was inappropriate, he followed up with, "I don't mean to demean psychiatrists or doctors," concluding, "the evidence supports . . . whatever disorders [Hinckley had] were certainly not severe ones."[51] Hinckley, as characterized by Adelman, was the spoiled, lazy son of wealthy parents whom he took advantage of in order to pursue his whims; Hinckley's interest in Foster was just a normal fantasy; his personality disorders were common.

For Adelman, the letter Hinckley wrote to Foster before leaving his hotel room on the day of the shooting—"perfectly rational, perfectly organized"—was evidence of his sanity: "The words are in order. There is nothing—run-on sentences, paragraphs very well, everything is logically written. Is this the letter of a man who is driven, who can't control his behavior, who has an inner rage . . . who is suffering from some problem in his inner world? Would a person who has that problem write a letter like this?"[52] Aside from the quality of Hinckley's writing, the fact that he didn't mail the letter showed, according to Adelman, that when he left the hotel that day, he wasn't yet sure that he was going to go through with his plans. Adelman wanted the jury to interpret this as evidence of "planning, consideration, reflection, appreciation of wrongfulness, conforming to the law,"[53] and that the real motivation was, as Dr. Dietz's diagnosis of narcissistic personality disorder would suggest, Hinckley's desire for fame. After recounting in detail the hours and minutes leading up to the shooting, Adelman told the jury that Hinckley was neither "out of control" nor "in a frenzy," that he made a decision to fire his gun six times, and that he should be held "criminally responsible for each and every one of these crimes."[54]

The Defense

Fuller urged the jury to take a more holistic approach to assessing Hinckley's mental state, saying they should not allow the prosecution's "suggestion that only [the events of] March 30, 1981, should be considered" to "mislead" them: "It took years and years of growth of the disease or disorder to lead to the state of mind" on that day, and "the question is not only what he was like then [on the day of the shooting], but to show what he was like, we must look how he got there."[55] Fuller wanted the jury to look at Hinckley's mental illness as a complex process that developed over a long period of time, suggesting that the prosecution's experts downplayed the deterioration of his mental state.

Pointing to the charts provided by the government depicting Hinckley's travel patterns in the months leading up to the shooting, Fuller said, "I think they [the prosecution's experts] also trivialized the frenetic behavior of the defendant over the months preceding the tragedy. . . . You look at the absolutely absurd travel patterns by this man. . . . On its face, it is irrational, purposeless, aimless."[56] Evidence the prosecution used to demonstrate Hinckley's careful planning and deliberation is characterized by the defense as frenzied and maniacal. Fuller summarized Hinckley's years leading up to the shooting, characterizing his life as anything but that of "an ordinary person like any other young man, and all American boy like any other fan," saying, "He lived a solitary life. He was a prisoner of himself for at least seven years before this tragedy. . . . To call him an ordinary boy . . . is silly."[57]

Fuller chose his words carefully, characterizing all of Hinckley's thoughts and actions as "bizarre," "psychotic," "delusional," and the "result of a serious mental illness in which [his] relation to reality . . . has been severed."[58] Confronting the stereotypical myth of the lunatic endorsed by the defense throughout the trial, Fuller argued:

> I think the evidence is clear from both sides . . . that the ability of a schizophrenic to maintain a contact with common reality is not unusual. . . . A severely ill psychotic schizophrenic may have a world of troubles unnoticed totally, unnoticed by us laymen, and bizarre conduct is not an indispensable ingredient to a diagnosis of schizophrenia. . . . The kind of frenzy we are talking about is an internal frenzy, an internal confusion, one that is going on in this man's inner world, all built upon false premises, false assumptions, false ideas. . . . Mr. Adelman suggested psychiatric influences, thought delusions, fantasies are not evidence you should consider in this case. That is precisely the kind of evidence you should consider in this case. That is why we are here.[59]

He went on to assert that "reconstruct[ing], as the government physicians have tried to do, the minute-by-minute progression of the defendant's thought processes" on the day of the shooting was impossible; he emphasized that in the "delusional state," Hinckley was not focused on the victims but on gaining "the love and affection and establish[ing] the relationship with Jodie Foster."[60] Fuller returned to the words of Dr. Dietz, who stated that Hinckley's actions "were not the reasonable acts of an entirely rational individual,"[61] concluding his remarks by assuring the jury that the prosecution had not met its burden of proof in establishing that Hinckley should be held criminally responsible for his actions.

Adelman took the opportunity to offer a rebuttal, attempting to draw the jury's attention back to the events on the day of the shooting: "How outrageous to say to you that nobody can reconstruct Mr. Hinckley's thoughts of March 30, 1981, like the Government doctors did. How did they do it? By talking to him and recording what he said. The doctors didn't make up these thoughts. John Hinckley told them, for goodness' sake."[62] Adelman suggested that all of the defense testimony regarding the years prior to the shooting had nothing to do with the crime, calling it "a parade of irrelevancies." He claimed that Hinckley's mental problems were common: "I think if we tried a lot of people's mental condition on New Year's Eve, it might be similar to John Hinckley on that date."[63] He argued that psychotic people demonstrate psychotic behavior, in spite of what the defense claimed; he did not, however, say what such behavior would be, leading the jury to conclude that psychosis can only mean raving, maniacal behavior that everyone can see. To support this claim, Adelman recalled the testimony of all the lay witnesses he had called: the hotel maids, the Secret Service and FBI agents, all of whom had interacted with Hinckley shortly before or after the shooting. The testimony of these witnesses, he argued, proved that there was no possibility that Hinckley was suffering from psychosis and that he most certainly possessed the ability to appreciate the wrongfulness of his act and conform his conduct to the requirements of the law.

Adelman trivialized Hinckley's erratic travel in the months preceding the shooting, calling his wanderings "the behavior of a desperate, bored young man with a pocket full of money . . . who likes Jodie Foster. Wouldn't we all like to be in this situation?"[64] Concluding his rebuttal, Adelman again emphasized that whatever personality defects Hinckley exhibited were not indicative of a serious mental disorder, that he did appreciate the wrongfulness of his actions, that he could conform his conduct to the law, and that they, the jury, were obligated to hold him criminally responsible for his actions in the name of justice.

Jury Instructions

Jury instructions in insanity defense trials have long been a source of controversy, and we should understand how the Hinckley jurors were told to make their decision. Judge Parker explained to them that the burden, as in all criminal trials, was on the government to prove the defendant guilty beyond a reasonable doubt. Specifically regarding the issue of legal insanity, he explained the burden of proving the defendant criminally responsible beyond a reasonable doubt. Outlining three possible verdicts for each of the thirteen counts of the indictment—guilty, not guilty, or not guilty by reason of insanity—he explained the parameters of the final option based on the language of the Model Penal Code: "The law provides that a jury shall bring a verdict of not guilty by reason of insanity if at the time of the criminal conduct the defendant, as a result of mental disease or defect, either lacked substantial capacity to conform his conduct to the requirements of the law or lacked substantial capacity to appreciate the wrongfulness of his conduct."[65] At this time, there was yet another brief debate over the use of the word "appreciate," even though it was part of the MPC standards. Adelman opposed its use as it opened up the possibility that the jury might consider both cognitive and emotional aspects of understanding (as if the two can be separated) and asked that the word be left undefined unless the court specified that it was strictly confined to cognitive understanding. Fuller asked that the word be defined to include emotional understanding or that such an interpretation be emphasized. Judge Parker opted to not define it at all.

Jury instructions regarding the definition of "mental disease or defect" are clearly of substantial importance in an insanity defense trial. Judge Parker explained that, while typically every defendant is presumed to be sane and responsible for his actions, when evidence of mental disease or defect is introduced, that presumption no longer holds. He said, "'insanity' does not require a showing that the defendant was disoriented in time or place," defining "mental disease or defect" as "any abnormal condition of the mind, regardless of its medical label, which substantially affects mental or emotional processes and . . . behavior controls"; he further provided the distinction between "disease" and "defect," the former being "capable of improving or deteriorating" and the latter capable of neither,[66] echoing the *Durham* court from some three decades prior. Parker instructed the jury that they could consider testimony regarding "the development, adaptation, and functioning of these mental and emotional processes and behavior controls" in deciding whether the defendant was suffering from a mental disease or defect at the time he committed the crime; he also permitted them to consider evidence regarding the defendant's mental condition on the day of the shooting as well as prior to and following the day of the shooting.

Judge Parker also instructed the jury on how to weigh the testimony of the many witnesses regarding the defendant's mental state. In terms of the experts, he explained that the jury should not be "bound by medical labels, definitions, or conclusions as to what is or is not a mental disease or defect" since the medical definitions, the purpose of which is deciding on treatment, may differ from the legal definitions, the purpose of which is determining criminal responsibility. The determination of criminal responsibility, he said, was the jury's alone to decide. In terms of the lay witnesses, he explained that the jury could consider that testimony but advised that they "bear in mind that an untrained person may not be readily able to detect mental disease or defect," suggesting that the testimony of witnesses without "prolonged and intimate contact with the defendant" who did not observe "abnormal acts"[67] need not be of significance to their decision.

Finally, Judge Parker explained if they did find the defendant not guilty by reason of insanity, he would be committed to St. Elizabeths Hospital; there, within fifty days, he would be permitted a hearing to determine his eligibility for release, but in this hearing, he would have the burden of proof.

He stated that the defendant would remain in custody unless "the Court finds by a preponderance of evidence that he is not likely to injure himself or other persons due to a mental disease."[68] The jury found Hinckley not guilty by reason of insanity, and he was committed to St. Elizabeths where he remained until 2016.

Public Reaction

The Hinckley verdict both shocked and angered the American public and provided a platform for political figures to express their moral outrage. The Associated Press cited an ABC News telephone poll that claimed 76 percent of those surveyed felt "justice had not been done in the Hinckley case."[69] Calls for abolition of the insanity defense were common, because, as one editorial writer wrote in the *New York Times*, the defense itself "is a prostitution of justice": "Since psychiatry has proven itself to be an abject failure in recognizing, treating, and predicting criminal behavior . . . psychiatry should be removed from the decision-making process. . . . The insanity defense has become an encouragement to crime, and so long as even one criminal can get away with murder by feigning insanity, the justice system will remain unable to protect citizens. . . . The insanity defense needs to be abolished, along with the practice of allowing psychiatrists to prostitute themselves and justice by pretending to be experts in court and acting as hired guns for both sides in a psychiatric showdown—their diagnoses and prognoses determined by who is paying their fees."[70] This statement is rife with the rhetoric of sanism, drawing on almost every trope I have identified. That psychiatry is deemed an "abject failure" and psychiatrists "prostitute themselves and justice by pretending to be experts and acting as hired guns" relies on the trope of illegitimacy. The trope of fakery also appears when the writer refers to criminals "get[ting] away with murder by feigning insanity." The suggestion that "the insanity defense has become an encouragement to crime" and renders "the justice system unable to protect citizens" illustrates the trope of pandemonium. These myths and their corresponding tropes make clear how sanism is deeply embedded in public discourse.

Many politicians were quick to jump on the bandwagon, as "tough on crime" policies had begun to gain traction in recent years. Texas Senator Ray Farabee stated that the insanity defense "undermines public confidence in our criminal justice system."[71] South Carolina Senator Strom Thurmond, then chairman of the Judiciary Committee, said he was troubled by the exoneration of "a defendant who obviously planned and knew exactly what he was doing," and that the Hinckley trial demonstrated that "there is something fundamentally wrong with the expanded modern insanity defense."[72]

Utah senator Orrin Hatch stated, "I don't find fault with the jury, I find fault with the law."[73] Treasury Secretary Donald Regan said, "Frankly, I'm outraged. I think when a person stalks a leading citizen of this country, shoots him, three of the people surrounding him, and then goes off scot-free, I think that's absolutely atrocious."[74]

Federal and State Reforms

In response to the massive public outcry following the Hinckley verdict, legislative movement was underway throughout the country at both the state and federal levels. These reforms included narrowing the substantive test of insanity, shifting the burden of proof to the defendant, supplementing the NGRI verdict with a verdict of "guilty but mentally ill," and abolishing the defense altogether.

In 1984, Congress passed the Insanity Defense Reform Act (IDRA). With endorsements from both the American Bar Association (ABA) and the American Psychiatric Association (APA), the first major change enacted by IDRA was that the substantive test for insanity was modified to change the requirement of a "mental disease or defect" to "severe mental disease" and to eliminate the volitional component or "control" test that had emerged in the late nineteenth century in *Parsons* and *Davis* and remained at the time the Model Penal Code was drafted. Advocating for the elimination of the volitional prong of the existing test, attorney Richard Bonnie argued that the "fluid and imprecise" medical definitions of insanity led to "an unacceptable risk of abuse and mistake" in insanity defense trials.[75] The APA agreed with this claim, asserting that "the line between an irresistible impulse and an impulse not resisted is probably no sharper than that between twilight and dusk," and "psychiatric testimony (particularly that of a conclusory nature) about volition is more likely to cause confusion for jurors," as opposed to testimony strictly confined to a defendant's appreciation of the wrongfulness of his conduct.[76]

The second major change came in the form of an alternative to the not guilty by reason of insanity verdict: guilty but mentally ill (GBMI). GBMI verdicts would result in a conviction and criminal sentence with the option for the inmate to receive psychiatric treatment at the discretion of the correctional facility in which he was incarcerated. Critics of this method argued it did not guarantee mental health care to mentally ill prisoners and, not surprisingly, they have thus far been correct. This is namely because, just as with NGRI verdicts, jury instructions and post-conviction procedures for GBMI verdicts vary widely from state to state. Even more interesting is that the definition of mental illness for a GBMI verdict "is typically drawn from the state's civil commitment statute and is usually much broader than the 'mental disease' required for the insanity defense."[77]

The third significant change IDRA brought was to procedures concerning the burden of proof. Before the Hinckley verdict, a slight majority of states placed the burden of proof on the prosecution, as was the case in Hinckley's trial, meaning that the onus was on the prosecutors to prove that the defendant was not legally insane at the time of the crime. IDRA officially reversed this procedure, shifting the burden to defendants wishing to plead insanity to prove beyond a reasonable doubt that they were legally insane at the time of the crime.[78]

Ultimately, four states—Idaho, Kansas, Utah, and Montana—abolished the insanity defense altogether. Courts in these states continue to allow evidence of a defendant's mental illness, but the scope is narrowed to the "purpose of proving that the defendant did not have any special knowledge or intent required for conviction."[79] Under such conditions, intent, regardless of capacity to appreciate wrongfulness or control conduct, becomes the prevailing factor. Had Hinckley's jury been given this instruction, his intention to kill the president would have been enough to convict him.

While the insanity defense continues to be contested and debated, particularly during high-profile trials—since Hinckley, just a few have included Andrea Yates, Lorena Bobbitt, and James Holmes—no major legislation has been enacted since IDRA. It should be noted that each state continues to determine which test or combination of tests are used; all states that still allow a defense of NGRI use some version of McNaughtan, some with consideration of "irresistible impulse," and the burden of proof is different from state to state. It is also interesting to know that in states that abolished the NGRI verdict in favor of GBMI, defendants who would have plead not guilty by reason of insanity are now, generally, being declared incompetent to stand trial, which has outcomes similar to a NGRI verdict.[80]

What we see in this history of the defense, as well as the continued challenges courts face when considering mental illness, is that it is best understood as an ideologic. By framing it in the language of rhetoric, we can more clearly see its landscape as that of competing discourses attempting to shore up their boundaries, continually smoothing over the narrative ruptures always threatening to break through. Hinckley's trial brought these issues to the forefront of public discourse on a national scale for the first time in the twentieth century, but as the cases that preceded it and those that have followed it show, the incompatible objectives of psychiatry and law seem to preordain ongoing conflict in locating a coherent legal procedure for mentally ill defendants.

Conclusion

The Insanity Defense Since Hinckley

> "The sanism . . . that drives mental disability law is rooted in prejudice. It is a prejudice that is invisible and hidden, is rarely recognized, and is largely socially acceptable. And this prejudice has corrupted all of us who are players in the system: lawyers, mental health professionals, judges, and forensic witnesses. And it is persons with mental disabilities who have suffered—and who continue to suffer."
>
> —Michael Perlin

> "The day will come when we look back at our current medicines . . . and the stories we tell to patients about their abnormal brain chemistry, and they will shake their heads in utter disbelief."
>
> —Robert Whitaker

Over thirty-five years have passed since the Hinckley verdict. Neither the legal standards for the insanity defense nor the conflict and controversy surrounding it have changed much. Legal scholars have continued to conduct a great deal of research to determine the effects of the varying tests for legal insanity on juror decision-making, and the results have repeatedly demonstrated that there is no significant difference in verdicts regardless of which version of the test is used; in fact, studies in which jurors are given no official test and instructed only to use their own best judgment yield results similar to those with each of the available iterations.[1] What this means, of course, is that a century and a half of debate between legal and mental health professionals, as well as shock and moral outrage from the public over any high-profile insanity defense trial, have had no significant effect on the insanity defense—how often it is used, how often it is successful, or what happens to successful NGRI acquittees after their verdicts. In fact, the only changes of note have occurred in states such as Montana that abolished the defense altogether in favor of the Guilty but Mentally Ill (GBMI) option. Data from those states have shown that defense attorneys for those defendants who would previously have entered a plea of not guilty by reason of insanity are now having their clients declared incompetent to stand trial;[2] this has roughly the same effect as a NGRI verdict, in that the defendants are confined to mental hospitals until they are judged competent for the purposes of participating in their defense. Basically, the number of defendants declared incompetent to stand trial is the same as the number of defendants who successfully pleaded NGRI when that was an option; it has been an even exchange, the legal and pragmatic results of which are largely identical. How can it be that over a century of linguistic wrangling has had almost no material impact on the function of the insanity defense? The rhetoric of sanism is a good explanation, along with the staying power of ideologic.

Few insanity defense trials since Hinckley have garnered as much public attention, but they continue to distort public sentiment about the use of the NGRI plea. Jeffrey Dahmer, accused of the murder of seventeen men, along with rape, dismemberment, and even cannibalism, pleaded not guilty by reason of insanity in his 1992 trial; he was unsuccessful, found guilty, sentenced to life in prison, and eventually murdered by another inmate.[3] Andrea Yates, who, in 2001, drowned her five children in the bathtub of her family home after years of well-documented, poorly managed mental illness, pleaded not guilty by reason of insanity; she was unsuccessful in her first trial, barely escaping the death penalty, and probably only because the jury was made aware that an expert for the prosecution lied on the stand before deciding on her sentence. Her appeal, however, was successful, and she remains institutionalized as recently as late 2017.[4] The trial of James Holmes for the 2012 Aurora movie theater mass shooting captured the nation's attention; he too was unsuccessful in his plea of not guilty by reason of insanity and was sentenced to life in prison in Colorado.[5] In all of these trials, similarly to Hinckley's, the prosecution emphasized the defendants' abilities to plan and act according to those plans as evidence of their sanity; after the public outcry over Hinckley and the shift in the legal standards for insanity (which still vary from state to state),[6] it appears that "knowing right from wrong" is once again the linchpin of the decision-making process. Here we are, back in England in 1843.

In 2017, a University of Texas, Austin, student named Kendrex White attacked fellow students with a hunting knife, killing one and wounding three others; as of this writing, his defense team has announced that they intend to offer a defense of NGRI. Whether they ultimately use it remains to be seen, though it would offer an interesting feature not present in the aforementioned cases, because the defendant is African American. Race is always a salient factor in the criminal justice system, but high-profile insanity defense cases rarely involve nonwhite defendants. In such cases, the insanity defense, in many ways, is an option for the (relatively) privileged, as are thorough and competent criminal defenses, more generally speaking.

Aside from these cases that loom large in the public memory, we rarely hear about the one percent of criminal cases in which an insanity defense is raised. I have had a Google alert for "insanity defense" set for some years now, since I've been working on this book, and there are mentions every day in local newspapers that never break through and make national headlines. A few recent headlines include: "Man Accused of Killing His Sisters Seeks Insanity Defense,"[7] "Man Who Killed Mother with Sword Committed After Guilty Plea, Insanity Finding,"[8] and "SC Mom Accused of Killing Kids Pleads Not Guilty, Uses Insanity Defense."[9] Even these cases, the ones that make it to smaller local newspapers, are still more bizarre or brutal than the vast majority of the cases that actually use the defense; most of those are not newsworthy at all, so public perception continues to be skewed by the media coverage.

Unlike the law, the medical study of the brain in the past few decades has yielded what seem to be tremendous insights into our understanding of mental illness and even criminality. For over two hundred years, attempts to learn the causes of and treatments for mental illness were hung up on a paradigm of nature versus nurture, biology versus socialization. Recent work has essentially shattered that paradigm and allowed us to understand that it is never "either/or" but rather, always "both/and." Who we are as individuals, our "decision-making and [our] desires . . . depend[s] on the intricate details of [our] neural machinery. Although acting on such drives [e.g., aggressiveness, sexual predilections] is popularly thought to be a free choice, the most cursory examination of the evidence demonstrates the limits of that assumption."[10] Lest we attempt to reduce human complexity to neurobiology, we must also recognize the influence of environmental and social structures on biological functions.

A popular book by neuroscientist Dr. James Fallon, *The Psychopath Inside*,[11] provides an interesting personal account of such a discovery. Fallon, who spent years studying "the psychopathic brain" by doing Functional Magnetic Resonance Imaging (fMRI)[12] on incarcerated populations, concluded that "the criminal mind" has a unique structure that shows a distinct difference from a "normal" brain in the frontal and temporal lobes, which are the areas that account for self-control and empathy. While using himself as a control group participant in an entirely different study, Dr. Fallon discovered, completely accidentally and much to his dismay, that he himself has the same neurological structure as the psychopaths he spent years studying. This revelation led him to conclude that biology cannot be the only explanation for criminality, since he is a prominent neuroscientist and by all accounts a functioning member of society. What he discovered in his subsequent efforts to understand himself and the research this new knowledge led him to conduct is that psychopathy, that is, antisocial behavior, is the result of both biology and socialization, nature and nurture. To put it simply, anyone can be born with the genetic makeup that will predispose them to antisocial behavior, which includes certain genes as well as brain structure (nature). What will determine whether or not certain traits are activated lies in how that individual is socialized, and this goes as far back as when the individual is in utero, but particularly during early childhood (nurture).

Similarly, changes to a person's neurobiology, such as developing a brain tumor, affect their behavior in what can be drastic and alarming ways. For example, Charles Whitman, more commonly known as the University of Texas Tower shooter,[13] "requested in his suicide note that an autopsy be performed to determine if [as he suspected] something had changed in his brain." An autopsy confirmed Whitman's suspicions when "a tumor the diameter of a nickel" known as a glioblastoma was discovered; the tumor was compressing the amygdala, the area of the brain responsible for regulating emotions such as fear and aggression. Scientists have known "that damage to the amygdala cause[s] emotional and social disturbances" for over a century,[14] yet this very significant revelation is rarely a serious consideration in discussions of criminality.

Numerous studies have supported Fallon's conclusions and demonstrated the fallacy of the nature/nurture distinction; nature and nurture are, in fact, one and the same. Prior to learning of Fallon's work, I came across a different study that made me think about my own work, one involving rats and parenting.[15] This study looked at the behavior of rat mothers: "good" mothers licked their babies a lot, while "bad" mothers did not. To nobody's surprise, the children of the "good" mothers exhibited "good" mothering behavior when they had babies, while the children of the "bad" mothers followed the behavior with which they were raised. What was very surprising was that the results were not simply the product of socialization or the rats mimicking their mothers' behavior but that the licking, or the lack thereof, sets off a hormonal domino effect that actually changes the chemical markers (epigenome) of certain areas of DNA.[16] Again, nature and nurture are indistinguishable in terms of their effects on animal behavior.

Social science research has yielded similar conclusions in multiple studies. As much as humanities scholars have sought to move away from biological determinism in favor of a social constructivist perspective, research on criminality has shown repeatedly that nature is as significant as nurture (if not more), or, more accurately, that the two cannot be separated into discrete strands for the purposes of understanding human behavior. Several studies have been conducted on children born to convicted criminals; the children were placed for adoption, and the eventual criminal conduct of the children suggests a heritable component to antisocial behavior.[17] Some of the more interesting and highly controversial research studies are "twin studies," research conducted on twins separated at birth and placed for adoption with different families. Dr. Peter Neubauer conducted one such study during the 1960s and '70s; families adopting each twin were told that their child would be part of a study, but they were never told that the child had a twin.[18] This study and others like it have become so controversial that the results of the Neubauer study are actually sealed until 2066 in an archive at Yale. The Minnesota Twin Family Study that ran from 1979 to 1999 followed 137 sets of twins separated at birth and reared apart. This study also confirmed the role of genetics in traits (such as religiosity, happiness and well-being, and social attitudes) that researchers hypothesized would be more strongly influenced by environment.[19] What I wish to emphasize here is that we now know that people are the product of their genetic makeup, but their genetic makeup is largely a product of their early life experiences; in other words, there is an infinite looping effect of nature and nurture, and the results are endlessly varied.

There are a number of predictors of criminality, and it is no coincidence that these predictors correspond to mental illness as well; these risk factors range from complications while in utero, to parental substance abuse, to poverty and exposure to violence (among many others).[20] What I primarily wish to point out is that understanding human behavior requires a massive accounting of infinite individual variables, while the law is designed as a one-size-fits-all institution and is not at all equipped to address the myriad conditions that influence mental illness or criminality, especially not when the two have to be considered together. That is the primary argument I have made in this book: psychiatry and law have fundamentally different ideological orientations, and this makes any criminal trial in which a defense involving mental illness is raised exceedingly complicated; approaching psychiatry and law as fundamentally rhetorical in nature helps us begin to untangle these knots.

The PBS series *Brains on Trial* hosted by Alan Alda[21] presents us with a glimpse into what it might look like if the criminal justice system adequately considered the neurological nuances of both the criminal behavior of the defendant as well as the unconscious biases of the judge and jury. Ultimately, we would need to conduct a full psychological and social history as well as fMRI on every defendant, judge, and juror in *every* trial, not just those involving an insanity plea, to screen for different neurological structures as well as varying biases in order to facilitate a truly fair legal process. While utterly fascinating, the institution of criminal justice is simply not designed to accommodate such demands. Imagining this as the new legal process is laughable; the time and money required are absurd, especially for a system that is already overburdened, underfunded, and constantly under attack for its many flaws.

Moreover, in spite of all of these advances in the understanding and treatment of mental illness that began with the advent in the 1950s of psychopharmaceuticals, the use of which skyrocketed during the 1980s and has been on a steady incline ever since, the number of adults and children in the United States classified as disabled due to mental illness has continued to rise. If we now better understand mental illness, and we have continued to develop pharmacological treatments that are more effective, the number of people disabled by their mental illness should have been decreasing steadily throughout this period.[22] This conundrum highlights a major flaw in this particular area of science.

Furthermore, during the time of this writing, a new study found that the software used to process the results of fMRI scans is flawed: the rate of false positives for most scientific research can be expected to be around five percent; the researchers who attempted to validate the results of the some forty thousand published studies whose results relied on fMRI data found a false positive rate of up to 70 percent in some cases.[23] This study now calls into question over two decades of research from which determinations regarding human behavior based on brain imaging have been made. These findings do not invalidate all of the aforementioned social science research, or even, necessarily, the fMRI research. What they do highlight, however, is the fragility of science itself. Like "The Law," we like to imagine capital-S "Science" as a stable and fixed entity. Again, the nature of discovery and innovation that inevitably brings about the debunking of previously held beliefs should dissuade this perception. Yet, so much in our daily lives is based on what we *know* from scientific discoveries, that upending our assumption of its correctness would have a destabilizing effect: this is the force of ideologic at work.

I have presented the history of the insanity defense by the major cases that define it, as acknowledged by legal scholars and historians. I have also provided some history of psychiatry as it intersected with these cases and influenced their legal outcomes. I have pointed out the influence of both moralism and widely accepted myths about mental illness on the law and psychiatry. What I hope is clear, then, is that both the law and psychiatry are endlessly interpretable and continually shifting, but both The Law and Psychiatry writ large are hegemonic discourses. As such, they serve particular social functions, and exposing the ruptures in either narrative of fixity is very costly to those it serves.

What I am describing here is an intractable problem; we are dealing with a jumble of what Sharon Crowley calls "densely articulated" ideologies[24] that attempt to function as a system: the law, psychiatry, public perception, mass media. Each has its own ideological orientation, and each serves a distinct purpose. It is no wonder that every high-profile case and every attempt to "fix" the problems with the insanity defense have, at best, had no significant effect, and, more often, have only served to further complicate the issue. Understanding the practices of both law and psychiatry as rhetorical by no means locates some elusive solution to the problem. Instead, it allows us to see more clearly *why* it is still a problem.

Appendix 1

Excerpts from *Parsons v. State*
Opinion by: Somerville
Decided July 28, 1887

In this case the defendants have been convicted of the murder of Bennett Parsons, by shooting him with a gun; one of the defendants being the wife and the other the daughter of the deceased. The defense set up in the trial was the plea of insanity, the evidence tending to show that the daughter was an idiot, and the mother and wife a lunatic, subject to insane delusions, and that the killing on her part was the offspring and product of those delusions.

The rulings of the court raise some questions of no less difficulty than of interest; for, as observed by a distinguished American judge, "of all medico-legal questions, those connected with insanity are the most difficult and perplexing." Per Dillon, G. J., in *State v. Felter*, 25 Iowa, 67. It has become of late a matter of comment among intelligent men, including the most advanced thinkers in the medical and legal professions, that the deliverances of the law courts on this branch of our jurisprudence have not heretofore been at all satisfactory, either in the soundness of their theories, or in their practical application. The earliest English decisions, striving to establish rules and tests on the subject, including alike the legal rules of criminal and civil responsibility, and the supposed tests of the existence of the disease of insanity itself, are now admitted to have been deplorably erroneous, and, to say nothing of their vacillating character, have long since been abandoned. The views of the ablest of the old text writers and sages of the law were equally confused and uncertain in the treatment of these subjects, and they are now entirely exploded. Time was in the history of our laws that the veriest lunatic was debarred from pleading his providential affliction as a defense to his contracts. It was said, in justilication of so absurd a rule, that no one could be permitted to stultify himself by pleading his own disability. So great a jurist as Lord Coke, in his attempted class incution of madmen, laid down the legal rule of criminal responsibility to be that one should "*wholly* have lost his memory and understanding;" as to which Mr. Erskine, when defending Hadfield for shooting the king, in the year 1800, justly observed: "No such madman ever existed in the world." After this great and historical case, the existence of delusion promised for a while to become the sole test of insanity, and, acting under the duress of such delusion, was recognized in effect as the legal rule of responsibility. Lord Kenyon, after ordering a verdict of acquittal in that case, declared with emphasis that there was "no doubt on earth" the law was correctly stated in the argument of counsel. But, as it was soon discovered that insanity often existed without delusions, as well as delusions without insanity, this view was also abandoned. Lord Hale had before declared that the rule of responsibility was measured by the mental capacity possessed by a child 14 years of age; and Mr. Justice Traoy, and other judges had ventured to decide that, to be non-punishable for alleged acts of crime, "a man must be totally deprived of his understanding and memory, so as not to know what he was doing, no more than an infant, a brute, or *a wild beast*." *Arnold's Cam*, 16 How. State Tr. 764. All these rules have necessarily been discarded in modern times in the light of the new scientific knowledge acquired by a more thorough study of the disease of insanity. In *Bellingham's Case*, decided in 1812, by Lord Mansfield at the Old Bailey, (Coll. Lun. 630,) the test was held to consist in a Knowledge that murder, the crime there committed, was "against the laws of God and nature," thus meaning an ability to distinguish between right and wrong in the abstract. This rule was not adhered to, but seems to have been modified so as to make the test rather a knowledge of right and wrong as applied to the particular act. Lawson, Insan. 231, § 7 *et seq*. The great leading case on this subject in England is *McNaghten's Case*, decided in 1843 before the English house of lords. 10 Clark & F. 200; Lawson, Crim. Def. 150. It was decided by the judges in that case that, in order to entitle the accused to acquittal, it must be clearly proved that, at the time of committing the offense, he was laboring under such a defect of reason, from disease of the mind, as not to know the nature and quality of the act he was doing, or, if he did, not to know that what he was doing was wrong. This rule is commonly supposed to have heretofore been adopted by this court, and has been followed by the general current of American adjudications. *Bostoell v. State*, 63 Ala, 307, 35

Amer. Rep. 20, and Lawson, Crim. Def. 352; *MeAllister v. State*, 17 Ala. 484; Lawson, Insan. 219–221. 231.

In view of these conflicting decisions, and of the new light thrown on the disease of insanity by the discoveries of modern psychological medicine, the courts of the country may well hesitate before blindly following in the unsteady footsteps found upon the old sandstones of our common-law jurisprudence a century ago. The trial court, with prudent propriety, followed the previous decisions of this court, the correctness of which, as to this subject, we are now requested to review.

We do not hesitate to say that we reopen the discussion of this subject with no little reluctance, having long hesitated to disturb our past decisions on this branch of the law. Nothing could induce us to do so except an imperious sense of duty, which has been excited by a protracted investigation and study, impressing our minds with the conviction that the law of insanity as declared by the courts on many points, and especially the rule of criminal accountability, and the assumed tests of disease, to that extent which wafers legal irresponsibility, have not kept pace with the progress of thought and discovery in the present advanced stages of medical science. Though science has led the way, the courts of England have declined to follow, as shown by their adherence to the rulings in *McNaghten's Case*, emphasized by the strange declaration made by the lord chancellor of England, in the house of lords, on so late a day as March 11, 1862, that "the introduction of medical opinions and medical theories into this subject has proceeded upon *the vicious principle of considering insanity as a disease*." It is not surprising that this state of affairs had elicited from a learned law writer, who treats of this subject, the humiliating declaration that, under the influence of these ancient theories, "the memorials of our Jurisprudence are written all over with cases in which those who are now understood to have been insane, have been executed as criminals." 1 Bish. Crim. Law, (7th Ed.) § 390. There is good reason, both for this fact, and for the existence of unsatisfactory rules on this subject. In what we say we do not intend to give countenance to acquittals of criminals, frequent examples of which have been witnessed in modern times, based on the doctrine of moral or emotional insanity, unconnected with mental disease, which is not yet sufficiently supported by psychology, or recognized by law as an excuse for crime. *Bostoell's Case, supra*; 1 Whart. Crim. Law, (9th Ed.) § 43.

In ancient times, lunatics were not regarded as "unfortunate sufferers from disease, but rather as subjects of demoniacal possession, or as self-made victims of evil passions." They were not cared for humanely in asylums and hospitals, but were incarcerated in jails, punished with chains and stripes, and often sentenced to death by burning or the gibbet. When put on their trial the issue before the court then was not as now. If acquitted, they could only be turned loose on the community to repeat their crimes without molestation or restraint. They could not be committed to hospitals, as at the present day, to be kept in custody, cared for by medical attention, and often cured. It was not until the beginning of the present century that the progress of Christian civilization asserted itself by the exposure of the then existing barbarities, and that the outcry of philanthropists succeeded in eliciting an investigation of the British parliament looking to their suppression. Up to that period the medical treatment of the insane is known to have been conducted upon a basis of ignorance, inhumanity, and empiricism. 9 Amer. Cyclop. (1874,) tit. "Insanity." Being punished for wickedness, rather than treated for disease, this is not surprising. The exposure of these evils not only led to the establishment of that most beneficent of modern civilized charities,—the hospital and asylum for the insane,—but also furnished hitherto unequaled opportunities to the medical profession of investigating and treating insanity on the pathological basis of its being a disease of the mind. Under these new and more favorable conditions, the medical jurisprudence of insanity has assumed an entirely new phase. The nature and exciting causes of the disease have been thoroughly studied and more fully comprehended. The result is that the "right and wrong test," as it is sometimes called, which, it must be remembered, itself originated with the medical profession, in the mere dawn of the scientific knowledge of insanity, has been condemned by the great current of modern medical authorities, who believe it to be "founded on an ignorant and imperfect view of the disease." 15 Encyclop. Brit. (9th Ed.) tit. "Insanity."

The question, then, presented seems to be whether an old rule of legal responsibility shall be adhered to, based on theories of physicians promulgated a hundred years ago, which refuse to recognize any evidence of insanity, except the single test, of mental capacity to distinguish right and wrong, or whether the courts will recognize as a possible fact, if capable of proof by clear and satisfactory testimony, the doctrine, now alleged by those of the medical profession who have made insanity a special subject of investigation, that the old test is wrong, and tout there is no single test by which the existence of the disease, to that degree which exempts from punishment, can in every case be infallibly detected. The inquiry must not be unduly obstructed by the doctrine of *stare decisis*, for the life of the common law system and the hope of its permanency consist largely in its power of adaptation to new scientize discoveries, and the requirements of an ever advancing civilisation. There is inherent in it the vital principle of juridical evolution, which preserves Itself by a constant struggle for approximation to the highest practical wisdom. It is not like the laws of the Medes and Persians, which could not be changed. In establishing any new rule, we should strive, however, to have proper regard for two opposite aspects of the subject, lest, in the words of Lord Hale, "on one side, there be a kind of inhumanity towards the defects of human nature, or, on the other, too great indulgence to great crimes."

It is everywhere admitted, and as to this there can be no doubt, that an Idiot, lunatic, or other person of diseased mind, who is afflicted to such extent as not to know whether he is doing right or wrong, is not punishable for any act which he may do while in that state. Can the courts justly say, however, that the only test or rule of responsibility in criminal cases is the power to distinguish right from wrong, whether in the abstract, or as applied to the particular case? Or may there not be insane persons, of a diseased brain, who, while capable of perceiving the difference between right and wrong, are, as matter of fact so far under *the duress of such disease* as to destroy *the power to choose* between right and wrong? Will the courts assume as a fact, not to be rebutted by any amount of evidence, or any new discoveries of medical science, that there is and can be no such state of mind as that described by a writer on psychological medicine as one "in which the reason has lost its empire over the passions, and the actions by which they are manifested, to such a degree that the individual can neither repress the former, nor abstain from the latter?" Dean, Mod. Jur. 497.

Much confusion can be avoided in the discussion of this subject by separating the duty of the jury from that of the court in the trial of a case of this character. The province of the Jury is to determine facts, that of the court to state the law. The rule in *McNaghten's Case* arrogates to the court, in legal effort, the right to assert, as matter of law, the following propositions: (1) That there is but a single test of the existence of that degree of insanity such as confers irresponsibility for crime; (2) that there does not exist any case of such insanity in which that single test—the capacity to distinguish right from wrong—does not appear; (3) that all other evidences of alleged insanity, supposed by physicians and experts to indicate a destruction of the freedom of the human will, and the irresistible duress of one's actions, do not destroy his mental capacity to entertain a criminal intent.

The whole difficulty, as justly said by the supreme Judicial court of New Hampshire, is that "courts have undertaken to declare that to be law which is *matter of fact*." "If," observes the same court, "the tests of insanity are matters of law, the practice of allowing experts to testify what they are should be discontinued; if they are matters of fact, the judge should no longer testify without being sworn as a witness, and showing himself to be qualified to testify as an expert." *State v. Pike*, 49 N. H. 399.

We first consider what is *the proper legal rule of responsibility in criminal case*. No one can deny that there must be two constituent elements of legal responsibility in the commission of every crime, and no rule can be just and reasonable which fails to recognize either of them: (1) Capacity of intellectual discrimination; and (2) freedom of will. Mr. Wharton, after recognizing this fundamental and obvious principle, observes: "If there be either incapacity to distinguish between right and wrong as to the particular act, or delusion as to the act, or inability to refrain from doing the act, there is no responsibility." 1 Whart. Crim. Law. (9th Ed.) § 33. Says Mr. Bishop, in discussing this subject: "There cannot be, and there is not, in any locality or age, a law punishing men for what they cannot avoid." 1 Bish. Crim. Law, (7th Ed.) § 383*b*. If therefore, it be true, as matter of fact, that the disease of insanity can, in its action on the human brain through a shattered nervous organization, or in any other mode, so affect the mind as to subvert the freedom of the will, and thereby destroy the power of the victim *to choose* between the right and wrong, although he perceive it,—by which we mean the power of volition to adhere in action to the right and abstain from the wrong,—is such a one criminally responsible for an act done under the influence of such controlling disease? We clearly think not, and such we believe to be the just, reasonable, and humane rule, towards which all the modern authorities in this country, legislation in England, and the laws of other civilized countries of the world, are gradually but surely tending, as we shall further on attempt more fully to show.

We next consider the question as to the *probable existence of such a disease*, and the *test of its presence*, in a given case, it will not do for the courts to dogmatically deny the possible existence of such *a disease*, or its pathological and psychical effects, because this is a matter of evidence, not of law, or judicial cognizance. Its existence, and effect on the mind and conduct of the patient, is a question of fact to be proved, just as much as the possible existence of cholera or yellow fever formerly was before these diseases became the subjects of common knowledge, or the effects of delirium from fever, or intoxication from opium and alcoholic stimulants would be. The courts could, with just as much propriety, years ago, have denied the existence of the Copernican system of the universe, the efficacy of steam and electricity as a motive power, or the possibility of communication in a few moments between the continents of Europe and America by the magnetic telegraph, or that of the instantaneous transmission of the human voice from one distant city to another by the use of the telephone. These are scientific facts, first discovered by experts before becoming matters of common knowledge. So, in like manner, must be every other unknown scientific fact in whatever profession or department of knowledge. The existence of such a cerebral disease as that which we have described is earnestly alleged by the superintendents of insane hospitals, and other experts, who constantly have experimental dealings with the insane, and they are permitted every day to so testify before juries. The truth of their testimony—or, what is the same thing, the existence or non-existence of such a disease of the mind—in each particular case is necessarily a matter for the determination of the jury from the evidence.

So it is equally obvious that the courts cannot, upon any sound principle undertake to say what are the invariable or infallible tests of such disease. The attempt has been repeatedly made, and has proved a confessed failure in practice. "Such a test," says Mr. Bishop, "has never been found, not because those who have searched for it have not been able and diligent, but because it does not exist." 1 Bish. Crim. Law (7th Ed.) § 381. In this conclusion, Dr. Ray, in his learned work on the Medical Jurisprudence of insanity, fully concurs. Ray, Med. Jur. Insan. 39. The symptoms and causes of insanity are so variable, and its pathology so complex, that no two cases may be just alike. "The fact of its existence," says Dr. Ray, "is never established by any single diagnostic symptom, but by the whole body of symptoms, no particular one of which is present in every case." Ray, Med. Jur. Insan. § 24. Its exciting causes being moral, psychical, and physical, are the especial subjects of specialists' study. What effect may be exerted on the given patient by age, sex, occupation, the seasons, personal surroundings, hereditary transmission, and other causes, is the subject of evidence based on investigation diagnosis, observation, and experiment. Peculiar opportunities, never before enjoyed in the history of our race, are offered in the present age for the ascertainment of these facts, by the establishment of asylums for the custody and treatment of the insane, which Christian benevolence and statesmanship have substituted for jails and gibbets. The testimony of these experts—differ as they may in many doubtful cases—would seem to be the best which can be obtained, however unsatisfactory it may be in some respects.

In the present state of our law, under the rule in *McNaghten's Case*, we are confronted with this practical difficulty, which itself demonstrates the defects of the rule. The courts, in effect, charge the juries, as matter of law, that no such mental disease exists as that often testified to by medical writers, superintendents of insane hospitals, and other experts; that there can be as matter of scientific fact, no cerebral defect, congenital or acquired, which destroys the patient's power of self control,—his liberty of will and action,—provided only he retains a mental consciousness of right and wrong. The experts are immediately put under oath, and tell the juries just the contrary as matter of evidence; asserting that no one of ordinary intelligence can spend an hour in the wards of an insane asylum without discovering such cases, and in fact that "the whole management of such asylums presupposes a knowledge of right and wrong on the part of their inmates." Guy

& F. Forensic Med. 220. The result in practice, we repeat, is that the courts charge one way, and the Jury, following an alleged higher law of humanity, and another, in harmony with the evidence.

In Bucknill on Criminal Lunacy, 59, it is asserted, as "the result of observation and experience, that in all lunatics, and in the most degraded idiots, whenever manifestations of any mental action can be educed, the feeling of right and wrong may be proved to exist."

"With regard to this test," says Dr. Russell Reynolds, in his work on the Scientific Value of the Legal Tests of insanity, 34, (London, 1872.) "I may say, and most emphatically, that it is utterly untrustworthy, because untrue to the obvious facts of nature."

In the learned treatise of Drs. Bucknill and Tube on Psychological Medicine, 269, (4th Ed., London, 1879,) the legal tests of responsibility are discussed, and the adherence of the courts to the right and wrong test is deplored as unfortunate; the true principle being stated to be "whether, in consequence of congenital defect or acquired disease, *the power of self-control* is absent altogether, or is so far wanting as to render the individual irresponsible." It is observed by the authors: "As has again and again been shown, the unconsciousness of right and wrong is one thing, and the powerlessness, through cerebral defect or disease, to do right, is another. To confound them in an asylum would have the effect of transferring a considerable number of the inmates thence to the treadmill or the gallows."

Dr. Peter Bryce, superintendent of the Alabama Insane Hospital for more than a quarter of a century past, alluding to the moral and disciplinary treatment to which the insane inmates are subjected, observes: "They are dealt with in this institution, as far as it is practicable to do so, as rational beings; and it seldom happens that we meet with an insane person who cannot be made to discern, to some feeble extent, his duties to himself and others, and his true relations to society." Sixteenth Ann. Rep. Ala. Insane Hosp. 1876, p. 22; Biennial Rep. 1686, pp. 12–18.

Other distinguished writers on the medical Jurisprudence of insanity have expressed like views, with comparative unanimity. And nowhere do we find the rule more emphatically condemned than by those who have the practical care and treatment of the insane in the various lunatic asylums of every civilized country. A notable instance is found in the following resolution, unanimously passed at the annual meeting of the British Association of Medical Officers of Asylums and Hospitals for the Insane, held in London, July 14, 1864, where there were present fifty-four medical officers: "Resolved, that so much of the legal test of the mental condition of an alleged criminal lunatic as renders him a responsible agent, because he knows the difference between right and wrong, is inconsistent with the fact, well known to every member of this meeting, that the power of distinguishing between right and wrong exists very frequently in those who are undoubtedly insane, and is often associated with dangerous and uncontrollable delusions." Judicial Aspects Insan. (Ordronaux, 1877.) 423, 424.

These testimonials as to a scientific fact are recognized by intelligent men in the affairs of every-day business, and are constantly acted on by juries. They cannot be silently ignored by judges. Whether established or not, there is certainly respectable evidence tending to establish it, and this is all the courts can require.

Nor are the modern law writers silent in their disapproval of the alleged test under discussion. It meets with the criticism or condemnation of the most respectable and advanced in thought among them, the tendency being to incorporate in the legal role of responsibility "not only *the knowledge* of good and evil, but the *power to choose* the one and refrain from the other." Browne, Insan. § 13 *et seq*., § 18; Ray, Med. Jur. §§ 16–19; 1 Whart. & S. Med. Jur. § 59; 1 Whart. Crim. Law, (9th Ed.) §§ S3. 43, 45; 1 Blah. Crim. Law, (7th Ed.) § 386 *et seq*.; Judicial Aspects Insan. (Ordronaux,) 419; 1 Greenl. Ev. § 372; 1 Steph. Hist. Crim. Law, § 168; 4 Amer. Law Rev. (1869–70.) 236 *et seq*.

The following practicable suggestion is made in the able treatise of Balfour Browne Above alluded to: "In a case of alleged insanity, then," he says, "if the individual suffering from enfeeblement of intellect, delusion, or any other form of mental aberration, was looked upon as, to the extent of this delusion, under the influence of duress, (the dire duress of disease,) and in so far *incapacitated to choose* the good and eschew the evil, in so far, it seems to as," he continues, "would the requirements of the law be fulfilled; and in that way it would afford an opening, by the evidence of experts, for the proof of the amount of self-duress in each individual case, and *thus alone can the criterion of law and the criterion of the inductive science of medical psychology be made to coincide*." Browne, Insan. § 18. This, in our judgment, is the practical solution of the difficulty before us, as it preserves to the courts and the juries, respectively, a harmonious field for the full assertion of their time-honored functions. So great, it may be added, are the embarrassments growing out of the old rule, as expounded by the judges in the house of English lords, that in March, 1874, a bill was brought before the house of commons, supposed to have been draughted by the learned counsel for the queen, Mr. Fitzjames Stephen, which introduced into the old rule the new element of an absence of the power of self-control, produced by diseases affecting the mind; and this proposed alteration of the law was cordially recommended by the late Chief Justice Cockburn, his only objection being that the principle was proposed to be limited to the case of homicide. 1 Whart. Crim. Law, (9th Ed.) § 45. p. 66. note 1; Browne, Insan. § 10, note 1.

There are many well-considered cases which support these views.

In the famous *Case of Hadfield*, 27 How. State Tr. 1282, 2 Lawson, Crim. Def. 201–215, who was indicted and tried for shooting the king, and who was defended by Mr. Erskine in an argument most able and eloquent, it clearly appeared that the accused understood the difference between right and wrong as applied to the particular act; yet he labored under the delusion that he had constant intercourse with the Divine Creator; that the world was coming to an end; and that, like Christ, he must be sacrificed for its salvation. He was so much under the duress of the delusion that he "must be destroyed, but ought not to destroy himself," that he committed the act for the specific purpose of being arrested and executed. He was acquitted on being tried before Lord Kenyon, and, no one ever doubted, justly so.

The case of *U.S. v. Lawrence*, 4 Cranch, C. C. 518, tried in 1835, presented another instance of delusion, the prisoner supposing himself to be the king of England, and of the United States as an appendage of England, and that General Jackson, then president, stood in his way in the enjoyment of the right. Acting under the duress of this delusion, the accused assaulted the president by attempting to shoot him with a pistol. He was, in five minutes, acquitted by the jury on the ground of insanity.

The case of *U.S. v. Guiteau*, 10 Fed. Rep. 161, Lawson, Crim. Def. 162, is still fresh in contemporary recollection, and a mention of it can scarcely be omitted in the discussion of the subject of insanity. The accused was tried, sentenced, and executed for the assassination of James A. Garfield, then president of the United States, which occurred in July, 1881. The accused himself testified that he was impelled to commit the act of killing by inspiration from the Almighty, in order, as he declared, "to unite the two factions of the republican party, and thereby save the government from going into the hands of the ex-rebels and their northern allies." There was evidence of various symptoms of mental unsoundness, and some evidence tending to prove such an alleged delusion, but there was also evidence to the contrary, strongly supported by the most distinguished experts, and looking to the conclusion that the accused entertained no such delusion, but that, being a very eccentric and immoral man, he acted from moral obliquity, the morbid love of notoriety, and with the expressed hope that the faction of the republican party, in whose interest he professed to act, would intervene to protect him. The case was tried before the United States district court, for the District of Columbia, before Mr. Justice Cox, whose charge to the jury is replete with interest and learning. While he adopted the right and wrong test of Insanity, be yet recognized the principle that, if the accused to fact entertained an insane delusion, which was the product of the disease of insanity, and not of a malicious heart and vicious nature, and acted solely under the induence of such delusion, he could not be charged with entertaining a criminal intent. An insane delusion was defined to be "an unreasoning and incorrigible belief in the existence of facts which are either impossible absolutely, or impossible under the circumstances of the individual;" and no doubt the case was largely determined by the application of this definition by the jury. It must ever be a mere matter of speculation what influence may have been exerted upon them by the high personal and political significance of the deceased, as the chief magistrate of the government, or other peculiar surroundings of a partisan nature. The case in its facts is so peculiar as scarcely to serve the purpose of a useful precedent in the future.

We note other adjudged cases, in this country, which support the modern rule for which we here contend, including one decided in England as far back as 1840, often referred to by the text writers. In *Reg. v. Oxford*, 9 Car. & P. 225, Lord Denman clearly had in mind this principle, when, after observing that one may commit a crime and not be responsible, he used this significant language: "If some *controlling disease* was in truth *the acting power within him*, which *he could not resist*, then he will not be responsible." The accused in that case acted under the duress of a delusion of an insane character.

In *State v. Fetter*, 25 Iowa, 68, the capacity to distinguish between right and wrong was held not to be a safe test of criminal responsibility in all cases; and it was accordingly decided that, if a person commit a homicide knowing it to be wrong, but do so under the influence of an uncontrollable and irresistible impulse, arising not from natural passion, but from an insane condition of the mind, he is not criminally responsible. "If," said Chief Justice Dillon, "by the observation and concurrent testimony of medical men who make the study of insanity a specialty, It shall be definitely established to be true that there is an unsound condition of the mind, that is, a diseased condition of the mind, in which, though a person abstractly knows that a given act is wrong, be is yet, by an *insane impulse*, that is, an impulse proceeding from a diseased Intellect, irresistibly driven to commit it, the law must modify its ancient doctrines, and recognize the truth, and give to this condition, when it is satisfactorily shown to exist, its exculpatory effect."

In *Hopps v. People*, 31 Ill. 385, which was an indictment for murder, the same rule was recognised in different words. It was there held that if, at the time of the killing, the defendant was not of sound mind, but affected with Insanity, and such disease was the *efficient cause* of the act, operating to create an uncontrollable impulse so as to deprive the accused of the power of volition in the matter, and he would not have done the act but for the existence of such condition of mind, he ought to be acquitted.

In *Bradley v. Stat**, 31 Ind. 492, a like modification of the old rule was announced, the court observing: "Men, under the influence of disease, may know the right, and yet be powerless to resist the wrong. The well-known exhibition of cunning by persons admitted to be insane, in the perpetration of an illegal act, would seem to indicate comprehension of its evil nature and legal consequences, and yet the power of self-control being lost from disease, there can be no legal responsibility."

In *Harris v. State*, 18 Tex. App. 287, 5 Amer. Crim. Rep. 857, this rule was applied to the disease known as "kleptomania," which was defined as a species of insanity producing an uncontrollable propensity to steal; and it was held, if clearly established by the evidence, to constitute a complete defense in a trial for theft.

State v. Pike, 49 N. H. 399, was an indictment for murder, to which the plea of insanity was set up as a defense. It was held to be a question of fact for the jury to determine, (1) whether there was such a mental disease as dipsomania, which is an irresistible craving for alcoholic liquors; and (2) whether the act of killing was the product of such disease. One of the most instructive discussions on the law of insanity, which can be found in legal literature, is the learned opinion of Mr. Justice Doe in that case. Lawson, Insan. 311, 312; Lawson, Crim. Def. 311 et seq.

This ruling was followed by the same court in *State v. Jones*, 60 N. H. 369, 9 Amer. Rep. 242, which was an indictment charging the defendant with murdering his wife. The evidence tended to show that the defendant was insane, and killed her under the delusive belief that she had been guilty of adultery with one French. The rule in *McNaghten's Case* was entirely repudiated, both on the subject of the right and wrong test, and that of delusions, and it was held that the defendant should be acquitted if he was at the time afflicted with a disease of the mind of such character as to take away the capacity to entertain a criminal intent, and that there could be no criminal intent imputed if, as matter of fact, the evidence showed that the killing was the offspring or product of such disease.

Numerous other cases could be cited, bearing on this particular phase of the law, and supporting the above views with more or less clearness of statement. That some of these cases adopt the extreme view, and recognize moral insanity as a defense to crime, and others adopt a measure of proof for the establishment of insanity more liberal to the defendant than our own rule, can neither lessen their weight as authority, nor destroy the force of their logic. Many of them go further on each of these points than this court has done and are therefore stronger authorities than they would otherwise be in support of our views. *Kriel v. Com.*, 5 Bush. 362; *Smith v. Com.*, 1 Duv. 224; *Dejarnette v. Com.*, 75 Va. 867; *Coyle v. Com.*, 100 Pa. St. 573; *Cunningham v. State*, 56 Miss. 269; *Com. v. Rogers*, 7 Metc. 500; *States v. Johnson*, 40 Conn.

136; *Andersen v. State*, 43 Conn. 514, 525; Busw. Insan. § 439 *et seq.; Stats v. Mewherter*, 46 Iowa, 88.

The law of Scotland is in accord with the English law on this subject, as might well be expected. The Criminal Code of Germany, however, contains the following provision, which is said to have been the formulated result of a very able discussion both by the physicians and lawyers of that country: "There is no criminal act when the actor at the time of the offense is in a state of unconsciousness, or morbid disturbance of the mind, *through which the free determination of his will is excluded*." 9 Encyclop. Brit. (9th Ed.) 112; citing Crim. Code Germ. (§ 51, R. G. B.)

The Code of France provides: "There can be no crime or offense if the accused was in a state of *madness* at the time of the act." For some time the French tribunals were inclined to Interpret this law in such a manner as to follow in substance the law of England. But that construction has been Abandoned, and the modern view of the medical profession is now adopted in that country.

It is no satisfactory objection to say that the rule above announced by us is of difficult application. The rule in *McNaghten's Case, supra*, is equally obnoxious to a like criticism. The difficulty does not lie in the rule, but is inherent in the subject of insanity itself. The practical trouble is for the courts to determine in what particular cases the party on trial is to be transferred from the category of sane to that of insane criminals; where, in other words, the border line of punishability is adjudged to be passed. But, as has been said in reference to an every-day fact of nature, no one can say where twilight ends or begins, but there is ample distinction nevertheless between *day* and *night*. We think we can safely rely in this matter upon the intelligence of our Juries, guided by the testimony of men who have practically made a study of the disease of insanity; and enlightened by a conscientious desire, on the one hand, to enforce the criminal laws of the land, and, on the other, not to deal harshly with any unfortunate victim of a diseased mind, acting without the light of reason or the power of volition.

Several rulings of the court, including especially the one given *ex mero motu*, and the one numbered 5, were in conflict with this view, and for these errors the judgment must be reversed. The charges requested by defendant were all objectionable on various grounds. Some of them were imperfect statements of the rules above announced; some were argumentative, and others were misleading by reason of ignoring one or more of the essentials of criminal irresponsibility, as explained in the foregoing opinion. It is almost needless to add that where one does not act under the duress of a diseased mind or insane delusion, but from motives of anger, revenge, or other passion, he cannot claim to be shielded from punishment for crime on the ground of insanity. Insanity proper is more or less a mental derangement, co-existing often, it is true, with a disturbance of the emotions, affections, and other moral powers. A mere moral or emotional insanity, so called, unconnected with disease of the mind, or irresistible impulse resulting from mere moral obliquity, or wicked propensities and habits, is not recognized as a defense to crime in our courts. 1 Whart. Crim. Law, (9th Ed.) § 46; *Boswell v. State*, 63 Ala. 307, 35 Amer. Rep. 20; *Ford v. State*, 71 Ala. 385.

The charges refused by the court raise the question as to how far one acting under the Influence of an insane delusion is to be exempted from criminal accountability. The evidence tended to show that one of the defendants, Mrs. Nancy J. Parsons, acted under the influence of an insane delusion that the deceased, whom she assisted in killing, possessed supernatural power to afflict her with disease, and to take her life by some "supernatural trick;" that by means of such power the deceased had caused defendant to be in bad health for a long time, and that she acted under the belief that she was in great danger of the loss of her life from the conduct of deceased operating by means of such supernatural power.

The rule in *McNaghten's Case*, as decided by the English judges, and supposed to have been adopted by the court, is that the defense of insane delusion can be allowed to prevail in a criminal case only when the imaginary state of facts would, if real, justify or excuse the act; or, in the language of the English judges themselves, the defendant "must be considered in the same situation as to responsibility as if the facts with respect to which the delusion exists were real." *Boswell's Com*, 63 Ala. 307. It is apparent, from what we have said, that this rule cannot be correct as applied to all cases of this nature, even limiting it as done by the English judges to cases where one "labors under partial delusion, and is not in other respects Insane." *McNaghten's Case*, 10 Clark & F. 200; Lawson, Crim. Def. 150. It holds a partially insane person as responsible as if he were entirely sane, and it ignores the possibility of crime being committed under the duress of an insane delusion, operating upon a human mind the integrity of which is destroyed or impaired by disease, except, perhaps, in cases where the imaginary state of facts, if real, would excuse or Justify the act done under their influence. Field, Med. Leg. Guide, 101–104; Guy & F. Forensic Med. 220. If the rule declared by the English judges be correct, it necessarily follows that the only possible instance of excusable homicide, in cases of delusional insanity, would be where the delusion, if real, would have been such as to create, in the mind of a reasonable man, a just apprehension of imminent peril to life or limb. The personal fear or timid cowardice of the insane man, although created by disease acting through a prostrated nervous organization, would not excuse undue precipitation of action on his part. Nothing would justify assailing his supposed adversary except an overt act, or demonstration on the part of the latter, such as, if the imaginary facts were real, would, under like circumstances, have justified a man perfectly sane in shooting or killing. If he dare fail to reason, on the supposed facts embodied in the delusion, as perfectly as a sane man could do on a like state of realities, he receives no mercy at the hands of the law. It exacts of him the last pound of flesh. It would follow also, under this rule, that the partially insane man, afflicted with delusions, would no more be excusable than a sane man would be, if, perchance, it was by his fault the difficulty was provoked, whether by word or deed; or if, in fine, he may have been so negligent as not to have declined combat when he could do so safely, without increasing his peril of life or limb. If this has been the law heretofore, it is time it should be so no longer. It is not only opposed to the known facts of modern medical science, but it is a hard and unjust rule to be applied to the unfortunate and providential victims of disease. It seems to be little less than inhumane, and its strict enforcement would probably transfer a large percentage of the inmates of our insane hospital from that institution to hard labor in the mines or the penitentiary. Its fallacy consists in the assumption that no other phase of delusion, proceeding from a diseased brain, can so destroy the volition of an insane person as to render him powerless to do what he knows to be right, or to avoid doing what he may know to be wrong. This inquiry, as we have said, and here repeat, is a question of fact for the determination of the jury in each particular case. It is not a matter of law to be decided by the courts. We think it sufficient if the insane delusion—by which we mean the delusion proceeding from a *diseased mind*—sincerely exists at the time of committing the alleged crime, and the defendant, believing it to be real, is so influenced by it as either to render him incapable of perceiving the true nature and quality of the set done, by reason of the depravation of the reasoning faculty, or so subverts his will as to destroy his free agency by rendering him powerless to resist by reason of *the duress of the disease*. In such a case, in other words, there must exist either one of two conditions: (1) Such mental defect as to render the defendant unable to distinguish between right and wrong in relation to the particular act; or (2) the overmastering of defendant's will in consequence of the insane delusion under the influence of which he acts, produced by disease of the mind or brain. *Rex v. Hadfield*, 27 How. State Tr. 1282, 2 Lawson, Crim. Def. 201; *Roberts v. State*, 3 Ga. 310; *Com. v. Rogers*, 7 Metc. 500; *State v. Windsor*, 5 Har. (Del.) 512; Busw. Insan. §§ 434, 440; 4 Amer. Law Rev. (1869–70.) pp. 236–252.

In conclusion of this branch of the subject, that we may not be misunderstood, we think it follows very clearly from what we have said that the inquiries to be submitted to the jury, then, in every criminal trial where the defense of insanity is interposed, are these: *First.* Was the defendant at the time of the commission of the alleged crime, as matter of fact, afflicted with a *disease of the mind*, so as to be either idiotic, or otherwise insane? *Second*, If such be the case, did he know right from wrong, as applied to the particular act in question? If he did not have such knowledge, he is not legally responsible. *Third*, If he did have such knowledge, he may nevertheless not be legally responsible if the two following conditions concur: (1) If, by reason of the duress of such mental disease, he had so far lost the *power to choose* between the right and wrong, and to avoid doing the act in question; as that his free agency was at the time destroyed; (2) and if, at the same time, the alleged crime was so connected with such mental disease, in the relation of cause and effect, as to have been the product of it *solely*.

The rule announced in *Boswell's Case*, 63 Ala. 308, *supra*, as stated in the fourth head-note, is in conflict with the foregoing conclusions, and to that extent is declared incorrect, and is not supported by the opinion in that case otherwise than by *dictum*. We adhere, however, to the rule declared by this court in *Boswell's Case, supra*, and followed in *Ford's Case*, 71 Ala. 385, holding that, when insanity is set up as a defense in a criminal case, it must be established, to the satisfaction of the jury, by a preponderance of the evidence; and a reasonable doubt of the defendant's sanity, raised by all the evidence, does not authorize an acquittal.

There was no error in overruling the objection taken by the defendants to the copy of the *venire* or list of jurors served on them. The act approved February 17, 1885, (Acts 1884–85, pp. 181, 185, § 10.) regulating the organization of juries, applies to this case, and provides that "the names of the jurors *so drawn*," in accordance with section 10 of the act, together with the panel of 36 jurors provided for by section 9, "shall constitute *the venire*" from which the jurors to try capital cases shall be selected. Acts 1684–85, pp. 185. 186. The rule on this subject declared in *Posey's Case*, 73 Ala. 490, and *Shelton's Case*, Id. 5, has no application under this act. These cases construe section 4872 of the Code, which contains different language from the law here construed.

Under the rule announced in *Ford v. State*, 71 Ala. 385, 397, and authorities there cited, there was no error in excluding the proposed statement of Mrs. Nail. This testimony was defective in not being preceded more fully by the facts and circumstances upon which the opinion of the witness as to the sanity of the accused was predicated, the witness not being an expert. Rogers, Exp. Test. § 61.

The other rulings of the court need not be considered by us.

The judgment is reversed, and the cause remanded. In the mean while the prisoners will be held in custody until discharged by due process of law.

Dissent by: Stone

Stone, C. J., (*dissenting.*) In *Boswell v. State*, 63 Ala. 307, two material questions arose, on the subject of insanity: *First*, whether or not, when that defense is set up, its existence must be proved by the accused, what measure of proof is required to establish it, and whether it is enough if the testimony raises a reasonable doubt of the prisoner's sanity. We held it was defensive in its nature, and that the proof did not come up to the required standard if it simply raised a reasonable doubt of its existence. As to the measure of proof, we applied the rule which obtains in civil cases, viz., that which reasonably satisfies the mind of a jury of the fact sought to be established. The *second* question presented and considered in that case was whether moral insanity was an excuse for an act otherwise punishable. We declared it was not; and in the category we included homicidal mania, irresistible impulse, and every other species of simply moral obliquity, provided the mental faculties were not shown to be unsound. Each of these principles were reaffirmed in *Ford v. State*, 71 Ala. 385.

The most important inquiry in *Boswell's Case*, the one chiefly relied on for reversal, was the first stated above,—the *onus* and measure of proof. The testimony scarcely raised any other. Our own decisions had left that question in deplorable uncertainty, as we attempted to show. The English authorities, particularly the older ones, had given way to a more enlightened understanding of mental disorders. It was on that question, namely, the presumption of sanity, and the burden and manner of overcoming that presumption, that the opinion of the judges in the *McNaghten Case*, was quoted and relied on. All the judges except Maule had concurred in advising the house of lords "that every man is to be presumed to be sane, and to possess a sufficient degree of reason to be responsible for his crimes, until the contrary is proved to their [the jury's] satisfaction." To this extent the advice of the judges was pertinent to *Boswell's Case*, and for this purpose it was used. Beyond this the cases were unlike. McNaghten's mental malady was presented to the judges as one of "mental delusion." Their answers were given on the postulate that his mental disease was "partial delusion only," and that he was not "in other respects insane." Hence we said in *Boswell's Case*: "It must not be overlooked that the judges were considering a case of partial insanity; the case of a person afflicted with insane delusion in respect to one or more particular subjects or persons." On the other hand in *Boswell's Case*, there was no pretense of mental delusion. What we said on that question was simply a statement and citation of authorities, supporting and following the views of the Judges given in the *McNaghten Case*. Its correctness or incorrectness was not material to a correct solution of the questions we were discussing; and, while the principle was quoted without dissent, there was nothing to cause us to inquire into or question its correctness. Our attention was not directed to the tests of criminal accountability, except to that phase of it which is classed as moral insanity, and which we explicitly declared was no defense to a prosecution for crime. I do not feel committed, by anything said in *Boswell's Case*, to any proposition beyond the two principles stated above.

I summarize my views of the questions I propose to discuss in the following brief paragraphs: (1) Insanity, when relied on as a defense to a prosecution for crime, is a mixed question of law and fact. (2) It is a perfect defense to an accusation of crime if the accused, at the time he committed the act, was afflicted with a mental disease to such extent as to render him incapable of determining between right and wrong, or of perceiving the true nature and quality of the act done. (3) When it is satisfactorily shown that the accused was mentally diseased at the time he did the act charged as an offense, and that he did the act in consequence solely of such mental disease, without which it would not have been done, this is a complete defense, even though the defendant knew the act was wrong. (4) When, at the time of committing the act charged, the defendant was laboring under a disease of the mind known as delusion, illusion, or hallucination, and the act done was solely the result of such mental disease, connected with and growing out of it as effect follows cause, and without which the act would not have been done, the defendant should be acquitted on the plea of insanity. Whart. Crim. Ev. § 336; 2 Greenl. Ev. § 372. (5) No form of moral or emotional insanity is a defense against a criminal accusation.

I have considered the very able opinion of my Brother Somerville with great care, and I differ from what I understand to be its declared principles only to a limited extent, to be commented upon further on. I have also read the legal authorities he relies on, but have not read, on this subject, the other authorities he refers to. Some of them, I fear, deal too much in the abstruse and metaphysical—refine too much—to become safe guides in judicial administration. Legal principles, when enunciated for the government of juries, should, if possible, be expressed so simply and clearly as to be easily understood by the class of men who generally perform that service. Less than this is not properly instructing juries on questions of law pertinent to the issues they are sworn to try.

I differ with my Brother Somerville in the interpretation of some of the legal authorities he relies on as supporting his views, and, as to others, in the estimate he places upon them as authority. This court has repudiated the doctrine of moral insanity as a defense for conduct otherwise criminal, and we hold that insanity is a defense to be affirmatively established by proof. It is not enough that a reasonable doubt of sanity is engendered. *Boswell's Case*, 63 Ala. 307; *Ford's Case*, 71 Ala. 885. Of the judicial authorities relied on by him, the following cases hold that the defense of insanity is made good, if the testimony raises a reasonable doubt of its existence. Some of them go so far as to hold that when any evidence of insanity is produced, the burden is then cast on the prosecution to establish sanity beyond a reasonable doubt. *State v. Jones*, 50 N. H. 369; *Bradley v. State*, 31 Ind. 492; *Hopps v. People*, 31 Ill. 385; *Cunningham v. State*, 56 Miss. 269; *State v. Johnson*, 40 Conn. 136.

In the opinion of my Brother Somerville, the *Case of Falter*, 25 Iowa, 68, is given a prominent place. The opinion in that case was prepared by the justly distinguished law writer and jurist, Chief Justice Dillon. The decision was in 1868. In considering the weight of that opinion, I remark, first, that it was pronounced by a court which holds that moral insanity is a defense to a criminal prosecution. Many of the expressions found in that opinion, and in the opinions of other courts entertaining similar views, are well chosen to express moral insanity and its workings. They are misleading, if not inappropriate, when used in description of intellectual unsoundness or mental insanity. The defense relied on in that case was homicidal manis, the existence of which, as mental disease, Chief Justice Dillon says, "both medicine and law now recognize." Yet in that case the distinguished judge said: "If this want of power to control arose from the insane condition of the mind of the accused, he should not be held responsible. But if want of power to control his actions arose from violent and ungovernable passions, in a mind not diseased or unsound, he would and ought to be punished for his acts."

In *Mecoherter's Case*, 46 Iowa, 88, decided in 1877, the following charge had been requested in behalf of the prisoner: "If the jury believe from the evidence that, at the time of the commission of the alleged homicide, the defendant was laboring under a diseased condition of the mind, that he was insane on the subject of the manner in which the deceased (a physician) had treated his wife, and on the subject of deceased, with others, having formed a conspiracy to take his (defendant's) life, then the jury should sequit the defendant." This charge the trial court had refused to give. The supreme court, in reference to it, said: "It will be at once observed that this instruction fails to present the condition that the mental disease must have destroyed the power of defendant to comprehend, rationally, the nature and consequences of his act and overpowered his will, which must exist in order to render him free from accountability for his acts." *Felter's Case* is cited in support of this principle.

In the still later case, *State v. Hockett*, 30 N. W. Rep. 742, the supreme court of Iowa expressed the principle as follows: "On the trial of an indictment for murder, where insanity is pleaded, and instruction to the jury that "the alleged insanity and the alleged crime must be connected, the one with the other, and the latter be the offspring of the former, in order to have the effect of rightfully declaring one irresponsible for his acts," is correct, where there is no evidence tending to show that the defendant was insane on all subjects, or was homicidally insane."

The case of *Hopps v. People*, 31 Ill. 385, is the next case relied on. The opinion in that case was by Judge Breese. The alleged insanity was in the form of mental illusions as to his wife's infidelity to him. Speaking for the court, Judge Breese said: "We have come to the conclusion that a safe and reasonable test, in all such cases would be, that whenever it shall appear from the evidence that at the time of doing the act charged, the prisoner was not of sound mind, but affected with insanity, and such affection was the efficient cause of the act, and that he would not have done the act but for that affection, he ought to be acquitted. But this unsoundness of mind, or affection of insanity, must be of such a degree as to create an uncontrollable impulse to do the act charged, by overruling the reason and judgment, and obliterating the sense of right and wrong as to the particular act done, and depriving the accused of the power of choosing between them." Let it be borne in mind that this summation of the principle was the utterance of a court which held that moral insanity precluded criminal accountability; and yet, to make the defense available, it was held necessary that the mental unsoundness should have so far progressed as to "obliterate the sense of right and wrong as to the particular act done."

That I am correct in my interpretation of the court's decision, I refer to the ruling of the same court made in *Dunn v. People*, 109 Ill. 635, decided in 1884. In that case the trial court had charged the Jury as follows: "If you believe from the evidence, beyond a reasonable doubt, that at the time of committing the alleged act the defendant was able to distinguish right from wrong, then you cannot acquit him on the ground of insanity." Two other charges were given, embodying the same thought, but expressed more in detail. In the opinion of the court is this language: "It is claimed that these instructions conflict with the law as declared in *Hopps v. People*, 31 Ill. 385, and *Chase v. People*, 40 Ill. 353. We do not so understand the instructions. In the *Hopps Vote*, in discussing the question of insanity, it said," etc. The court then proceeds to repeat that part of the opinion which I have copied above. It was added: "If, at the time the crime was committed, the defendant knew that it was wrong to commit such a crime, and had the power of mind to choose either to do or not to do that act, and of controlling his conduct in accordance with such choice, then he ought to be held responsible, although he was not entirely and perfectly sane. * * * Where a man knows that it is wrong to do a certain act, and possesses the power of mind to do or not to do that act, it would be a dangerous doctrine to hold that such person should not be held responsible because he might not be regarded entirely and perfectly sane."

The case of *Bradley v. State*, 31 Ind. 492, comes next in order. The opinion in that case, which was pronounced in 1869, shows that the writer had read considerably on the subject of mental disorders. Viewed from the standpoint that, like the cases we have cited, that opinion was delivered by a court which holds that moral insanity is a defense to a criminal charge, and that, if a reasonable doubt of sanity is engendered, an acquittal must follow, there is nothing remarkable in that case, except that it expresses disapprobation of the simply right and wrong test.

In *Walker v. State*. 102 Ind. 602, 1 N. E. Rep. 856, decided in 1885, the supreme court of that state again considered the question of insanity as a defense for crime. The trial court had charged the jury that "only persona of sound mind in law can be convicted of crime. * * * When considered [insanity] in relation to crime, it is general rule that persons who are in that condition which the law recognizes as of unsound mind are not responsible criminally for their acts when in that condition. But it is also true that mere weakness of mind alone, or slight mental ailments which do not exclude that knowledge of right and wrong, and the power to net in accordance with the plain dictates of reason and justice, do not constitute unsoundness of mind in the law. * * * In cases of partial insanity, when the mind may be clouded and weakened, but not remembering, reasoning, and judging, or so perverted by insane delusions as to act under false impressions or influences,—in these cases the rule is this: A man is not to be excused from responsibility if he has capacity and reason sufficient to enable him to distinguish between right and wrong as to the particular act he is then doing, [to have] a knowledge and consciousness that the act he is then doing is criminal and wrong, and will subject him to punishment. In order to be responsible, he must have sufficient power of memory to recollect the relations in which he stands to others, and in which others stand to him; that the act he is doing is contrary to the plain dictates of justice and right, injurious to others, and in violation of the dictates of duty. On the contrary, although he may be laboring under partial insanity, if he still understands the nature and character of his act, and its consequences, if he has a knowledge that it is wrong and criminal, and a mental power sufficient to apply that knowledge to his own case, and to know that if he does the act he will do wrong and receive punishment, such partial insanity is not sufficient to exempt him from responsibility for criminal acts. He is then not insane. The true test is this: Has the defendant in a criminal case the power to distinguish right from wrong, and the power to adhere to the right and avoid the wrong? Has the defendant, in addition to this, the power to govern his mind, his body, and his estate? If he has these powers, he must exercise them. He is then in law not a person of unsound mind, and the law will hold him answerable for his acts. But if his mind be so unsound that he has them not, then the law will excuse his act by reason of the unsoundness of his mind." Speaking of the ruling on these charges, and another not material to the inquiry before us, the revising court said: "Considered as a whole, * * * it contains nothing materially injurious to the appellant."

The case of *Harris v. State*, 18 Tex. App. 287, presented the question of moral insanity—kleptomania. Held a valid defense by that court. There was nothing decided material to the question we have in hand.

Smith v. Com. 1 Duv. 224, declares two propositions: *First*, that moral insanity is a defense to a prosecution for crime. The insanity relied on was that the prisoner, when he perpetrated the homicide, was drunk, and that "such a condition superinduced moral Insanity." The *second* proposition of the opinion was that a reasonable doubt of the prisoner's sanity justified an acquittal. This case was decided in 1864.

In the later case of *Kriel v. Com.*, 5 Bush, 362, the defense of reasonable doubt of sanity was expressly held insufficient. In the opinion is the following clause: "If there be mental or moral insanity, however recent, to such an extent as to destroy free agency and moral responsibility, on being established by satisfactory evidence, this will excuse." In the same opinion, after stating that drunkenness may be of such a character and to such a degree as to repel all idea of malice, and to reduce homicide from murder to manslaughter, it is added: "But as this state of mind is superinduced by the wrongful act of the perpetrator, a due regard for the interest of society, and the personal security of every one, precludes it from being a satisfactory excuse, and an entire exemption from punishment. Indeed, if it appeared that intoxication excited the animal passions and aroused a destructive propensity in the accused, why should even drunkenness in such a case be considered a mitigating cause, any more than the unchaining a mad dog in the streets of the town, or the riding a vicious animal into a crowd, merely because the perpetrator had no particular malice at any one, or indeed expected death at all to ensue? yet if, by reason thereof, any one should lose his life, this recklessness is set down as malice towards mankind in general, and the perpetrator criminally responsible in the highest degree."

The case of *Cunningham v. State*, 56 Miss. 269, declares principles which I am unable fully to reconcile. It first allows a reasonable doubt of sanity, engendered by the evidence, to be a defense against a charge of crime, but declares that the burden of proving insanity is on the defendant. It next adopts the right and wrong theory, or capacity to perceive the difference between right and wrong as the test of insanity. It then adopts the rule declared by the Judges in the *McNaghton Case* as applicable to cases of mental delusion. The views of Justice Chalmers, in the latter part of his opinion rendered in this case, I reproduce entire. The court below had been requested to instruct the jury that "there is no responsibility for an act committed under the uncontrollable impulse resulting from mental disease." On this clause of the charge the court expresses itself as follows:

> The second clause declares that there is no responsibility for "an act committed under the uncontrollable impulse resulting from mental disease. If the impulse meant is the direct result of such mental disease as destroys the perception of right and wrong, this is only a reaffirmation of the doctrine announced in several preceding charges, and it derives no additional strength from the prefix of the word "uncontrollable." But there is said to be an uncontrollable impulse springing from a mental condition quite different from this,—a state of the mind which perfectly perceives the true relations of the party, and recognizes all the obligations thereby imposed, but which is unable to control the will. This character of insanity is variously styled moral or emotional or impulsive or paroxysmal insanity. It is known among medical writers as lesion of the will. Its peculiarity is said to be that, while the mental perception is unimpaired, the mind is powerless to control the will; that while its unhappy subject knows the right and desires to pursue it, some mysterious and uncontrollable impulse compels him to commit the wrong. This kind of insanity, if insanity it can be called, though sometimes recognized by respectable courts, and still oftener, perhaps, by juries seeking an excuse to evade the stern dictates of the law, is properly rejected by the authorities generally. The possibility of the existence of such a mental condition is too doubtful, the theory is too problematical, and too incapable of a practical solution, to afford a safe basis of legal adjudication. It may serve as a metaphysical or psychological problem, to interest and amuse the speculative philosopher, but it must be discarded by the jurist and the law-giver in the practical affairs of life. To it may well be applied the language of Judge Curtis, who, in speaking of this and similar questions, says: "They are an important as well as a deeply interesting study, and they find their place in that science which ministers to diseases of the mind. * * * But the law is not a medical nor a metaphysical science. Its search is after those practical rules which may be administered without inhumanity, for the security of civil society by protecting it from crime. And therefore it inquires, not into the peculiar consti-

> tution of mind of the accused, or what weakness, or even disorders, he was afflicted with, but solely *whether he was capable of having, and did have, a criminal intent*. If he had, it punishes him; if not, it holds him dispunishable." *U.S. v. McGlue*, 1 Curt. 1. The latter clause of the instruction in question is copied—as, indeed, the whole instruction is—from the syllabus, or head-notes of *Com. v. Rogers*, 7 Metc. 500, but it fails to embody the qualification and restriction thrown around the doctrine in the opinion itself. The uncontrollable impulse which the learned chief justice declares will excuse the act is said to be that which "overwhelms reason, conscience, and judgment." "If so," says he, "then the act was not the act of a voluntary agent, but the involuntary act of the body, without the concurrence of the mind directing it." In other words, it is the uncontrollable act of a mind destitute of reason, conscience, or judgment as to the particular object, however sane as to other matters. The latter clause of the instruction, therefore, should have been restricted by words conveying the idea that the act was the direct result of an uncontrollable impulse, springing from mental disease, existing to so high a degree that for the time it overwhelmed the reason, judgment, and conscience.

In *Com. v. Rogers*, 7 Metc. 500, a case tried before Shaw, C. J., the defense was rested on mental delusion. The sum of the instructions is contained in the following extract: "The questions, then, in the present case, will be these: (1) Was there such a delusion and hallucination? (2) Did the accused act under a false but sincere belief that the warden had a design to shut him up, and, under that pretext, destroy his life, and did he take this means to prevent it? (3) Are the facts of such a character, taken in connection with the opinions of the professional witnesses, as to induce the jury to believe that the accused had been laboring for several days under monomania, attended with delusion, and did this indicate such a diseased state of the mind that the act of killing the warden was to be considered as an outbreak or paroxysm of disease, which for the time being overwhelmed and superseded reason and judgment, so that the accused was not an accountable agent? If such was the case, the accused is entitled to an acquittal; otherwise, as the evidence proves beyond all doubt, the fact of killing, without provocation, by the use of a deadly weapon, and attended with circumstances of violence, cruelty, and barbarity, he must undoubtedly be convicted of willful murder."

In the case of *Dejarnette v. Com.*, 75 Va. 867, the principle declared is embodied in the following extract from the opinion: "In every case, although the accused may be laboring under partial insanity, if he still understands the nature and character of his act, and its consequences, and has a knowledge that it is wrong and criminal, and a mental power sufficient to apply that knowledge to his own case, and to know that if he does the act he will do wrong and receive punishment, and possesses withal a will sufficient to restrain the impulse that may arise from a diseased mind, such partial insanity is not sufficient to exempt him from responsibility to the law for his crimes." This court recognized moral insanity as a defense.

So, in Pennsylvania, the court receives the defense of moral insanity as an answer to a criminal accusation. In *Boswell's Case* we commented on Chief Justice Gibson's language, as used in *Com. v. Mosler*, 4 Pa. St. 264, and disapproved it. In *Coyle v. Com.*, 100 Fa. St. 573, decided in 1882, the trial court had repeated to the jury the language of Chief Justice Gibson, which we copied in *Boswell's Case*. This was urged as a ground of reversal in the supreme court. In reply, the court said: "The able argument of counsel has failed to convince us that this was not a correct declaration of the law, or that it has since been ruled otherwise by this court. The validity of such a defense is admitted, but the existence of such a form of mania must not be assumed without satisfactory proof. Care must be taken not to confound it with acts of reckless frenzy. When interposed as a defense to the commission of a high crime, its existence should be clearly manifested. Such defense is based on an unsound state or condition of the mind, proved by acts and declarations of violence. It certainly is not requiring too much to hold that it shall be shown in more than a single instance. We know no later case in this state where the precise question has been ruled otherwise." Nothing else is said in that case which is material to the subject I am considering, except that the court repudiates the right of acquittal, if the testimony simply raises a reasonable doubt of sanity. The insanity relied on in that case was homicidal mania, a so-called form of insanity which this court declines to recognize as a mental disease.

The Connecticut cases need but a passing notice. *State v. Johnson*, 40 Conn. 136, presented the defense of dipsomania. In that case they not only permitted the defense of moral insanity, but, when insanity was the defense, the state was at that time required to prove sanity beyond a reasonable doubt. A discussion of the questions there considered would present no new features.

The case of *Anderson v. State*, 43 Conn. 514, scarcely raises a question material to the line of thought I am pursuing. The majority of the revising court—three to two—granted petitioner a new trial, rather against legal rules, because in their judgment he had not had his case fully and sufficiently represented in the court below. The profession, on reading it, would not esteem it a safe or valuable precedent.

In the later case of *State v. Hoyt*, 46 Conn. 330, that court qualified its rulings by holding that proof of the insanity of a person accused of crime is a matter of defense wholly, and the burden of proving it rests on the accused.

The case of *State v. Pike*, 49 N. H. 399, was decided in 1870. The defense relied on was dipsomania,—an inordinate craving of alcoholic stimulants. The defendant was convicted of murder in the first degree. The chief questions discussed on error arose on the refusal of the court to give the following instruction to the jury: "The defendant requested the court to instruct the jury that the sanity—the mental capacity of the defendant to commit any crime charged in the indictment—is a fact to be proved by the state beyond all reasonable doubt; that there is no legal presumption of sanity which can have any weight with the jury as a matter of law; that there is no legal presumption of sanity which is a substitute for evidence, or which, as a matter of law, affects the burden of proof in criminal cases." An offer had been made, in the court below, to prove, by non-expert witnesses, their naked opinion that the accused was insane when he committed the homicide. This testimony had been rejected, and it was claimed that in this ruling there was error. The majority opinion of the court was delivered by Smith, J., affirming the judgment, in which all the justices, except Justice Doe, appear to have concurred. Then follows a most elaborate opinion by Justice Doe, which I can but regard as a dissenting opinion, although not so expressed in the book. It covers 36 pages, discloses much thought, reading, and research, and is expressed in a bright, incisive, combative style. He first devoted many pages to prove that all witnesses—non-experts as well as experts—should be allowed alike to testify to their opinions of a prisoner's insanity. In this he opposed the views of his brother justices, and he stands opposed to our uniform rulings, which I need not cite. He also declared, in terms, that "there was error in the refusal of the court to instruct the jury that there is no legal presumption of sanity; and also in the instruction that every person of mature age is presumed to be sane until there is evidence tending to show insanity." In this he also stood opposed to his brother judges. He did more. He antagonized every authority I have ever seen or heard of on the subject. And, as I understand his position, he took the ground that there are no legal tests on the subject of sanity or insanity; that the judges can give no directions for determining such issue, and that it is solely and purely a question of fact, to be determined by the jury on the sworn testimony before them. The presiding judge must give no instructions or directions as to the constituents or classifications of mental disorders, nor as to the dividing line which separates accountable sanity from irresponsible insanity. To allow him to do so would be to receive unsworn testimony from a non-expert witness. The result of this is that the judge must sit quietly by in his supposed ignorance, as a silent looker on, while the forensic battle is waged between opposing counsel, with their expert opinion testimony, before the jury, as the sole triers and arbiters of the facts. Who is to determine the pertinency of the evidence offered? Not the presiding judge, for, not knowing, what constitutes insanity, he can not know what facts and circumstances tend to prove its existence. Can there be judicial administration without a presiding umpire to determine the disputes of opposing litigants? As well put a locomotive engine in motion without an engineer, or launch a ship without a pilot or rudder.

The error of judge Doe's position, as I understand it, and, in fact, of the whole New Hampshire court, lies in the assumption that the question of sanity or insanity is one purely of fact. I admit it is largely so; but no question of judicial contestation can ever become solely a question of fact. Law pervades every human transaction, every question of *status*, every inquiry of right and wrong, as vital force pervades every fibre, every corpuscle, of the living animal. The legal element may be agreed between the contestants, and hence may not be visible; still it is there, and defines and determines what the issue is, and how the suit is to be maintained or defeated.

It is my opinion that the inquiry of insanity, like most others in judicial administration, is a mixed question of law and fact. Of law, as to the extent and measure of mental disorder which absolves from legal accountability; of law, necessarily, in determining the pertinency of testimony offered in proof or disproof of the alleged mental disorder. Like most if not all other courts whose utterances on these questions have fallen under my observation, this court stands unmistakably committed to this doctrine. Hence we have held that what is called emotional, or moral insanity is not a disease of the intellect, but sheer depravity,—a surrender of the higher teachings of conscience to baser and debased passions, instincts, and appetites. This, we hold, the intellectual faculties remaining sound, is no defense to a criminal accusation. Hence we have held (and I understand my brothers as asserting it in this case) that to excuse conduct otherwise criminal, on the plea of insanity, the mind proper, as distinguished from the emotions, must be diseased, and the act charged must have been connected with that disease as effect with cause. Hence we have held, and so decide in this case, that, on the trial of such issue in the primary court, the presiding judge is within proper bounds when he determines what testimony is and what is not pertinent to the issue.

It will be observed that the cases I have collated and considered were decisions made by courts which hold that moral insanity is a defense to a criminal prosecution. I think this fact should be considered in weighing their value as authority. The phrases, "sudden impulse," and "overpowering or subverting the will," are frequently encountered in the opinions delivered in those cases. Impulse is emotional rather than intellectual. It is a sudden emotional influence brought to bear on the will as an intellectual faculty, and, as a rule, not the offspring of the reasoning faculties. It is rather the antithesis of a formed judgment. It differs from the cognitive or knowing faculty, and not infrequently so dominates the latter as to acquire, for the time, the mastery of the will. The will, the executive faculty of the mind, cannot, with propriety be said to be subverted. To be subverted or overturned is to cease to have purpose,—to cease to act; for without the function of the will there can be no physical action. The will retains all its power, but, for the time, ceases to act in harmony with the knowledge possessing faculty. It is *perverted*, but not subverted. I am speaking in common parlance, and employing language in its popular sense. When the will is perverted by a disease of the brain or intellectual faculties, then any act caused thereby is blameless in the sight of the law. On the other hand, if there be no disease of the intellectual faculties, and the act done, though by a very perverted will, is nevertheless the offspring of moral depravity, debauched appetite, blunted sense of right, or other kindred prompting of a wicked heart, then for such an act there is a moral and legal accountability in the amplest sense of those terms. The murderer, the assassin, the burglar, the incendiary, can truthfully plead that their wills have ceased to be the executors of their intellectual promptings. Criminal passion or appetite has obtained mastery over their higher and purer intellectual endowments, and perverted their wills to its baser uses. I have indulged in these reflections, because I think the expressions "sudden impulse" and "subversion of the will" are inaccurate and misleading; at least, under our jurisprudence.

Keeping myself reasonably abreast with advanced thought, and with the later and better understanding of mental disorders, I am willing to disclaim, as untenable, one of the tests of legal accountability declared by the Judges in the McNaghten Case. That was a case of partial insanity, called "mental delusion." There can be no difference, in a legal point of view, between delusion, illusion, and hallucination. In that case it was said that the delusion would be a defense only when the supposed facts, if real, would have justified the act done. This rule is too exacting. At the head of this opinion I have presented my views of the questions discussed in the form of syllabi.

In the present case the wife and daughter were tried and convicted of the murder of the husband and father. The homicide was perpetrated with a gun, in the hands of the daughter, at the alleged instigation of the wife. The defense interposed for the daughter was idiocy. The wife's defense was insanity, in the form of mental delusion. The delusion or hallucination was her alleged belief in a supernatural power and influence the husband had and exercised over her, by which he could bring sickness and even death upon her. That, by the exercise of this power, he had brought on her protracted sickness, and she feared and believed he would ultimately destroy her life. Of course, this fear and belief could only be gathered from her own conduct, and expressions of belief and fear. If this delusion proceeded from mental disorder, or defective mental organism, it is questionable if the case does not fall directly within the rule declared in the *McNaghten Case*. If the wife believed her husband possessed supernatural power over her, by which, through unseen influences, he could bring upon her disease, and even death; that he had exerted that power, and caused her to be sick for a great length of time, and she believed, intended ultimately to take her life,—in what manner could she rid herself of such impending peril? She could not flee away from it if she would; for, the power being supernatural, it could pursue her whithersoever she fled. Supposing her delusion to be a fact, how could she save her own life by any preventive measures short of taking his?

Was her alleged delusion insanity? Was it, if it existed, a disease of the reasoning faculty? What say psychological experts on this subject? It is believed that the delusion claimed for her is a very common superstition with the grossly ignorant, particularly among the colored population. Less than three centuries ago the whole English-speaking people labored under this delusion or superstition, and called it witchcraft. So firmly did they believe it that they made the practice of it a capital felony. Many unfortunates to whom this dark art was imputed paid the penalty by the most torturing of all known methods of inflicting the death sentence. Were our ancestors, from the king on his throne to the laboring peasant, all insane? Even the great and good Sir Matthew Hale was a believer in witchcraft He said "that there were such creatures as witches he made no doubt at all; for,—*First*, the Scriptures had affirmed so much; *secondly*, the wisdom of all nations had provided laws against such persons, which is an argument of their confidence in such crime." On the other hand, if the great, the noble, and the learned, two or three centuries ago, slaughtered men and women indiscriminately as the imputed possessors of this demoniacal power, and under all the forms of law and for the public welfare, is it right to make an example of one ignorant, superstitious woman, if she destroyed one life as the only means, to her benighted vision, of saving her own? Of course this is stated on the hypothesis that she really believed her husband possessed and was exercising this dangerous power.

Let us pursue this line of thought a little further. In the world are very many religious faiths, each, perhaps, asserting a divine or supernatural inspiration. Take three of the most prominent, the Christian, the Mohammedan, and the Buddhist, each numbering its adherents by the hundred millions. With each of these faiths the profession of the other two are mere superstitions or hallucinations. Are the invocations to Allah and to the Enlightened One any more an illusion to our comprehension than Christian worship is to theirs? Our faith, we maintain, is founded alike on Divine revelation and the inherent evidences of its purity and truth. Is their mental delusion a species of partial insanity? And if, in the zeal of the religion of Mohammed, propagation by the sword is believed to be a duty, is such act to be excused on the score of mental illusion? What of the believers in spiritualistic materializations, mind-reading, and the many other isms which live their brief day, and are not without a following? Are the believers in such supernatural power mentally diseased? Such inquiries may be amusing, if not interesting, to the visionary and speculative. They can only bewilder, when applied to the actual transactions of business life. Judicial administration is too real to enter upon such doubtful and dangerous speculations. In the language of Judge Curtis: "It searches after those practical rules which may be administered without inhumanity, for the security of civil society, by protecting it from crime. It inquires not into the peculiar constitution of mind of the accused, or what weakness or even disorders he was afflicted with, but solely whether he was capable of having and did have a criminal intent." I hold we should take our steps cautiously, in adopting the theories of psychological enthusiasts, lest we disarm retributive justice of all its restraining energy.

This is a dissenting opinion, and I wish to be understood as intimating no opinion, either one way or the other, on the sufficiency or insufficiency of the asserted insanity relied on in this case. It being, under the opinion of my brothers, a question of fact for the jury, I will leave it to them, without any attempt to bias them by anything I may say. I regret the necessity I have felt resting on me of differing with my brothers in this case. I regret what I conceived to be a duty to express my views so much at length. On a question of less importance, I would not have done so. I have feared, however, and still fear, that the effect of their ruling will be to let in many of the evils which result from allowing the defense of emotional insanity. I acquit them of all intention to alter the rule of this court on that subject. Still. I think the line cannot be too clearly and sharply drawn which separates the pitiable, unfortunate victims of diseased mental faculties from the recklessly depraved, whose chief evidence of insanity is found in the causeless atrocity of their crimes. Human life has become all too cheap; and, while we spread the mantle of mercy over the criminally irresponsible, the lawless should be made to feel that the way of the transgressor is hard. The terror of the law may thus become a minister of peace.

Appendix 2

Excerpts from *Davis v. United States*
Opinion by: Harlan
Submitted: October 30, 1895
Decided: December 16, 1895

• MR. JUSTICE HARLAN delivered the opinion of the court.

Dennis Davis was indicted for the crime of having, on the 18th day of September, 1894, at the Creek Nation, in the Indian Territory, within the Western District of Arkansas, feloniously, wilfully, and of his malice aforethought, killed and murdered one Sol Blackwell.

He was found guilty of the charge in the indictment. A motion for a new trial having been overruled, and the court having adjudged that the accused was guilty of the crime of murder, as charged, he was sentenced to suffer the penalty of death by hanging.

At the trial below the government introduced evidence which, if alone considered, made it the duty of the jury to return a verdict of guilty of the crime charged.

But there was evidence tending to show that at the time of the killing the accused, by reason of unsoundness or weakness of mind, was not criminally responsible for his acts. In addition to the evidence of a practising physician of many years standing, and who, for the time, was physician at the jail in which the accused was confined previous to his trial, "other witnesses," the bill of exceptions states, "testified that they had been intimately acquainted with the defendant for a number of years, lived near him, and had been frequently with him, knew his mental condition, and that he was weak-minded, and regarded by his neighbors and people as being what they called half crazy. Other witnesses who had known the defendant for ten to twenty years, witnesses who had worked with him and had been thrown in constant contact with him, said he had always been called half crazy, weak-minded; and in the opinion of the witnesses defendant was not of sound mind."

The issue, therefore, was as to the responsibility of the accused for the killing alleged and clearly proved.

In its elaborate charge the court instructed the jury as to the rules by which they were to be guided in determining whether the accused took the life of the deceased feloniously, wilfully, and with malice aforethought. "Where," the court said, "a man has been shot to death, where the facts, as claimed by the government here, show a lying in wait, show previous preparation, show the selection of a deadly weapon, and show concealment to get an opportunity to do the act, where that state of case exists, if there is a mental condition of the kind that renders a man accountable—why, there is crime, and that crime is murder."

Referring to the evidence adduced to show that the accused was incompetent in law to commit crime, the court observed: "Now when a man premeditates a wicked design that produces death, and executes that design, if he is a sane being, if he is what the law calls a sane man, not that he may be partially insane, not that he may be eccentric, and not that he may be unable to control his will power if he is in a passion or rage because of some real or imaginary grievance he may have received—I say, if you find him in that condition and you find these other things attending the act, you would necessarily find the existence of the attributes of the crime of murder known as 'wilfulness' and malice aforethought." But, the court said, the law "presumes every man is sane, and the burden of showing it is not true is upon the party who asserts it. The responsibility of overturning that presumption, that the law recognizes as one that is universal, is with the party who sets it up as a defence. The government is not required to show it. The law presumes that we are all sane; therefore the government does not have to furnish any evidence to show that this defendant is sane. It comes in here with the fact established in legal contemplation until it is overthrown. The government takes and keeps that attitude until the evidence brought in the case overthrows this presumption of sanity. Now, let us see what the nature of this defence is. The defendant interposes the plea of insanity, and he says by this plea that he did the killing, but the act is not one for which he can be held responsible. In other words, that the act was and is excusable in the law, because he was insane at the time of its commission. Now, I say to you in this connection, and it is a fact admitted in argument by the counsel, that under the evidence there is nothing that justifies the act of the killing; nor was it such an act that the law upholds it or mitigates it, or reduces it to a grade lower than murder. If it was committed by the defendant while he was actually insane it is excusable."

Again: "Now, I will undertake or endeavor to tell you, and I bespeak your most earnest attention especially upon this proposition of 'insanity.' The term 'insanity,' as used in this defence, means such a perverted and deranged condition of the mental and moral faculties as to render a person incapable of distinguishing between right and wrong, or unconscious at the time of the nature of the act he is committing; or where, though conscious of the nature of the act and able to distinguish between right and wrong, and know that the act is wrong, yet his will, by which I mean the governing power of his mind, has been, otherwise than voluntarily, so completely destroyed that his actions are not subject to it, but are beyond his control. Such insanity, if proved to your reasonable satisfaction to have existed at the time of the commission of the act—that is the test—at the time of its commission, is in the law an excuse for it, however brutal or atrocious it may have been. For a person to be excused from criminal responsibility it is not necessary that he be a raving maniac, but ordinarily it requires something more than mere eccentricity of a natural character. Such insanity does not excuse."

Later in the charge the court recurred to the defence of insanity and said: "Now, as I have already told you, the law presumes every person who has reached the years of discretion to be of sane mind, and this presumption continues until the contrary is shown. So that when, as in this case, insanity is interposed as a defence, the fact of the existence of such insanity at the time of the commission of the offence charged, must be established by the evidence to the reasonable satisfaction of a jury, and the burden of proof of the insanity rests with the defendant. Although you may believe and find from the evidence that the defendant did commit the act charged against him, yet, if you further find that at the time he did so he was in such an insane condition of mind that he did not and could not understand and comprehend the nature of the act; or that thus knowing and understanding it, he was so far deprived of his will, not by his own passion conceived for the purpose of spurring him on to commit the violence, not by his own passion of mind engendered by some real or fancied grievance; but that he was so far deprived of his will by disease or other cause over which he had no control, as to render him unable to control his actions, then such killing was not a malicious killing, and you will acquit him of the crime charged against him."

In concluding its charge the court thus summarized the principles by which the jury were to be guided in their deliberations:

> Now, gentlemen, the propositions are few in this case. First, inquire whether there was a killing; then whether the act of killing was done by the defendant, and what was his condition of mind under the law at that time, as I have given it to you. See what his mental condition was at that time under the law as I have given it to you, and if he is to be held responsible for his actions. If so, you are then to take a step further and see whether these attributes of the crime of murder existed as I have defined them to you; that is, that the killing was done wilfully and with malice aforethought.
>
> Gentlemen, I have given you the law in the case, and you are to take it as the law and by this law and the testimony you are to make up your verdict. You are to be satisfied beyond a reasonable doubt of the guilt of this defendant before you convict. When you start into a trial of a case, as I have already told you, you start in with the presumption of sanity. Then comes in the responsibility resting upon the defendant to show his condition; to show his irresponsibility under the law. He is required to show that—to your reasonable satisfaction, I say, to your reasonable satisfaction—that it is a state of case where he is excusable for the act.

These extracts from the charge of the court present this important question: If it appears that the deceased was killed by the accused under circumstances which—nothing else appearing—made a case of murder, can the jury properly return a verdict of guilty of the offence charged if upon the whole evidence from whatever side it comes they have a reasonable doubt whether at the time of killing the accused was mentally competent to distinguish between right and wrong or to understand the nature of the act he was committing? If this question be answered in the negative the judgment must be reversed; for the court below instructed the jury that the defence of insanity could not avail the accused unless it appeared affirmatively, to the reasonable satisfaction of the jury, that he was not criminally responsible for his acts. The fact of killing being clearly proved, the legal presumption, based upon the common experience of mankind, that every man is sane, was sufficient, the court in effect said, to authorize a verdict of guilty, although the jury might entertain a reasonable doubt upon the evidence, whether the accused, by reason of his mental condition, was criminally responsible for the killing in question. In other words, if the evidence was in equilibrio as to the accused being sane, that is, capable of comprehending the nature and effect of his acts, he was to be treated just as he would be if there were no defence of insanity or if there were an entire absence of proof that he was insane.

This exposition of criminal law is not without support by adjudications in

England and in this country. In *Regina v. Stokes*, 3 Car. & K. 185, 188, a case of murder, Baron Rolfe said: "If the prisoner seeks to excuse himself upon the plea of insanity, it is for him to make it clear that he was insane at the time of committing the offence charged. The onus rests on him; and the jury must be satisfied that he actually was insane. If the matter is left in doubt, it will be their duty to convict him; for every man must be presumed to be responsible for his acts until the contrary is clearly shown." The same judge, in *Regina v. Layton*, 4 Cox C.C. 149, 155, which was also a case of murder and the defence insanity, after observing that in cases of that description it was a cardinal rule "that the burden of proving innocence rested on the party accused," said that the question for the jury was "not whether the person was of sound mind, but whether he had made out to their satisfaction that he was not of sound mind."

But the most deliberate and careful statement of the doctrine in the English courts is to be found in McNaghten's case, 10 Cl. & Fin. 200, 203, 210, decided in 1843. The accused having been found not guilty, on the ground of insanity, his trial became the subject of discussion in the House of Lords, and much was said about insane delusions and partial insanity, as giving or not giving immunity for acts which, being committed by sane persons, were punishable criminally. The judges were summoned to give their opinion on that question, although there was no case pending before the House. Hansard's Parliamentary Debates, vol. 67, 3d series, 714 to 743. Among the questions propounded to the judges were these: "What are the proper questions to be submitted to the jury, when a person alleged to be afflicted with insane delusions respecting one or more particular subjects or persons is charged with the commission of a crime (murder, for example), and insanity is set up as a defence? In what terms ought the question to be left to the jury, as to the person's state of mind at the time when the act was committed?" Mr. Justice Maule delivered a separate opinion, in which he expressed great difficulty in answering the questions put to the judges, because they did not appear to arise out of, and were not propounded with reference to, a particular case, or for a particular purpose, which might explain or limit the generality of these terms, and also, because he had heard no argument, at the bar or elsewhere, on the subject referred to in the questions. He expressed fear that any answers made would embarrass the administration of justice in criminal cases. He, nevertheless, said that "to render a person irresponsible for crime on account of unsoundness of mind, the unsoundness should, according to law as it has long been understood and held, be such as rendered him incapable of knowing right from wrong;" and that the judge, in the particular case on trial, should employ such terms in his instructions as, in his discretion, would be proper to assist the jury in coming to a right conclusion as to the guilt of the accused. Lord Chief Justice Tindal, speaking for himself and the other judges, said, in response to the questions propounded, that the jurors ought to be told in all cases where insanity is set up as a defence that "every man is presumed to be sane, and to possess a sufficient degree of reason to be responsible for his crimes, until the contrary be proved to their satisfaction; and that to establish a defence on the ground of insanity it must be clearly proved that, at the time of the committing of the act, the party accused was laboring under such a defect of reason, from disease of the mind, as not to know the nature and quality of the act he was doing; or, if he did know it, that he did not know he was doing what was wrong."

In *Commonwealth v. Rogers*, 7 Met. (Mass.) 500, 504, 506, (1844) it was said by Chief Justice Shaw, in his charge to the jury, that "the ordinary presumption is, that a person is of sound mind, until the contrary appears; and in order to shield one from criminal responsibility, the presumption must be rebutted by proof of the contrary, satisfactory to the jury. Such proof may arise, either out of the evidence offered by the prosecutor to establish the case against the accused, or from distinct evidence offered on his part; in either case it must be sufficient to establish the fact of insanity; otherwise the presumption will stand." The jury, after being in consultation for several hours, came into court and asked whether they must be satisfied beyond a doubt of the insanity of the prisoner to entitle him to an acquittal. The court responded that if the preponderance of the evidence was in favor of the insanity of the prisoner, the jury would be authorized to find him insane. A verdict was returned of not guilty, by reason of insanity. In *Commonwealth v. York*, 9 Met. (Mass.) (1845) 93, 116, the charge was murder, and the defence provocation or mutual combat, making the offence, at most, only manslaughter. The court held that the guilt of malicious homicide was established beyond reasonable doubt, by proof, beyond reasonable doubt, of the fact of voluntary killing, without excuse or justification apparent upon the evidence introduced in behalf of the prosecution; that, in such case, the proof must preponderate in favor of the fact of sudden and mutual combat, in order to justify a finding in favor of the prisoner in respect to the fact, it not being sufficient to raise a doubt, even though it be a reasonable doubt, of the fact of extenuation. In that case Mr. Justice Wilde dissented in an able opinion, holding that "the burden of proof, in every criminal case, is on the Commonwealth to prove all the material allegations in the indictment; and if, on the whole evidence, the jury have a reasonable doubt whether the defendant is guilty of the crime charged, they are bound to acquit him." p. 134. In *Commonwealth v. Eddy*, 7 Gray, (1856) 583, in which the crime charged was murder and the defence insanity, Mr. Justice Metcalf, speaking for himself and Justices Bigelow and Merrick, said: "The burden is on the Commonwealth to prove all that is necessary to constitute the crime of murder. And as that crime can be committed only by a reasonable being—a person of sane mind—the burden is on the Commonwealth to prove that the defendant was of sane mind when he committed the act of killing. But it is a presumption of law that all men are of sane mind; and that presumption of law sustains the burden of proof, unless it is rebutted and overcome by satisfactory evidence to the contrary. In order to overcome the presumption of law and shield the defendant from legal responsibility, the burden is on him to prove, to the satisfaction of the jury, by a preponderance of the whole evidence in the case, that, at the time of committing the homicide, he was not of sane mind."

It would seem that later cases in Massachusetts do not go to the extent indicated by the above cases. In *Commonwealth v. Heath* etc., 11 Gray, 303, which was tried before Justices Dewey, Metcalf, and Thomas, the charge was murder, and one question was whether the defendants were of sufficient intelligence to be responsible for a homicide. Upon this point, and as to the burden of proof, the court said: "The law presumes men and women of the age of the prisoners to be sane, to be responsible agents. Where therefore a homicide is proved to have been committed in such way and under such circumstances as, when done by a person of sane mind, would constitute murder, the presumption of law, as of common sense and general experience, supplies that link. It presumes men to be sane till the contrary is shown. The presumption of law stands until it is met and overcome by the evidence in the case. This evidence may come, of course, as well from the witnesses for the Government as the witnesses for the defence; and when the evidence is all in, the jury must be satisfied, in order to convict the prisoner, not only of the doing of the acts which constitute murder, but that they proceeded from a responsible agent, one capable of committing the offence. This is the rule to be applied to a case where the defence is idiocy, an original defect and want of capacity. Whether the rule is modified where the defence relied upon is insanity, disease of the mind or delusion, it is not necessary now to inquire." In respect to that case we observe that, upon principle, the rule as to the burden of proof in criminal cases cannot be materially different, where the defence is insanity, disease of the mind or delusion, from the rule obtaining when the defence is an original defect and want of capacity. In *Commonwealth v. Pomeroy*, (reported in Wharton on Homicide, 2d ed. 753, Appendix,) which was tried in 1874 before Mr. Justice Gray (then Chief Justice of the Supreme Judicial Court of Massachusetts) and Mr. Justice Morton, afterwards Chief Justice of the same court, it was contended by the prosecution that the question of sanity, raised by the defendant, was to be determined by the preponderance of proof; that the Commonwealth was not bound to prove the sanity of the accused beyond a reasonable doubt. But the court said: "The burden is upon the government to prove everything essential beyond reasonable doubt; and that burden, so far as the matter of sanity is concerned, is ordinarily satisfactorily sustained by the presumption that every person of sufficient age is of sound mind and understands the nature of his acts. But when the circumstances are all in, on the one side and on the other; on the one side going to show a want of adequate capacity, on the other side going to show usual intelligence; when the whole is in, the burden rests where it was in the beginning—upon the government to prove the case beyond a reasonable doubt."

In *State v. Spencer*, 1 Zabriskie, 196, 202, 212 (1846), which was a case of murder tried before Chief Justice Hornblower, it was said that "when the evidence of sanity on the one side, and of insanity on the other, leaves the scale in equal balance, or so nearly poised that the jury have a reasonable doubt of his sanity, then a man is to be considered sane and responsible for what he does;" and that the "proof of insanity at the time of committing the act, ought to be as clear and satisfactory, in order to acquit him on the ground of insanity, as the proof of committing the act ought to be, in order to find a sane man guilty." Again, in the same case: "If, in your opinion, it is clearly proved that the prisoner at the bar, at the time of the homicide, was unconscious that what he did was wrong, and that he ought not to do it, you must acquit him on the ground of insanity; but if in your opinion this is not clearly established beyond a reasonable doubt, then you must find him guilty of the act and proceed to investigate the nature of the homicide." There are other cases to the same general effect, some of them holding that the presumption of sanity will prevail, and that the jury may properly convict, unless the defence of insanity is established beyond a reasonable doubt; others, that it is the duty of the jury to convict unless it appears by a preponderance of evidence that the accused was insane when the killing occurred.

We are unable to assent to the doctrine that in a prosecution for murder, the defence being insanity, and the fact of the killing with a deadly weapon being clearly established, it is the duty of the jury to convict where the evidence is equally balanced on the issue as to the sanity of the accused at the time of the killing. On the contrary, he is entitled to an acquittal of the specific crime charged if upon all the evidence there is reasonable doubt whether he was capable in law of committing crime.

No one, we assume, would wish either the courts or juries when trying a case of murder to disregard the humane principle, existing at common law and recognized in all the cases tending to support the charge of the court below, that, "to make a complete crime cognizable by human laws, there must be both a will and an act;" and "as a vicious will without a vicious act is no civil crime, so, on the other hand, an unwarrantable act without a vicious will is no crime at all. So that to constitute a crime against human laws, there must be, first, a vicious will; and, secondly, an unlawful act consequent upon such vicious will." 4 Bl. Com. 21. All this is implied in the accepted definition of murder; for it is of the very essence of that heinous crime that it be committed by a person of "sound memory and discretion," and with "malice aforethought," either express or implied. 4 Bl. Com. 195; 3 Inst. 47; 2 Chitty's Cr. Law, 476. Such was the view of the court below which took care in its charge to say that the crime of murder could only be committed by a sane being, although it instructed the jury that a reasonable doubt as to the sanity of the accused would not alone protect him against a verdict of guilty.

One who takes human life cannot be said to be actuated by malice aforethought, or to have deliberately intended to take life, or to have "a wicked, depraved, and malignant heart," or a heart "regardless of society duty and fatally bent on mischief," unless at the time he had sufficient mind to comprehend the criminality or the right and wrong of such an act. Although the killing of one human being by another human being with a deadly weapon is presumed to be malicious until the contrary appears, yet, "in order to constitute a crime, a person must have intelligence and capacity enough to have a criminal intent and purpose; and if his reason and mental powers are either so deficient that he has no will, no conscience, or controlling mental power, or if, through the overwhelming violence of mental disease, his intellectual power is for the time obliterated, he is not a responsible moral agent, and is not punishable for criminal acts." *Commonwealth v. Rogers*, 7 Met. (Mass.) 501. Neither in the adjudged cases nor in the elementary treatises upon criminal law is there to be found any dissent from these general propositions. All admit that the crime of murder necessarily involves the possession by the accused of such mental capacity as will render him criminally responsible for his acts.

Upon whom then must rest the burden of proving that the accused, whose life it is sought to take under the forms of law, belongs to a class capable of committing crime? On principle, it must rest upon those who affirm that he has committed the crime for which he is indicted. That burden is not fully discharged, nor is there any legal right to take the life of the accused, until guilt is made to appear from all the evidence in the case. The plea of not guilty is unlike a special plea in a civil action, which, admitting the case averred, seeks to establish substantive ground of defence by a preponderance of evidence. It is not in confession and avoidance, for it is a plea that controverts the existence of every fact essential to constitute the crime charged. Upon that plea the accused may stand, shielded by the presumption of his innocence, until it appears that he is guilty; and his guilt cannot in the very nature of things be regarded as proved, if the jury entertain a reasonable doubt from all the evidence whether he was legally capable of committing crime.

This view is not at all inconsistent with the presumption which the law, justified by the general experience of mankind as well as by considerations of public safety, indulges in favor of sanity. If that presumption were not indulged the government would always be under the necessity of adducing affirmative evidence of the sanity of an accused. But a requirement of that character would seriously delay and embarrass the enforcement of the laws against crime, and in most cases be unnecessary. Consequently the law presumes that every one charged with crime is sane, and thus supplies in the first instance the required proof of capacity to commit crime. It authorizes the jury to assume at the outset that the accused is criminally responsible for his acts. But that is not a conclusive presumption, which the law upon grounds of public policy forbids to be overthrown or impaired by opposing proof. It is a disputable or, as it is often designated, a rebuttable presumption resulting from the connection ordinarily existing between certain facts—such connection not being "so intimate, nor so nearly universal, as to render it expedient that it should be absolutely and imperatively presumed to exist in every case, all evidence to the contrary being rejected; but yet it is so general, and so nearly universal, that the law itself, without the aid of a jury, infers the one fact from the proved existence of the other, in the absence of all opposing evidence." 1 Greenl. Ev. § 38. It is therefore a presumption that is liable to be overcome or to be so far impaired in a particular case that it cannot be safely or properly made the basis of action in that case, especially if the inquiry involves human life. In a certain sense it may be true that where the defence is insanity, and where the case made by the prosecution discloses nothing whatever in excuse or extenuation of the crime charged, the accused is bound to produce some evidence that will impair or weaken the force of the legal presumption in favor of sanity. But to hold that such presumption must absolutely control the jury until it is overthrown or impaired by evidence sufficient to establish the fact of insanity beyond all reasonable doubt or to the reasonable satisfaction of the jury, is in effect to require him to establish his innocence, by proving that he is not guilty of the crime charged.

In considering the distinction between the presumption of innocence and reasonable doubt, this court, in *Coffin v. United States*, upon full consideration, said: "The presumption of innocence is a conclusion drawn by the law in favor of the citizen, by virtue whereof, when brought to trial upon a criminal charge, he must be acquitted, unless he is proven to be guilty. In other words, this presumption is an instrument of proof created by the law in favor of one accused, whereby his innocence is established until sufficient evidence is introduced to overcome the proof which the law has created. This presumption on the one hand, supplemented by any other evidence he may adduce, and the evidence against him on the other, constitute the elements from which the legal conclusion of his guilt or innocence is to be drawn." Reasonable doubt it was also said was "the result of the proof, not the proof itself; whereas the presumption of innocence is one of the instruments of proof, going to bring about the proof, from which reasonable doubt arises; thus one is a cause, the other an effect. To say that the one is the equivalent of the other is, therefore, to say that legal evidence can be excluded from the jury, and that such exclusion may be cured by instructing them correctly in regard to the method by which they are required to reach their conclusion upon the proof actually before them." *Coffin v. United States*, 156 U.S. 432, 459, 460.

Strictly speaking, the burden of proof, as those words are understood in criminal law, is never upon the accused to establish his innocence or to disprove the facts necessary to establish the crime for which he is indicted. It is on the prosecution from the beginning to the end of the trial and applies to every element necessary to constitute the crime. Giving to the prosecution, where the defence is insanity, the benefit in the way of proof of the presumption in favor of sanity, the vital question from the time a plea of not guilty is entered until the return of the verdict, is whether upon all the evidence, by whatever side adduced, guilt is established beyond reasonable doubt. If the whole evidence, including that supplied by the presumption of sanity, does not exclude beyond reasonable doubt the hypothesis of insanity, of which some proof is adduced, the accused is entitled to an acquittal of the specific offence charged. His guilt cannot be said to have been proved beyond a reasonable doubt—his will and his acts cannot be held to have joined in perpetrating the murder charged—if the jury, upon all the evidence, have a reasonable doubt whether he was legally capable of committing crime, or (which is the same thing) whether he wilfully, deliberately, unlawfully, and of malice aforethought took the life of the deceased. As the crime of murder involves sufficient capacity to distinguish between right and wrong, the legal interpretation of every verdict of guilty as charged is that the jury believed from all the evidence beyond a reasonable doubt that the accused was guilty, and was therefore responsible, criminally, for his acts. How then upon principle or consistently with humanity can a verdict of guilty be properly returned, if the jury entertain a reasonable doubt as to the existence of a fact which is essential to guilt, namely, the capacity in law of the accused to commit that crime?

The views we have expressed are supported by many adjudications that are entitled to high respect. If such were not the fact, we might have felt obliged to accept the general doctrine announced in some of the above cases; for it is desirable that there be uniformity of rule in the administration of the criminal law in governments whose constitutions equally recognize the fundamental principles that are deemed essential for the protection of life and liberty.

In *People v. McCann*, 16 N.Y. 58, a case of murder, the jury were instructed that if any reasonable doubt existed as to the proof of the deed itself the prisoner should be acquitted; "but as sanity is the natural state, there is no presumption of insanity, and the defence must be proved beyond a reasonable doubt." This instruction was held to be erroneous by the unanimous judgment of the Court of Appeals of New York, of which, at the time, Judges Denio, Johnson, Comstock, and Selden were members. The judges who delivered opinions concurred in the view that, while there was no presumption of insanity, and while the law presumes a sufficient understanding and will to do the act, the fact of the killing by the accused being established by proof, the burden was upon the prosecution to show from all the evidence the existence of the requisites or elements constituting the crime, one of which was the sanity of the prisoner. In that case Mr. Justice Brown said: "If there be a doubt about the act of killing, all will concede that the prisoner is entitled to the benefit of it; and if there be any doubt about the will, the faculty of the prisoner to discern between right and wrong, why should he be deprived of the benefit of it, when both the act and the will are necessary to make out the crime?" And, "If he is entitled to the benefit of the doubt in regard to the malicious intent, shall he not be entitled to the same benefit upon the question of his sanity, his understanding? For, if he was without reason and understanding at the time, the act was not his, and he is no more responsible for it than he would be for the act of another man." pp. 67, 68. So in *Brotherton v. People*, 75 N.Y. 159, 162, Chief Justice Church, speaking for the court, after observing that crimes can only be committed by human beings in a condition to be responsible for their acts, and that the burden of overthrowing the presumption of sanity and of showing insanity is upon the person who alleges it, says: "If evidence is given tending to establish insanity, then the general question is presented to the court and jury whether the crime, if committed, was committed by a person responsible for his acts, and upon this question the presumption of sanity, and the evidence, are all to be considered, and the prosecutor holds the affirmative, and if a reasonable doubt exists as to whether the prisoner is sane, or not, he is entitled to the benefit of the doubt, and to an acquittal." To the same effect are *O'Connell v. People*, 87 N.Y. 377, 380, and *Walker v. People*, 88 N.Y. 81, 88.

In *Chase v. People*, 40 Illinois, 352, 358, reaffirming the rule announced in the case of *Hopps v. People*, 31 Illinois, 385, 392, the court, speaking by Chief Justice Breese, said: "Sanity is an ingredient in crime as essential as the overt act, and if sanity is wanting there can be no crime, and if the jury entertain a reasonable doubt on the question of insanity, the prisoner is entitled to the benefit of the doubt. We wish to be understood as saying, as in that case, that the burden of proof is on the prosecution to prove guilt beyond a reasonable doubt, whatever the defence may be. If insanity is relied on and evidence given tending to establish that unfortunate condition of mind, and a reasonable well-founded doubt is thereby raised of the sanity of the accused, every principle of justice and humanity demands that the accused shall have the benefit of the doubt."

The same principle is recognized in New Hampshire. Bellows, J., speaking for the court, after observing that a plea of not guilty, in a criminal cause, puts in issue all the allegations of the indictment, said: "A system of rules, therefore, by which the burthen is shifted upon the accused of showing that any of the substantial allegations are untrue, or, in other words, to prove a negative is purely artificial and formal, and utterly at war with the humane principle which, in favorem vitoe, requires the guilt of the prisoner to be established beyond reasonable doubt." Again, in the same case, after saying that to justify a conviction, all the elements of the crime charged must be shown to exist, and to a moral certainty, including the facts of a sound memory, an unlawful killing and malice, he proceeded: "As to the first, the natural presumption of sanity is prima facie proof of a sound memory, and that must stand unless there is other evidence tending to prove the contrary; and then whether it come from the one side or the other in weighing it, the defendant is entitled to the benefit of all reasonable doubt, just the same as upon the point of an unlawful killing or malice. Indeed, the want of sound memory repels the proof of malice in the same way as proof that the killing was accidental, in self-defence, or in heat of blood; and there can be no solid distinction founded upon the fact that the law presumes the existence of a sound memory. So the law infers malice from the killing when that is shown, and nothing else; but in both cases the inference is one of fact, and it is for the jury to say whether, on all the evidence before them, the malice or the sanity is proved or not. Indeed, we regard these inferences of fact as not designed to interfere in any way with the obligation of the prosecutor to remove all reasonable doubt of guilt; but they are applied as the suggestions of experience, and with a view to the convenience and expedition of trials, leaving the evidence, when adduced, to be weighed without regard to the fact whether it comes from the one side or the other." "The criminal intent must be proved as much as the overt act, and without a sound mind such intent could not exist; and the burthen of proof must always remain with the prosecutor to prove both the act and criminal intent." *State v. Bartlett*, 43 N.H. 224, 231.

So in *People v. Garbutt*, 17 Michigan, 9, 22, the court, speaking by Chief Justice Cooley, after observing that the prosecution may rest upon the presumption of sanity until that presumption is overthrown by the defendant's evidence, said: "Nevertheless, it is a part of the case for the government; the fact which it supports must necessarily be established before any conviction can be had; and when the jury come to consider the whole case upon the evidence delivered to them, they must do so upon the basis that on each and every portion of it they are to be reasonably satisfied before they are at liberty to find the defendant guilty."

In *Cunningham v. State*, 56 Mississippi, 269, the question was carefully examined and the rule was stated by Chalmers, J., to be, that whenever the condition of the prisoner's mind is put in issue by such facts proved on either side as create a reasonable doubt of his sanity, it devolves upon the State to remove it and to establish the sanity of the prisoner to the satisfaction of the jury beyond all reasonable doubt arising out of all the evidence in the case.

In *Dove v. State*, 3 Heiskell 348, 371, Chief Justice Nicholson, delivering the unanimous opinion of the Supreme Court of Tennessee, thus stated its view of the question: "When the proof of insanity makes an equipoise, the presumption of sanity is neutralized—it is overturned, it ceases to weigh, and the jury are in reasonable doubt. How, then, can a presumption, which has been neutralized by countervailing proof, be resorted to to turn the scale? The absurdity to which this doctrine leads will be more obvious by supposing that the jury should return a special verdict. It would be as follows: 'We find the defendant guilty of the killing charged, but the proof leaves our minds in doubt whether he was of such soundness of memory and discretion as to have done the killing wilfully, deliberately, maliciously, and premeditatedly.' Upon such a verdict no judge could pronounce the judgment of death upon the defendant." So, in *Plake v. State*, 121 Indiana, 433, 435, Judge Elliott, speaking for the Supreme Court of Indiana, said: "If the evidence is of such a character as to create a reasonable doubt whether the accused was of unsound mind at the time the crime was committed, he is entitled to a verdict of acquittal. *Polk v. State*, 19 Indiana, 170; *Bradley v. State*, 31 Indiana, 492; *McDougal v. State*, 88 Indiana, 24." To the same effect are many other American cases cited in argument. The principle is accurately stated by Mr. Justice Cox of the Supreme Court of the District of Columbia as follows: "The crime, then, involves three elements, viz., the killing, malice, and a responsible mind in the murderer. But after all the evidence is in, if the jury, while bearing in mind both these presumptions that I have mentioned—i.e. that the defendant is innocent until he is proved guilty, and that he is and was sane, unless evidence to the contrary appears—and considering the whole evidence in the case, still entertain what is called a reasonable doubt, on any ground, (either as to the killing or the responsible condition of mind,) whether he is guilty of the crime of murder, as it has been explained and defined, then the rule is that the defendant is entitled to the benefit of that doubt and to an acquittal." Guiteau's case, 10 Fed. Rep. 161, 163.

It seems to us that undue stress is placed in some of the cases upon the fact that, in prosecutions for murder the defence of insanity is frequently resorted to and is sustained by the evidence of ingenious experts whose theories are difficult to be met and overcome. Thus it is said, crimes of the most atrocious character often go unpunished, and the public safety is thereby endangered. But the possibility of such results must always attend any system devised to ascertain and punish crime, and ought not to induce the courts to depart from principles fundamental in criminal law, and the recognition and enforcement of which are demanded by every consideration of humanity and justice. No man should be deprived of his life under the forms of law unless the jurors who try him are able, upon their consciences, to say that the evidence before them, by whomsoever adduced, is sufficient to show beyond a reasonable doubt the existence of every fact necessary to constitute the crime charged.

For the reason stated, and without alluding to other matters in respect to which error is assigned, the judgment is reversed and the cause remanded with directions to grant a new trial, and for further proceedings consistent with this opinion.

Reversed.

Appendix 3

Excerpts from *Durham v. United States*
Opinion by: Bazelon

Monte Durham was convicted of housebreaking,[1] by the District Court sitting without a jury. The only defense asserted at the trial was that Durham was of unsound mind at the time of the offense. We are now urged to reverse the conviction (1) because the trial court did not correctly apply existing rules governing the burden of proof on the defense of insanity, and (2) because existing tests of criminal responsibility are obsolete and should be superseded.[2]

I.

Durham has a long history of imprisonment and hospitalization. In 1945, at the age of 17, he was discharged from the Navy after a psychiatric examination had shown that he suffered "from a profound personality disorder which renders him unfit for Naval service." In 1947 he pleaded guilty to violating the National Motor Theft Act[3] and was placed on probation for one to three years. He attempted suicide, was taken to Gallinger Hospital for observation, and was transferred to St. Elizabeths Hospital, from which he was discharged after two months. In January 1948, as a result of a conviction in the District of Columbia Municipal Court for passing bad checks, the District Court revoked his probation and he commenced service of his Motor Theft sentence. His conduct within the first few days in jail led to a lunacy inquiry in the Municipal Court where a jury found him to be of unsound mind. Upon commitment to St. Elizabeths, he was diagnosed as suffering from "psychosis with psychopathic personality." After 15 months of treatment, he was discharged in July 1949 as "recovered" and was returned to jail to serve the balance of his sentence. In June 1950 he was conditionally released. He violated the conditions by leaving the District. When he learned of a warrant for his arrest as a parole violator, he fled to the "South and Midwest obtaining money by passing a number of bad checks." After he was found and returned to the District, the Parole Board referred him to the District Court for a lunacy inquisition, wherein a jury again found him to be of unsound mind. He was readmitted to St. Elizabeths in February 1951. This time the diagnosis was "without mental disorder, psychopathic personality." He was discharged for the third time in May 1951. The housebreaking which is the subject of the present appeal took place two months later, on July 13, 1951.

According to his mother and the psychiatrist who examined him in September 1951, he suffered from hallucinations immediately after his May 1951 discharge from St. Elizabeths. Following the present indictment, in October 1951, he was adjudged of unsound mind in proceedings under Sec. 4244 of Title 18 U.S.C., upon the affidavits of two psychiatrists that he suffered from "psychosis with psychopathic personality." He was committed to St. Elizabeths for the fourth time and given subshock insulin therapy. This commitment lasted 6 month—until February 1953—he was released to the custody of the District Jail on the certificate of Dr. Silk, Acting Superintendent of St. Elizabeths, that he was "mentally competent to stand trial and able to consult with counsel to properly assist in his own defense."

He was thereupon brought before the court on the charge involved here. The prosecutor told the court: "So I take this attitude, in view of the fact that he has been over there (St. Elizabeths) a couple of times and these cases that were charged against him were dropped, I don't think I should take the responsibility of dropping these cases against him; then Saint Elizabeths would let him out on the street, and if that man committed a murder next week then it is my responsibility. So we decided to go to trial on one case, that is the case where we found him right in the house, and let him bring in the defense, if he wants to, of unsound mine at the time the crime was committed, and then Your Honor will find him on that, and in your decision send him back to Saint Elizabeths Hospital, and then if they let him out on the street it is their responsibility."

Shortly thereafter, when the question arose whether Durham could be considered competent to stand trial merely on the basis of Dr. Silk's ex parte statement, the court said to defense counsel: "I am going to ask you this, Mr.

Ahern: I have taken the position that if once a person has been found of unsound mind after a lunacy hearing, an ex parte certificate of the superintendent of Saint Elizabeths is not sufficient to set aside that finding and I have held another lunacy hearing. That has been my custom. However, if you want to waive that you may do it, if you admit that he is now of sound mind."

The court accepted counsel's waiver on behalf of Durham, although it had been informed by the prosecutor that a letter from Durham claimed need of further hospitalization, and by defense counsel that "the defendant does say that even today he thinks he does need hospitalization; he told me this morning."[4] Upon being so informed, the court said, "Of course, if I hold he is not mentally competent to stand trial I send him back to Saint Elizabeths Hospital and they will send him back again in two or three months."[5] In this atmosphere Durham's trial commenced.

His conviction followed the trial court's rejection of the defense of insanity in these words:

> I don't think it has been established that the defendant was of unsound mind as of July 13, 1951, in the sense that he didn't know the difference between right and wrong or that even if he did, he was subject to an irresistible impulse by reason of the derangement of mind.
>
> While, of course, the burden of proof on the issue of mental capacity to commit a crime is upon the Government, just as it is on every other issue, nevertheless, the Court finds that there is not sufficient to contradict the usual presumption of (sic) the usual inference of sanity.
>
> There is no testimony concerning the mental state of the defendant as of July 13, 1951, and therefore the usual presumption of sanity governs.
>
> While if there was some testimony as to his mental state as of that date, the burden of proof would be on the Government to overcome it. There has been no such testimony, and the usual presumption of sanity prevails.
>
> Mr. Ahern, I think you have done very well by your client and defended him very ably, but I think under the circumstances there is nothing that anybody could have done.

We think this reflects error requiring reversal.

In *Tatum v. United States* we said, "when lack of mental capacity is raised as a defense to a charge of crime, the law accepts the general experience of mankind and presumes that all people, including those accused of crime, are sane."[6] So long as this presumption prevails, the prosecution is not required to prove the defendant's sanity, like any other fact, must be proved as part of the prosecution's case beyond a reasonable doubt."[7] Here it appears that the trial judge recognized this rule but failed to find "some evidence." We hold that the court erred and that the requirement of "some evidence" was satisfied.[8]

In Tatum we held that requirement satisfied by considerably less than is present here. Tatum claimed lack of memory concerning the critical events and three lay witnesses testified that he appeared to be in "more or less of a trance," or "abnormal," but two psychiatrists testified that he was of "sound mind" both at the time of examination and at the time of the crime. Here, the psychiatric testimony was unequivocal that Durham was of unsound mind at the time of the crime. Dr. Gilbert, the only expert witness heard,[9] so stated at least four times. This crucial testimony is set out in the margin.[10] Intensive questioning by the court failed to produce any retraction of Dr. Gilbert's testimony that the "period of insanity would have embraced the date July 13, 1951." And though the prosecution sought unsuccessfully in its cross- and recross-examination of Dr. Gilbert to establish that Durham was a malingerer who feigned insanity whenever he was trapped for his misdeeds, it failed to present any expert testimony to support this theory. In addition to Dr. Gilbert's testimony, there was testimony by Durham's mother to the effect that in the interval between his discharge from St. Elizabeths in May 1951, and the crime "he seemed afraid of people" and had urged her to put steel bars on his bedroom windows.

Apparently the trial judge regarded this psychiatric testimony as "no testimony" on two grounds: (1) it did not adequately cover Durham's condition on July 13, 1951, the date of the offense; and (2) it was not directed to Durham's capacity to distinguish between right and wrong. We are unable to agree that for either of these reasons the psychiatric testimony could properly be considered "no testimony."

(1) Following Dr. Gilbert's testimony that the condition in which he found Durham on September 3, 1951 was progressive and did not "arrive overnight," Dr. Gilbert responded to a series of questions by the court:

Q. (Court). Then is it reasonable to assume that it is not possible to determine how far this state of unsound mind had progressed by July 13th? Isn't that so? A. (Dr. Gilbert). As to the seriousness of the symptoms as compared with them and the time I observed him, that's true, except that his travels were based, according to his statement to me, on certain of the symptoms and his leaving Washington, his giving up his job and work and leaving the work that he had tried to do.

Q. But you can't tell, can you, how far those symptoms had progressed and become worse by the 13th of July? A. No, not how far they were, that is correct.

Thereafter, when the prosecutor on recross asked Dr. Gilbert whether he would change his opinion concerning Durham's mental condition on July 13, 1951, if he knew that Durham had been released from St. Elizabeths just two months before as being of sound mind, the court interrupted to say: "Just a minute. The Doctor testified in answer to my question that he doesn't know and he can't express a definite opinion as to his mental condition on the 13th of July:" This, we think, overlooks the [witness's] unequivocal testimony on direct and cross-examination,[11] and misconceives what he had said in response to questioning by the court, namely, that certain symptoms of mental disorder antedated the crime, although it was impossible to say how far they had progressed.

Moreover, any conclusion that there was "no testimony" regarding Durham's mental condition at the time of the crime disregards the testimony of his mother. Her account of his behavior after his discharge from St. Elizabeths in May 1951, was directly pertinent to the issue of his sanity at the time of the crime.

(2) On re-direct examination, Dr. Gilbert was asked whether he would say that Durham "knew the difference between right and wrong on July 13, 1951; that is, his ability to distinguish between what was right and what was wrong." He replied: "As I have stated before, if the question of the right and wrong were propounded to him he could give you the right answer." Then the court interrupted to ask:

The Court. No, I don't think that is the question, Doctor—not whether he could give a right answer to a question, but whether he, himself, knew the difference between right and wrong in connection with governing his own actions. If you are unable to answer, why, you can say so; I mean, if you are unable to form an opinion.

The Witness. I can only answer this way: That I can't tell how much the abnormal thinking and the abnormal experiences in the form of hallucinations and delusions—delusions of persecution—had to do with his antisocial behavior.

I don't know how anyone can answer that question categorically, except as one's experience leads him to know that most mental cases can give you a categorical answer of right and wrong, but what influence these symptoms have on abnormal behavior or anti-social behavior—

The Court. Well, your answer is that you are unable to form an opinion, is that it?

The Witness. I would say that that is essentially true, for the reasons that I have given.

Later, when defense counsel sought elaboration from Dr. Gilbert on his answers relating to the "right and wrong" test, the court cut off the questioning with the admonition that "you have answered the question, Doctor."

The inability of the expert to give categorical assurance that Durham was unable to distinguish between right and wrong did not destroy the effect of his previous testimony that the period of Durham's "insanity" embraced July 13, 1951. It is plain from our decision in Tatum that this previous testimony was adequate to prevent the presumption of sanity from becoming conclusive and to place the burden of proving sanity upon the Government. None of the testimony before the court in Tatum was couched in terms of "right and wrong."

Finally, even assuming arguendo that the court, contrary to the plain meaning of its words, recognized that the prosecution had the burden of proving Durham's sanity, there would still be a fatal error. For once the issue of insanity is raised by the introduction of "some evidence." so that the presumption of sanity is no longer absolute, it is incumbent upon the trier of fact to weigh and consider "the whole evidence, including that supplied by the presumption of sanity" on the issue of "the capacity in law of the accused to commit" the crime.[12] Here, manifestly, the court as the trier of fact did not and could not weigh "the whole evidence," for it found there was "no testimony concerning the mental state" of Durham.

For the foregoing reasons, the judgment is reversed and the case is remanded for a new trial.

II.

It has been ably argued by counsel for Durham that the existing tests in the District of Columbia for determining criminal responsibility, i.e., the so-called right-wrong test supplemented by the irresistible impulse test, are not satisfactory criteria for determining criminal responsibility. We are argued to adopt a different test to be applied on the retrial of this case. This contention has behind it nearly a century of agitation for reform.

A. The right-wrong test, approved in this jurisdiction in 1882,[13] was the exclusive test of criminal responsibility in the District of Columbia until 1929 when we approved the irresistible impulse test as a supplementary test in *Smith v. United States*.[14] The right-wrong test has its roots in England. There, by the first quarter of the eighteenth century, an accused escaped punishment if he could not distinguish "good and evil," i.e., if he "doth not know what he is doing, no more than a wild beast."[15] Later in the same century, the "wild beast" test was abandoned and "right and wrong" was substituted for "good and evil."[16] And toward the middle of the nineteenth century, the House of Lords in the famous M'Naghten case[17] restated what had become the accepted "right-wrong" test[18] in a form which has since been followed, not only in England[19] but in most American jurisdictions[20] as an exclusive test of criminal responsibility: "the jurors ought to be told in all cases that every man is to presumed to be sane, and to possess a sufficient degree of reason to be responsible for his crimes, until the contrary be proved to their satisfaction; and that, to establish a defence on the ground of insanity, it must be clearly proved that, at the time of the committing of the act, the party accused was labouring under such a defect of reason, from disease of the mind, as not to know the nature and quality of the act he was doing, or, if he did know it, that he did not know he was doing what was wrong."[21]

As early as 1838, Isaac Ray, one of the founders of the American Psychiatric Association, in his now classic *Medical Jurisprudence of Insanity*, called knowledge of right and wrong a "fallacious" test of criminal responsibility.[22] This view has long since been substantiated by enormous developments in knowledge of mental life.[23] In 1928 Mr. Justice Cardozo said to the New York Academy of Medicine: "Everyone concedes that the present (legal) definition of insanity has little relation to the truths of mental life."[24]

Medico-legal writers in large number,[25] The Report of the Royal Commission on Capital Punishment 1949–1953,[26] and The Preliminary Report by the Committee on Forensic Psychiatry of the Group for the Advancement of Psychiatry[27] present convincing evidence that the right-and-wrong test is "based on an entirely obsolete and misleading conception of the nature of insanity."[28] The science of psychiatry now recognizes that a man is an integrated personality and that reason, which is only one element in that personality, is not the sole determinant of his conduct. The right-wrong test, which considers knowledge or reason alone, is therefore an inadequate guide to mental responsibility for criminal behavior. As Professor Sheldon Glueck of the Harvard Law School points out in discussing the right-wrong tests, which he calls the knowledge tests:

> It is evident that the knowledge tests unscientifically abstract out of the mental make-up but one phase or element of mental life, the cognitive, which, in this era of dynamic psychology, is beginning to be regarded as not the most important factor in conduct and its disorders. In brief, these tests proceed upon the following questionable assumptions of an outworn era in psychiatry: (1) that lack of knowledge of the "nature or quality" of an act (assuming the meaning of such terms to be clear), or incapacity to know right from wrong, is the sole or even the most important symptom of mental disorder; (2) that such knowledge is the sole instigator and guide of conduct, or at least the most important element therein, and consequently should be the sole

> criterion of responsibility when insanity is involved; and (3) that the capacity of knowing right from wrong can be completely intact and functioning perfectly even though a defendant is otherwise demonstrably of disordered mind.[29]

Nine years ago we said: "The modern science of psychology does not conceive that there is a separate little man in the top of one's head called reason whose function it is to guide another unruly little man called instinct, emotion, or impulse in the way he should go."[30]

By its misleading emphasis on the cognitive, the right-wrong test requires court and jury to rely upon what is, scientifically speaking, inadequate, and most often, invalid[31] and irrelevant testimony in determining criminal responsibility.[32]

The fundamental objection to the right-wrong test, however, is not that criminal irresponsibility is made to rest upon an inadequate, invalid or indeterminable symptom or manifestation, but that it is made to rest upon any particular symptom.[33] In attempting to define insanity in terms of a symptom, the courts have assumed an impossible role,[34] not merely one for which they have no special competence.[35] As the Royal Commission emphasizes, it is dangerous "to abstract particular mental faculties, and to lay it down that unless these particular faculties are destroyed or gravely impaired, an accused person, whatever the nature of his mental disease, must be held to be criminally responsible."[36] In this field of law as in others, the fact finder should be free to consider all information advanced by relevant scientific disciplines.[37]

Despite demands in the name of scientific advances, this court refused to alter the right-wrong test at the turn of the century. [38] But in 1929, we reconsidered in response to "the cry of scientific experts" and added the irresistible impulse test as a supplementary test for mining criminal responsibility. Without "hesitation" we declared, in *Smith v. United States*, "it to be the law of this District that, in cases where insanity is interposed as a defense, and the facts are sufficient to call for the application of the rule of irresistible impulse, the jury should be so charged."[39] We said:

> The modern doctrine is that the degree of insanity which will relieve the accused of the consequences of a criminal act must be such as to create in his mind an uncontrollable impulse to commit the offense charged. This impulse must be such as to override the reason and judgment and obliterate the sense of right and wrong to the extent that the accused is deprived of the power to choose between right and wrong.

> The mere ability to distinguish right from wrong is no longer the correct test either in civil or criminal cases, where the defense of insanity is interposed. The accepted rule in this day and age, with the great advancement in medical science as an enlightening influence on this subject, is that the accused must be capable, not only of distinguishing between right and wrong, but that he was not impelled to do the act by an irresistible impulse, which means before it will justify a verdict of acquittal that his reasoning powers were so far dethroned by his diseased mental condition as to deprive him of the will power to resist the insane impulse to perpetrate the deed, though knowing it to be wrong.[40]

As we have already indicated, this has since been the test in the District.

Although the Smith case did not abandon the right-wrong test, it did liberate the fact finder from exclusive reliance upon that discredited criterion by allowing the jury to inquire also whether the accused suffered from an undefined "diseased mental condition (which) deprive(d) him of the will power to resist the insane impulse."[41] The term "irresistible impulse," however, carries the misleading implication that "diseased mental condition(s)" produce only sudden, momentary or spontaneous inclinations to commit unlawful acts.[42]

As the Royal Commission found: "In many cases this is not true at all. The sufferer from (melancholia, for example) experiences a change of mood which alters the whole of his existence. He may believe, for instance, that a future of such degradation and misery awaits both him and his family that death for all is a less dreadful alternative. Even the thought that the acts he contemplates are murder and suicide pales into insignificance in contrast with what he otherwise expects. The criminal act, in such circumstances, may be the reverse of impulsive. It may be coolly and carefully prepared; yet it is still the act of a madman. This is merely an illustration; similar states of mind are likely to lie behind the criminal act when murders are committed by persons suffering from schizophrenia or paranoid psychoses due to disease of the brain."[43]

We find that as an exclusive criterion the right-wrong test is inadequate in that (a) it does not take sufficient amount of physic realities and scientific knowledge, and (b) it is based upon one symptom and so cannot validly be applied in all circumstances. We find that the "irresistible impulse" test is also inadequate in that it gives no recognition to mental illness characterized by brooding and reflection and so relegates acts caused by such illness to the application of the inadequate right-wrong test. We conclude that a broader test should be adopted.[44]

B. In the District of Columbia, the formulation of tests of criminal responsibility is entrusted to the courts[45] and, in adopting a new test, we invoke our inherent power to make the change prospectively.[46]

The rule we now hold must be applied on the retrial of this case and in future cases is not unlike that followed by the New Hampshire court since 1870.[47] It is simply that an accused is not criminally responsible if his unlawful act was the product of mental disease or mental defect.[48]

We use "disease" in the sense of a condition which is considered capable of either improving or deteriorating. We use "defect" in the sense of a condition which is not considered capable of either improving or deteriorating and which may be either congenital, or the result of injury, or the residual effect of a physical or mental disease.

Whenever there is "some evidence" that the accused suffered from a diseased or defective mental condition at the time the unlawful act was committed, the trial court must provide the jury with guides for determining whether the accused can be held criminally responsible. We do not, and indeed could not, formulate an instruction which would be either appropriate or binding in all cases. But under the rule now announced, any instruction should in some way convey to the jury the sense and substance of the following: If you the jury believe beyond a reasonable doubt that the accused was not suffering from a diseased or defective mental condition at the time he committed the criminal act charged, you may find him guilty. If you believe he was suffering from a diseased or defective mental condition when he committed the act, but believe beyond a reasonable doubt that the act was not the product of such mental abnormality, you may find him guilty. Unless you believe beyond a reasonable doubt either that he was not suffering from a diseased or defective mental condition, or that the act was not the product of such abnormality, you must find the accused not guilty by reason of insanity. Thus your task would not be completed upon finding, if you did find, that the accused suffered from a mental disease or defect. He would still be responsible for his unlawful act if there was no causal connection between such mental abnormality and the act.[49] These questions must be determined by you from the facts which you find to be fairly deducible from the testimony and the evidence in this case.[50]

The questions of fact under the test we now lay down are as capable of determination by the jury as, for example, the questions juries must determine upon a claim of total disability under a policy of insurance where the state of medical knowledge concerning the disease involved, and its effects, is obscure or in conflict. In such cases, the jury is not required to depend on arbitrarily selected "symptoms, phases or manifestations"[51] of the disease as criteria for determining the ultimate questions of fact upon which the claim depends. Similarly, upon a claim of criminal irresponsibility, the jury will not be required to rely on such symptoms as criteria for determining the ultimate question of fact upon which such claim depends. Testimony as to such "symptoms, phases or manifestations," along with other relevant evidence, will go to the jury upon the ultimate questions of fact which it alone can finally determine. Whatever the state of psychiatry, the psychiatrist will be permitted to carry out his principal court function which, as we noted in *Holloway v. U.S.*, "is to inform the jury of the character of (the accused's) mental disease (or defect)."[52] The jury's range of inquiry will not be limited to, but may include, for example, whether an accused, who suffered from a mental disease or defect did not know the difference between right and wrong, acted under the compulsion of an irresistible impulse, or had "been deprived of or lost the power of his will."[53]

Finally, in leaving the determination of the ultimate question of fact to the jury, we permit it to perform its traditional function which, as we said in Holloway, is to apply "our inherited ideas of moral responsibility to individuals prosecuted for crime."[54] Juries will continue to make moral judgments, still operating under the fundamental precept that "Our collective conscience does not allow punishment where it cannot impose blame."[55] But in making such judgments, they will be guided by wider horizons of knowledge concerning mental life. The question will be simply whether the accused acted because of a mental disorder, and not whether he displayed particular symptoms which medical science has long recognized do not necessarily, or even typically, accompany even the most serious mental disorder.[56]

The legal and moral traditions of the western world require that those who, of their own free will and with evil intent (sometimes called *mens rea*), commit acts which violate the law, shall be criminally responsible for those acts. Our traditions also require that where such acts stem from and are the product of a mental disease or defect as those terms are used herein, moral blame shall not attach, and hence there will not be criminal responsibility.[57] The rule we state in this opinion is designed to meet these requirements.

Reversed and remanded for a new trial.

Appendix 4

Hinckley Letter to Jodie Foster

3/30/81
12:45 P.M.
Dear Jodie,

There is a definite possibility that I will be killed in my attempt to get Reagan. It is for this very reason that I am writing you this letter now.

As you well know by now I love you very much. Over the past seven months I've left you dozens of poems, letters and love messages in the faint hope that you could develop an interest in me. Although we talked on the phone a couple of times I never had the nerve to simply approach you and introduce myself. Besides my shyness, I honestly did not wish to bother you with my constant presence. I know the many messages left at your door and in your mailbox were a nuisance, but I felt that it was the most painless way for me to express my love for you.

I feel very good about the fact that you at least know my name and know how I feel about you. And by hanging around your dormitory, I've come to realize that I'm the topic of more than a little conversation, however full of ridicule it may be. At least you know that I'll always love you.

Jodie, I would abandon this idea of getting Reagan in a second if I could only win your heart and live out the rest of my life with you, whether it be in total obscurity or whatever.

I will admit to you that the reason I'm going ahead with this attempt now is because I just cannot wait any longer to impress you. I've got to do something now to make you understand, in no uncertain terms, that I am doing all of this for your sake! By sacrificing my freedom and possibly my life, I hope to change your mind about me. This letter is being written only an hour before I leave for the Hilton Hotel. Jodie, I'm asking you to please look into your heart and at least give me the chance, with this historical deed, to gain your respect and love.

I love you forever,
John Hinckley

Notes

Introduction

Epigraph. *Game of Thrones*. Season 5, episode 8, "Hardhome," directed by Miguel Sapochnik, written by David Benioff and D. B. Weiss, featuring Peter Dinklage, Lena Headey, and Emilia Clarke, aired May 31, 2015, on HBO.

1. I should emphasize that this is generally only when the perpetrator is white; for example, mass murders committed by people of Middle Eastern descent are inevitably attributed to "radical Islamic terrorism."

2. In December 2012, Adam Lanza fatally shot twenty children and six adults at Sandy Hook Elementary in Newtown, Connecticut. In May 2014, Elliot Rodger killed six people and injured fourteen near UC Santa Barbara. In June 2015, Dylan Roof killed nine parishioners and injured one at a Charleston, South Carolina, church. In June 2015, John Russell Houser killed two people and wounded nine at a Lafayette, Louisiana, movie theater. In 2015, Vester Flanagan shot and killed a reporter and a cameraman during a live broadcast in Roanoke, Virginia. In October 2017, Stephen Paddock killed 58 people and injured over 500 at a country music festival in Las Vegas.

3. McNaughtan is almost always spelled "M'Naghten" or "M'Naughten," but there are a number of variations in the existing literature across disciplines. One comprehensive book, Moran's *Knowing Right from Wrong*, that deals solely with this trial has identified a single extant signature belonging to the person in question; it provides what is argued to be the correct spelling, McNaughtan, which is the version I use in this book.

4. The idea that the law and legal decision-making, as well as the mental health professions, are influenced by popular culture is not new or novel; it is, however, problematic and rarely acknowledged within those disciplinary practices. Two books

that take up this issue are Richard Sherwin's 2002 *When Law Goes Pop: The Vanishing Line Between Law and Popular Culture* from University of Chicago Press and Otto F. Wahl's *Media Madness: Public Images of Mental Illness* (1997) from Rutgers University Press.

5. For example, philosopher Jonathan Westphal's book *The Mind-Body Problem* (2016) from MIT Press; the 2013 PBS series *Brains on Trial with Alan Alda*; David Eagleman's article in *The Atlantic*, "The Brain on Trial" (2011); Scott O'Lilienfield and Robert Byron's article in *Scientific American*, "Your Brain on Trial" (2013).

Chapter 1

Epigraph. Tarika Daftary-Kapur, et al., "Measuring Knowledge of the Insanity Defense: Scale Construction and Validation," *Behavioral Sciences and the Law* 29: 40.

1. Omri Berger, Dale E. McNiel, and Renée L. Binder, "PTSD as a Criminal Defense: A Review of Case Law," *Journal of the American Academy of Psychiatry and the Law* 40, no. 4 (2012): 509–21; Landy F. Sparr and Roland M. Atkinson, "Posttraumatic Stress Disorder as an Insanity Defense: Medicolegal Quicksand," *The American Journal of Psychiatry* (1986).

2. Jessie Manchester, "Beyond Accommodation: Reconstructing the Insanity Defense to Provide an Adequate Remedy for Postpartum Psychotic Women," *The Journal of Criminal Law and Criminology (1973–)* 93, no. 2/3 (2003): 713–52.

3. Nicholas J. Schweitzer and Michael J. Saks, "Neuroimage Evidence and the Insanity Defense," *Behavioral Sciences and the Law* 29, no. 4 (2011): 592–607.

4. Jennifer Eno Louden and Jennifer L. Skeem, "Constructing Insanity: Jurors' Prototypes, Attitudes, and Legal Decision-Making," *Behavioral Sciences and the Law* 25 (2007): 449–70.

5. This brief list of examples are just a few of thousands: Michael L. Perlin, "Unpacking the Myths: The Symbolism Mythology of Insanity Defense Jurisprudence," *Case Western Reserve Law Review* 40 (1989): 599; Richard J. Bonnie, "The Moral Basis of the Insanity Defense," *American Bar Association Journal* 69, no. 2 (1983): 194–97; Eric Silver, Carmen Cirincione, and Henry J. Steadman, "Demythologizing Inaccurate Perceptions of the Insanity Defense," *Law and Human Behavior* 18, no. 1 (1994): 63–70; Caton F. Roberts, Stephen L. Golding, and Frank D. Fincham, "Implicit Theories of Criminal Responsibility: Decision Making and the Insanity Defense," *Law and Human Behavior* 11, no. 3 (1987): 207; James R. P. Ogloff, "A Comparison of Insanity Defense Standards on Juror Decision Making," *Law and Human Behavior* 15, no. 5 (1991): 509; Valerie P. Hans, "An Analysis of Public Attitudes toward the Insanity Defense," *Criminology* 24, no. 2 (1986): 393–414.

6. These revisions to the standards are the subjects of chapters 5 and 6.

7. Jennifer Eno Louden and Jennifer L. Skeem, "Constructing Insanity: Jurors' Prototypes, Attitudes, and Legal Decision-Making," 449–50.

8. Ibid., 465.

9. Ibid.

10. Ibid.

11. Ibid.

12. Ibid.

13. Ibid., 466.

14. Ibid.

15. Aristotle, *On Rhetoric*, trans. George Kennedy (New York: Oxford University Press, 2006).

16. Perlin attributes the term to Morton Birnbaum in "The Right to Treatment: Some Comments on Its Development" in *Medical Moral and Legal Issues*, Vol. 97, pgs. 106–7; Birnbaum was a pioneer in advocating the constitutional basis for the right to treatment for institutionalized mental patients.

17. Michael Perlin, *The Hidden Prejudice: Mental Disability on Trial* (Washington, DC: American Psychological Association, 2000), 21–23.

18. Ibid., 27.

19. Ibid., 29.

20. Ibid., 23.

21. Ibid., 36.

22. Iris Marion Young, *Justice and the Politics of Difference* (Princeton University Press, 1990), 124.

23. For current scholarship on affect, see the work of Lauren Berlant, Lawrence Grossberg, Brian Massumi, Ann Cvetkovich, among others.

24. Ibid., 124.

25. Wayne C. Bartee and Alice Fleetwood Bartee, *Litigating Morality: American Legal Thought and Its English Roots* (New York: Praeger, 1992), xiii.

26. Perlin, *The Hidden Prejudice: Mental Disability on Trial*, 224.

27. Sharon Crowley, *Toward a Civil Discourse: Rhetoric and Fundamentalism* (University of Pittsburgh Press, 2006), 59.

28. Ibid., 60.

29. Ibid., 62.

30. Young, *Justice and the Politics of Difference*, 131.

31. Crowley, *Toward a Civil Discourse: Rhetoric and Fundamentalism*, 77.

32. I am thinking of Ian Haney Lopéz's analysis of citizenship and naturalization cases in which courts were forced to reckon with the arbitrariness of "white" as a racial category.

33. Crowley, *Toward a Civil Discourse: Rhetoric and Fundamentalism*, 78–79.

34. Ibid., 70–71.

35. Ibid., 64–65.

36. Ibid., 63.

37. Ian Haney Lopéz explains how legal precedent naturalized "whiteness" in the US in his book *White by Law: The Legal Construction of Race* (1996) from New York University Press.

38. Crowley, *Toward a Civil Discourse: Rhetoric and Fundamentalism*, 72.

39. Ibid.

40. Ibid., 73.

41. Ibid.

42. Ibid.

43. Perlin, *The Hidden Prejudice: Mental Disability on Trial*, 26.

44. Crowley, *Toward a Civil Discourse: Rhetoric and Fundamentalism*, 73.

45. See, for example, Zizek's *Plague of Fantasies*.

46. Joshua Gunn, "Refiguring Fantasy: Imagination and Its Decline in US Rhetorical Studies," *Quarterly Journal of Speech* 89, no. 1 (2003): 48.

47. Crowley, *Toward a Civil Discourse: Rhetoric and Fundamentalism*, 97.

48. Ibid., 97.

49. Ibid., 98.
50. Ibid., 98–99.
51. Ibid., 98.
52. Young, *Justice and the Politics of Difference*, 131.
53. Ibid.,132.
54. Ibid.,130. This book was written prior to Donald Trump's election, which seems to have upended, among many things, the idea that public expressions of various "isms" are unacceptable.
55. Ibid.,133.
56. Perlin, *The Hidden Prejudice: Mental Disability on Trial*, 30.
57. Young, *Justice and the Politics of Difference*, 142.
58. Perlin, *The Hidden Prejudice: Mental Disability on Trial*, 24–25.
59. Young, *Justice and the Politics of Difference*, 146.
60. Julia Kristeva, *The Powers of Horror: Essays on Abjection* (Columbia University Press, 1982), 1–4.
61. Young, *Justice and the Politics of Difference*, 142.
62. Ibid., 145.
63. Bartee and Bartee, *Litigating Morality*, xi.
64. George Lakoff, *Moral Politics: How Liberals and Conservatives Think* (Chicago: University of Chicago Press, 1996), 41.
65. Ibid., 44.
66. Ibid.
67. Ibid., 66.
68. Ibid., 108.
69. Ibid., 109.
70. Michel Foucault, *Discipline and Punish: The Birth of the Prison*, trans. Alan Sheridan (New York: Random House, 1977), 92.
71. Ibid., 93.
72. Clarke Rountree, *Judging the Supreme Court: Constructions of Motives in "Bush v. Gore"* (East Lansing: Michigan State University Press, 2007), 3.
73. Ibid.
74. Ibid.
75. This leads logically to the conclusion that those beings that lack the capacity to reason are not fully human, which resulted in early standards for legal insanity such as the "wild beast test."
76. Bartee and Bartee, *Litigating Morality*, 84.
77. Michel Foucault, *Madness and Civilization: A History of Insanity in the Age of Reason*, trans. Richard Howard (New York: Random House, 1965), 242–44.
78. Ibid., 246.
79. Ibid., 247.
80. Ibid., 248.
81. Ibid., 250–51.
82. Ibid., 252–59.
83. Ibid., 266.
84. Ibid., 268–69, emphasis mine.
85. Patricia E. Erickson and Steven K. Erickson, *Crime, Punishment, and Mental Illness: Law and the Behavioral Sciences in Conflict* (New Brunswick: Rutgers University Press, 2008), 2.

Chapter 2

Epigraph. Thomas Maeder, *Crime and Madness: The Origins and Evolution of the Insanity Defense* (New York: Harper Collins, 1985): 2.

1. Roy Porter, *Madness* (Oxford: Oxford University Press, 2003) 12.
2. Ibid., 10; Alan A. Baumeister, Mike F. Hawkins, Joni Lee Pow, and Alex S. Cohen, "Prevalence and Incidence of Severe Mental Illness in the United States: An Historical Overview," *Harvard Review of Psychology* (2012): 247.
3. Theodore Millon, *Masters of the Mind* (Hoboken, NJ: Wiley, 2004) 4.
4. Daniel N. Robinson, *Wild Beasts and Idle Humours* (Cambridge, Harvard University Press, 1996) 9.
5. Porter, *Madness*, 13.
6. Ibid., 4.
7. Millon, *Masters of the Mind*, 12.
8. Porter, *Madness*, 16; Robinson, *Wild Beasts and Idle Humours*, 32; Millon, 14–15.
9. Ibid., 37.
10. Ibid., 41.
11. Robinson, *Wild Beasts and Idle Humours*, 23.
12. Ibid., 20.
13. Ibid., 16.
14. Ibid., 19.
15. Porter, *Madness*, 35.
16. Ibid., 35.
17. Plato, *Laws*, Book XI, pg. 266.
18. Robinson, *Wild Beasts and Idle Humours*, 21.
19. Ibid., 22.
20. Aristotle, *Nichomachean Ethics*, Book V, Chapter VIII , 138.
21. Ibid., 139.
22. Millon, *Masters of the Mind*, 26.
23. Ibid., 27.
24. Judith Bonzol, "The Medical Diagnosis of Demonic Possession in an Early Modern English Community," *Parergon* 26, no. 1 (2009): 121.
25. Millon, *Masters of the Mind*, 31.
26. Ibid.
27. Bonzol, Judith, "The Medical Diagnosis of Demonic Possession," 121.
28. Millon, *Masters of the Mind*, 31–32.
29. Robinson, *Wild Beasts and Idle Humours*, 38.
30. Ibid., 39.
31. Ibid., 45.
32. Ibid., 34–35.
33. Ibid., 41.
34. Ibid., 43.
35. Ibid., 57.
36. Ibid., 49.
37. Carlos Espí Forcén and Fernando Espí Forcén, "Demonic Possession and Mental Illness: Discussion of Selected Cases in Late Medieval Hagiographical Literature," *Early Science in Medicine*, 19 (2014): 258–79.
38. Millon, *Masters of the Mind*, 34.

39. Ibid., 33.
40. Ibid.
41. Ibid., 33–34.
42. Ibid., 35.
43. Robinson, *Wild Beasts and Idle Humours*, 54.
44. Ibid., 54–55.
45. Ibid., 55.
46. Ibid.
47. Ibid., 56.
48. Ibid., 57.
49. Ibid., 61–62.
50. Wayne C. Bartee and Alice Fleetwood Bartee, *Litigating Morality: American Legal Thought and Its English Roots* (New York: Praeger, 1992), 84.
51. Porter, *Madness*, 17.
52. Bartee and Bartee, *Litigating Morality*, 84.
53. Robinson, *Wild Beasts and Idle Humours*, 63–64.
54. Ibid., 51.
55. *The Lombard Laws*, 84.
56. *The Lombard Laws*, 115.
57. Robinson, *Wild Beasts and Idle Humours*, 51.
58. Ibid., 62.
59. Porter, *Madness*, 25.
60. Judith Bonzol, "The Medical Diagnosis of Demonic Possession in an Early Modern English Community," 117–18.
61. Ibid., 138.
62. Millon, *Masters of the Mind*, 52.
63. Annie Borthwick, Chris Holman, David Kennard, Mark McFetridge, Karen Messruther, and Jenny Wilkes, "The Relevance of Moral Treatment to Contemporary Mental Health Care," *Journal of Mental Health* 10, no. 4 (2001): 428.
64. Porter, *Madness*, 127.
65. Ibid., 127.
66. Millon, *Masters of the Mind*, 59.
67. Whitaker, *Mad in America*, 6.
68. Ibid.
69. Ibid.
70. Ibid.
71. Porter, *Madness*, 127.
72. Ibid., 128.
73. Ibid., 90.
74. Ibid., 90.
75. Ibid., 97.
76. Porter, *Madness*; Shorter, *A History of Psychiatry*; Foucault, *Discipline and Punish*.
77. Foucault, *Discipline and Punish*.
78. Ibid.
79. This practice is the origin of the phrase "certifiably insane" (Whitaker, 9).
80. Ibid., 9.
81. Foucault, *Discipline and Punish*.
82. Ibid., 11.
83. Ibid.

Chapter 3

Epigraph. From Jean-Baptiste Molière, *L'Amour Medicin* (*The Love Doctor*), 1665, as cited in Edward Shorter, *A History of Psychiatry from the Era of the Asylum to the Age of Prozac* (New York: Wiley and Sons, 1997), 20.

1. Richard Moran, *Knowing Right from Wrong: The Insanity Defense of Daniel McNaughtan* (New York: The Free Press, 1981), 7.
2. This book's conclusion covers the current statutes from state to state in more detail.
3. Edward Shorter, *A History of Psychiatry: From the Era of the Asylum to the Age of Prozac*, 18.
4. Allan V. Horwitz and Gerald N. Grob, "The Checkered History of American Psychiatric Epidemiology," *The Milbank Quarterly* 89, no. 4 (2011): 631.
5. Porter, *Madness*.
6. Ibid.
7. Shorter, *A History of Psychiatry*.
8. Porter, *Madness*, 102.
9. Shorter, *A History of Psychiatry*, 10.
10. Ibid., 97.
11. Millon, *Masters of the Mind*.
12. Ibid., 92.
13. Annie Borthwick, Chris Holman, David Kennard, Mark McFetridge, Karen Messruther, and Jenny Wilkes, "The Relevance of Moral Treatment to Contemporary Mental Health Care," *Journal of Mental Health* 10, no. 4 (2001): 428.
14. Millon, *Masters of the Mind*, 100.
15. The asylums under Pinel's direction, Bicêtre and Salpêtrière, are the major focus of Foucault's criticism in *Discipline and Punish* of the bourgeois morality that drove asylum reforms of the time. According to Foucault, "moral treatment was merely a form of repression of deviant individuals, based on a regime that instilled fears and anxiety as its main agents of control" (Borthwick, et al.). Other historians, such as Edward Shorter and Roy Porter, have critiqued Foucault's assessment of any sort of grand confinement for the purposes of policing the troublesome as a vast oversimplification of the complex social and economic processes under which the lunatic asylums and the corresponding discipline of psychiatry developed.
16. Shorter, *A History of Psychiatry*, 12.
17. Bicêtre was the asylum for men, and Salpêtrière for women.
18. Whitaker, *Mad in America*, 20.
19. Shorter, *A History of Psychiatry*.
20. Whitaker, *Mad in America*, 21.
21. Shorter, *A History of Psychiatry*.
22. Annie Borthwick et al., "The Relevance of Moral Treatment to Contemporary Mental Health Care," 429.
23. Shorter, *A History of Psychiatry*, 20.
24. Ibid., 11.
25. Ibid., 11–12.
26. Ibid., 13.
27. Ibid.
28. Ibid.
29. Shorter, *A History of Psychiatry*, 17.

30. Porter, *Madness*, 105.
31. Millon, *Masters of the Mind*, 96.
32. Bartee and Bartee, *Litigating Morality*, 85.
33. Ibid., 85.
34. Ibid.
35. Bartee and Bartee, *Litigating Morality*.
36. Ibid., 86.
37. Ibid.
38. Ibid.
39. Ibid., 87.
40. Bartee and Bartee, *Litigating Morality*, 87.
41. Rafiq Memon, "Legal Theory and Case Law Defining the Insanity Defence in English and Welsh Law," *The Journal of Forensic Psychiatry and Psychology* 17(2): 233 [230–52].
42. It is important to note that Hadfield's insanity was based on what we would now call Traumatic Brain Injury, and that perhaps it was easier for the jury to comprehend a more tangible injury to the brain as opposed to a more amorphous "mental disease or defect."
43. Bartee and Bartee, *Litigating Morality*, 88.
44. Rafiq Memon, "Legal Theory and Case Law."
45. Richard Moran, *Knowing Right from Wrong*, 487.
46. Bartee and Bartee, *Litigating Morality*, 89.
47. Ibid.
48. Rafiq Memon, "Legal Theory and Case Law."
49. Bartee and Bartee, *Litigating Morality*, 91; Rafiq Memon, "Legal Theory and Case Law," 234.
50. Rafiq Memon, "Legal Theory and Case Law," 234.
51. Ibid., 10.
52. Richard Moran, *Knowing Right from Wrong*, 11.
53. Ibid., 11, emphasis added.
54. Ibid., 12.
55. Ibid.
56. Ibid., 12.
57. Ibid., 14.
58. Ibid., 15.
59. Ibid., 16.
60. Stephen Allnutt, Anthony Samuels, and Colman O'Driscoll, "The Insanity Defence: From Wild Beasts to M'Naghten," *Australus Psychiatry* 15(4): 293.
61. Richard Moran, *Knowing Right from Wrong*, 16.
62. Ibid., 16.
63. Ibid., 16–17.
64. Ibid., 17.
65. Ibid., 18, emphasis added.
66. Ibid., 19.
67. Ibid.
68. Ibid., 19; Richard J. Bonnie, John C. Jeffries Jr., and Peter W. Low, *A Case Study in the Insanity Defense: The Trial of John Hinckley, Jr.* (New York: Thomson/Foundation Press, 1986), 10–11.

69. Richard Moran, *Knowing Right from Wrong*, 9.
70. Ibid., 10.
71. Ibid.
72. Ibid., 13.
73. Ibid.
74. Ibid.
75. Ibid.
76. Ibid., 20.
77. Ibid.
78. Ibid.
79. Ibid.
80. Ibid., 19–20.
81. Ibid., 21.
82. Ibid., 22.
83. Ibid., 22–23.
84. Ibid., 23.
85. As mentioned in the introduction, Moran's spelling is based on an extant signature.
86. Bonnie, Jeffries, and Low, *A Case Study in the Insanity Defense*, 11.

Chapter 4

Epigraph. Michel Foucault, *History of Madness* (New York: Routledge, 2013), 483.
1. Margarita Tartakovsky, "How the DSM Developed: What You Might Not Know," World of Psychology, https://psychcentral.com/blog/archives/2011/07/02/how-the-dsm-developed-what-you-might-not-know/.
2. Whitaker, *Mad in America*.
3. Ibid.
4. Ibid.
5. Millon, *Masters of the Mind*, 104.
6. Ibid., 105.
7. Ibid., 104.
8. Ibid., 108.
9. Ibid., 105.
10. Ibid.
11. Ibid., 106.
12. Ibid.
13. Ibid.
14. Ibid., 107.
15. Ray, *Treatise*, iii, preface to the fifth edition.
16. *Parsons v. State*, para. 2, pg. 1.
17. The full text of the opinion is included as appendix 1 in this book.
18. Ibid., para. 2, pg. 1.
19. Ibid., para. 2, pg. 1.
20. Ibid., para. 2, pg. 1.
21. Ibid., para. 3, pg. 1.
22. Ibid., para. 4, pg. 2.
23. Ibid., para. 5, pg. 2.

24. Goldstein, *The Insanity Defense*, 68–69.
25. *Parsons v. State*, 4.
26. Ibid., 5.
27. Ibid.
28. Ibid.
29. Ibid.
30. Ibid., 5, emphasis in original.
31. Ibid., 5.
32. Ibid., 6.
33. Ibid.
34. Ibid.
35. Ibid.
36. Ibid.
37. Ibid.
38. Ibid.
39. Ibid.
40. Ibid., 6–7.
41. Ibid., 7.
42. Ibid.
43. Ibid.
44. Ibid., 10.
45. Ibid., 11–12, emphases in original.
46. Ibid., Stone (dissenting), 13.
47. Ibid.
48. Ibid., Stone (dissenting), 18.
49. Ibid.
50. Ibid., Stone (dissenting), 20.
51. Davis v. United States, United States Supreme Court, Brief for the United States, 1.
52. Ibid., 1895, Opinion by Harlan, 1.
53. *Davis v. United States*, 25.
54. The full text of the opinion is included as appendix 2 in this book.
55. *Davis v. United States*, 1897, Opinion by Brewer, para. 1.
56. *Davis v. United States*, 1895, Opinion by Harlan, para. 4.
57. *Davis v. United States*, 1897, Opinion by Brewer, para. 3.
58. Ibid., para. 4.
59. *Davis v. United States*, 18.
60. Ibid., 19.
61. Ibid.
62. Ibid., 13.
63. *Davis v. United States*, 1895, Opinion by Harlan, para. 13.
64. Ibid., para. 24.
65. *Com. v. Rogers*; *Com. v. Eddy*; *Com. v. Heath*; *People v. McCann*; *Brotherton v. People*; *Chase v. People*; *State v. Bartlett*; *Cunningham v. State*; *Dove v. State*; *Plake v. State*; Guiteau.
66. *Davis v. United States*, 1897, Opinion by Brewer, para. 5.
67. I would like to express my deep gratitude to Dr. Kerr Norwood at the Alabama State Archives and Lauren Jarvis at the Arkansas History Commission for their assistance in locating and bringing these pieces to my attention.

68. "In the County Jail," *Weekly Iron Age*, February 4, 1895.
69. "A Foul Murder: A Horrible Crime Committed Near Jonesboro," *Weekly Iron Age*, February 4, 1895.
70. Ibid.
71. Ibid.
72. Ibid.
73. Ibid.
74. F. Smith, "The Indian Territory: Items of Interest from Correspondence and Exchanges," *Weekly Elevator*, September 28, 1894, p. 2.
75. Goldstein, *The Insanity Defense*, 69.
76. Ibid., 75.
77. As cited in Goldstein, *The Insanity Defense*, 76.
78. Goldstein, *The Insanity Defense*, 77.

Chapter 5

Epigraph. As cited in *Durham v. United States*, 214 F.2d 862, 1954 (see appendix 3 in this book).
1. Kirk and Kutchins, *The Selling of the DSM*.
2. Porter, *Madness*.
3. Ibid., 186.
4. Ibid.
5. Ibid., 152
6. Ibid.
7. Ibid., 188.
8. Ibid.
9. Steven Reidbord, "A Brief History of Psychiatry: Biology and Psychology Wrestle for the Upper Hand," *Psychology Today*, Web.
10. Porter, *Madness*, 197.
11. Margarita Tartakovsky, "How the DSM Developed: What You Might Not Know," World of Psychology, Web.
12. The full text of the opinion is included as appendix 3 in this book.
13. *Durham v. United States*, 2.
14. Ibid., 2–3. "After the Civil War, [the name] St. Elizabeths was used with increasing frequency until the title was officially changed by Congress in 1916. For some reason, Congress did not use an apostrophe S in the legislation that changed the name of the hospital, and so to this day an apostrophe is not used in the hospital's name": Thomas Otto, "St. Elizabeths Hospital: A History" (Washington, DC: United States General Services Administration, National Capital Region, 2013), http://www.stelizabethsdevelopment.com/docs/Full_History_of_St_Elizabeths.pdf.
15. *Durham v. United States*, 3. The diagnosis of "without mental disorder" meant that he was not mentally ill (just "bad"), and therefore they could incarcerate him without having to treat him.
16. Ibid., 1.
17. Ibid., 3.
18. Ibid., 3; Subshock Insulin Therapy, or Insulin Shock Therapy, involves injecting patients with large doses of insulin in order to induce a coma daily for extended periods of time; it was used primarily to treat schizophrenia and was popular in the 1940s and '50s.

19. An ex parte statement is one decided by a judge that does not require all parties to be present; in this case, Dr. Silk's statement was made without Durham or his counsel present to object or cross examine the opposing party.
20. Ibid., 3.
21. Ibid.
22. Ibid.
23. Ibid.
24. Ibid.
25. Ibid.
26. Ibid.
27. Ibid.
28. Ibid.
29. Ibid., 4.
30. Ibid., 1, emphasis mine.
31. Mr. Ahern was counsel for the defense representing Monty Durham.
32. *Durham v. United States*, 3.
33. As cited in *Durham v. United States: Tatum v. United States* says, "When lack of mental capacity is raised as a defense to a charge of crime, the law accepts the general experience of mankind and presumes that all people, including those accused of crime, are sane." However, "as soon as 'some evidence of mental disorder is introduced, sanity, like any other fact, must be proved as part of the prosecution's case beyond a reasonable doubt.'"
34. *Durham v. United States*, 3.
35. Ibid.
36. Ibid.
37. Ibid.
38. Ibid., 3–4.
39. Ibid., 4.
40. Ibid., 5.
41. Goldstein, *The Insanity Defense*, 80.
42. Ibid., 81.
43. Ibid.
44. *Durham v. United States*, 5.
45. Ibid.
46. Ibid.
47. Ibid.
48. Ibid., 6.
49. Ibid.
50. Ibid., 6.
51. Ibid.
52. Ibid., 7.
53. Goldstein, *The Insanity Defense*, 83.
54. *Durham v. United States*, 7.
55. Goldstein, *The Insanity Defense*, 84
56. Ibid., 85.
57. Ibid., 83.
58. Ibid., 84.
59. Bruce A. Arrigo, "Insanity Defense Reform and the Sign of Abolition," *International Journal for the Semiotics of Law* 10(29), 1997: 191–211

60. Goldstein, *The Insanity Defense*, 86.

61. Lawrence Meyer, "Judge Bazelon; Activist Federal Judge Here Decides to Take Semi-Retired Status on Bench; Author of 'Durham Rule' Decides to 'Step Back,'?" *The Washington Post*, May 15, 1979, A1.

62. Goldstein, *The Insanity Defense*.

63. Ibid., 87.

64. Ibid.

65. Ibid., 88.

66. Ibid., 89.

67. *Durham v. United States*, 7.

68. Ibid., 87.

Chapter 6

Epigraph. C. David Mortensen, *Violence and Communication: Public Reactions to an Attempted Presidential Assassination* (Lanham, MD: University Press of America, 1987), xiii.

1. Bonnie et al., *A Case Study*.

2. Shorter, *A History of Psychiatry*; Whitaker, *Anatomy of an Epidemic*.

3. Brett J. Deacon, "The Biomedical Model of Mental Disorder: A Critical Analysis of its Validity, Utility, and Effects on Psychotherapy Research," *Clinical Psychology Review* 33 (2013): 847.

4. Porter, *Madness*.

5. Kirk and Kutchins, *The Selling of the DSM*, 10–11.

6. Maxmen, Gerald, *The New Psychiatry*, emphasis mine.

7. Kirk and Kutchins, *The Selling of the DSM*, 11.

8. Bonnie et al. Most of the information in this chapter, particularly evidence from the trial transcripts, comes from this book, which is still the most accessible document that provides comprehensive coverage of the trial. In full, the trial transcripts are approximately seven thousand pages in length, which are both difficult and costly to obtain, and Bonnie et al. provide access to the most significant aspects of the prosecution and defense arguments.

9. Bonnie et al., *A Case Study*.

10. *Taxi Driver*.

11. Bonnie et al., *A Case Study*.

12. Foster has been very adamant about not publicly discussing her ordeal. She has addressed it only twice: in an article published in *Esquire* (December 1982), "Why Me?" and in a 1999 interview with Charlie Rose. She has been known to turn down interviews if she is told it will be brought up or even walk out of interviews if it is mentioned.

13. Bonnie et al., *A Case Study*.

14. Ibid.

15. Ibid.

16. Ibid., 27.

17. Ibid., 28.

18. Kimberly Collins, Gabe Hinkebein, and Staci Schorgl, "The John Hinckley Trial: Key Figures," *Famous Trials*.

19. A copy of this letter is included as appendix 4 in this book.

20. Collins, Hinkebein, and Schorgl, "The John Hinckley Trial."

21. Bonnie, et al., *A Case Study*, 50.
22. Ibid., 29.
23. Ibid. 30.
24. Ibid., 41.
25. Ibid., 42–43.
26. Ibid., 46–47.
27. According to Hinckley, as Reagan walked into the hotel, he looked at Hinckley and smiled and waved.
28. Collins, Hinkebein, and Schorgl, "The John Hinckley Trial," 39.
29. Ibid., 47–49.
30. Ibid., 66.
31. Ibid., 85.
32. Ibid., 31.
33. Ibid.
34. Ibid., 34–35.
35. Ibid., 36.
36. Ibid., 36–37.
37. Ibid., 37–38.
38. Ibid., 38.
39. Ibid., 51.
40. *United States v. Brawner* (1972) was the decision in which the Model Penal Code was adopted in the District of Columbia. Adelman argued that the justices in Brawner were "silent on the meaning of 'appreciate,' and that the court therefore should consider the intentions of the drafters of the Model Penal Code" (Bonnie et al., *A Case Study*, 49), whereas the defense characterized the Brawner court as broadening the right-from-wrong test.
41. Ibid., 51–52.
42. Ibid., 52.
43. In *Washington v. United States* (1967), the issue of "conclusory" expert testimony was addressed. The opinion was appended to include "guidelines for jury instructions designed to emphasize the proper scope of the witnesses' expertise and the jury's ultimate responsibility to find the facts and apply the law" (Bonnie et al., *A Case Study*, 53).
44. Ibid., 53.
45. Ibid., 55.
46. Ibid., 56.
47. Ibid., 57–59.
48. Ibid., 70.
49. Ibid., 70.
50. Ibid., 87–88.
51. Ibid., 88.
52. Ibid., 92.
53. Ibid.
54. Ibid., 95–96.
55. Ibid., 96.
56. Ibid.
57. Ibid., 97.
58. Ibid., 99–102.

59. Ibid., 104.
60. Ibid., 105.
61. Ibid., 106.
62. Ibid., 108.
63. Ibid., 111.
64. Ibid.
65. Ibid., 116.
66. Ibid., 117.
67. Ibid., 118.
68. Ibid., 119.
69. Associated Press, "Hinckley Acquittal Brings Moves to Change Insanity Defense," *New York Times*, June 24, 1982.
70. Burns, "If All Criminal Acts," *New York Times*, July 1, 1982.
71. Associated Press. "Hinckley Acquittal Brings Moves to Change Insanity Defense."
72. Steven V. Roberts, "High US Officials Express Outrage, Asking for New Laws on Insanity Plea," *New York Times*, June 23, 1982.
73. Ibid.
74. Taylor, "Insanity Laws Seen as Hurting Society," *New York Times*, July 1, 1982.
75. Bonnie et al., *A Case Study in the Insanity Defense*, 128.
76. Ibid., 129.
77. Ibid., 131.
78. Ibid.
79. Ibid., 135.
80. Bruce A. Arrigo, "Insanity Defense Reform and the Sign of Abolition: Re-Visting Montana's Experience," *International Journal for the Semiotics of Law* 10(29), (1997): 191–211.

Conclusion

Epigraph 1. Michael J. Perlin, *The Hidden Prejudice: Mental Disability on Trial*, Washington, DC: American Psychological Association, 2000, 309.
Epigraph 2. Robert Whitaker, *Mad in America: Bad Science, Bad Medicine, and the Enduring Mistreatment of the Mentally Ill*, New York: Basic Books, 2010, 291.

1. Norman J. Finkel, "The Insanity Defense Reform Act of 1984: Much Ado About Nothing," *Behavioral Sciences and the Law* 7(3), (1989): 403–19.
2. Bruce A. Arrigo, "Insanity Defense Reform and the Sign of Abolition: Re-Visting Montana's Experience."
3. Jeffrey Dahmer Biography. Biography.com.https://www.biography.com/people/jeffrey-dahmer-9264755.
4. Suzanne O'Malley, "*Are You There Alone?": The Unspeakable Crimes of Andrea Yates*, New York: Simon and Schuster, 2004.
5. James Holmes Biography. Biography.com. https://www.biography.com/people/james-holmes-20891561.
6. For a recent breakdown of insanity defense standards by state, see Paul H. Robinson and Tyler Scot Williams, "Mapping American Criminal Law: Variations Across the 50 States: Ch. 14 Insanity Defense" (2017). *Faculty Scholarship*. 1718. http://scholarship.law.upenn.edu/faculty_scholarship/1718; 6 states abolished the defense

entirely; 6 states use "substantial capacity to appreciate the criminality of conduct" as their measurement; 11 jurisdictions (10 states plus the District of Columbia) use "substantial capacity to appreciate the criminality of conduct" as their measurement; 28 states, the vast majority, still rely on the most narrow (and outdated) test, a complete loss of understanding, as their standard by which to assess legal insanity.

7. Kevin Grasha, "Man Accused of Killing His Sisters Seeks Insanity Defense," Cincinatti.com, July 5, 2016. http://www.cincinnati.com/story/news/2016/07/05/man-accused-killing-his-sisters-seeks-insanity-defense/86710210/.

8. Ed Treleven, "Man Who Killed Mother with Sword Committed After Guilty Plea, Insanity Finding," *Wisconsin State Journal*, June 29, 2016.

9. "SC Mom Accused of Killing Kids Pleads Not Guilty, Uses Insanity Defense," WBTW News 13, Web, June 21, 2016.

10. David Eagleman, "The Brain on Trial," *The Atlantic*, July/August 2011, https://www.theatlantic.com/magazine/archive/2011/07/the-brain-on-trial/308520/.

11. James Fallon, *The Psychopath Inside: A Neuroscientist's Personal Journey into the Dark Side of the Brain* (New York: Penguin, 2013).

12. According to RadiologyInfo.org, "Functional magnetic resonance imaging (fMRI) measures the metabolic changes that occur within the brain. It may be used to examine the brain's anatomy, determine which parts of the brain are handling critical functions, evaluate the effects of stroke or disease, or guide brain treatment. fMRI may detect abnormalities within the brain that cannot be found with other imaging techniques."

13. It was August 1966 when Whitman, a student and former Marine, first murdered his wife and mother and then went to the campus tower and opened fire on people below; he killed 14 people there and wounded 31 more. He was shot by police, which was the only reason the assault ended when it did. A fifteenth victim died from injuries sustained in the shooting in 2001. A recent documentary, "Tower," provides a detailed account of the events on campus through interviews with survivors: "'Tower' Pays Tribute to a 1966 Campus Shooting that was 'Pushed Aside.'" http://www.npr.org/2017/02/08/514001421/tower-pays-tribute-to-a-1966-campus-shooting-that-was-pushed-aside.

14. David Eagleman, "The Brain on Trial," *The Atlantic*, July/August 2011.

15. Radiolab, "Inheritance." http://www.radiolab.org/story/251876-inheritance/.

16. Molly Webster, "The Great Rat Mother Switcheroo," January 10, 2013, http://www.radiolab.org/story/261176-the-great-mother-switcheroo/.

17. Caitlin M. Jones, "Genetic and Environmental Influences on Criminal Behavior," 2005, http://www.personalityresearch.org/papers/jones.html.

18. Joe Richman, "Identical Strangers," *Explore Nature vs. Nurture*. Podcast audio, Oct. 25, 2007, https://www.npr.org/2007/10/25/15629096/identical-strangers-explore-nature-vs-nurture.

19. Tanya Lewis, "Twins Separated at Birth Reveal Staggering Influence of Genetics," Live Science, August 11, 2014, http://www.livescience.com/47288-twin-study importance-of-genetics.html.

20. J. David Hawkins, Todd I. Herrenkohl, David P. Farrington, Devon Brewer, Richard F. Catalano, Tracy W. Harachi, and Lynn Cothern, "Predictors of Youth Violence," *Juvenile Justice Bulletin*, April 2000, http://www.crim.cam.ac.uk/people/academic_research/david_farrington/predviol.pdf.

21. *Brains on Trial with Alan Alda*, PBS, Sept. 18, 2013, http://www.pbs.org/program/brains-trial/.

22. Robert Whitaker, *Anatomy of an Epidemic: Magic Bullets, Psychiatric Drugs, and the Astonishing Rise of Mental Illness in America* (New York: Broadway Books, 2015).

23. Anders Eklund, Thomas E. Nichols, and Hans Knutsson, "Cluster Failure: Why fMRI Inferences for Spatial Extent Have Inflated False Positive Results," *Proceedings of the National Academy of Sciences of the United States Early Edition* (2016), http://www.pnas.org/content/113/28/7900.full.

24. Sharon Crowley, *Toward a Civil Discourse.*

Appendix 3

1. D.C. Code Secs. 22–1801, 22–2201 and 22–2202 (1951). (*Note: all appendix notes are original to* Durham v. United States. *—Andrea L. Alden.*)

2. Because the questions raised are of general and crucial importance, we called upon the Government and counsel whom we appointed for the indigent appellant to brief and argue this case a second time. Their able presentations have been of great assistant to us. On the question of the adequacy of prevailing tests of criminal responsibility, we received further assistance from the able brief and argument of Abram Chayes, amicus curiae by appointment of this Court, in *Steward v. United States*, 94 U.S.App.D.C.—, 214 F.2d 879.

3. 18 U.S.C. § 408 (1946). 1948 Revision, 18 U.S.C. §§ 10, 2311–2313.

4. Durham showed confusion when he testified. These are some examples:

Q. Do you remember writing it? A. No. Don't you forget? People get all mixed up in machines.
Q. What kind of a machine? A. I don't know, they just get mixed up.
Q. Are you cured now? A. No, sir.
Q. In your opinion? A. No, sir.
Q. What is the matter with you? A. You hear people bother you.
Q. What? You say you hear people bothering you? A. Yes.
Q. What kind of people? What do they bother you about? A. (No response.)

Although we think the court erred in accepting counsel's admission that Durham was of sound mind, the matter does not require discussion since we reverse on other grounds and the principles governing this issue are fully discussed in our decision today in *Gunther v. United States*, U.S. App.D.C. . . . , 215 F.2d 493.

5. The court also accepted a waiver of trial by jury when Durham indicated, in response to the court's question, that he preferred to be tried without a jury and that he waived his right to a trial by jury.

6. 1951, 88 U.S.App.D.C. 386, 389, 190 F.2d 612, 615.

7. 88 U.S.App.D.C. at page 389, 190 F.2d at page 615, quoting Glueck, *Mental Disorder and the Criminal Law* 41–42 (1925).

8. In its brief, the prosecution confounds the "some evidence" test with the "evidence sufficient to create a reasonable doubt" test, despite our explanation in Tatum that the "evidence sufficient to create a reasonable doubt" test applies only after the issue has been raised by "some evidence" and the burden is already upon the Gov-

ernment to prove the defendant's sanity beyond a reasonable doubt. 88 U.S.App.D.C. at page 390, 190 F.2d at page 616.

9. Dr. Amino Perretti, who also examined Durham in connection with those proceedings and furnished an affidavit that Durham was of unsound mind, was unable to testify due to illness.

10. (1) Q. (Mr. Ahern). As a result of those examinations did you reach a conclusion as to the sanity or insanity of the defendant? A. Yes, I did arrive at an opinion as to his mental condition.

Q. And what is that opinion? A. That he at that time was of unsound mind.

Q. Can you tell us what disorder he was suffering from, Doctor? A. The report of his case at the time, as of October 9, 1951, I used the diagnosis of undifferentiated psychosis, but according to the record the diagnosis was at the time of commitment psychosis with psychopathic personality.

Q. At that time were you able to make a determination as to how long this condition had existed? A. According to the record I felt at the time that he had been in that attitude or mental disorder for a period of some few to several months.

(2) Q. (Mr. Ahern). Directing your attention specifically to July 13, 1951, will you give us your opinion as to the mental condition of the defendant at that time? A. From my previous testimony and previous opinion, to repeat it, it was my opinion that he had been of unsound mind from sometime not long after a previous release from Saint Elizabeths Hospital (i.e., May 14, 1951).

(3) Q. (Mr. Ahern). In any event, Doctor, is it your opinion that that period of insanity would have embraced the date July 13, 1951? A. Yes. My examination would antedate that; that is, the symptoms obtained, according to my examinations, included that—the symptoms of the mental disorder.

Q. Can you tell us what symptoms you found, Doctor? A. Well, he was trying to work for a while, he stated, and while he was working at one of these People's Drug Stores he began to hear false voices and suffer from hallucinations and believed that the other employees and others in the store talked about him, watched him, and the neighbors did the same, watching him from their windows, talking about him, and those symptoms continued and were present through the time that I examined him in September and October.

Q. (Mr. McLaughlin). You were asked the specific question, Doctor, whether or not in your opinion on July 13, 1951, this defendant was of unsound mind and didn't know the difference between right and wrong. Can you express an opinion as to that? A. Yes. It is my opinion he was of unsound mind.

(4) Q. (Mr. McLaughlin). Can you tell us—this is for my own information, I would like to know this—you say that this defendant, at the time you examined him in 1951 was of unsound mind and had been of unsound mind sometime prior to that; is that your statement? A. Yes, sir.

Q. Can you tell us how long prior to that time he was of unsound mind? A. Well, while he was working in People's Drug Store the symptoms were present, and how long before that, I didn't get the date of that.

Q. When was he working in People's Drug Store? A. Sometime after his discharge from Saint Elizabeths Hospital.

Q. In 1947? A. Oh, no; 1951.

11. See note 10, supra.

12. Davis v. United States, 1895, 160 U.S. 469, 488, 16 S.Ct. 353, 358, 40 L.Ed. 499.

13. 1882, 12 D.C. 498, 550, 1 Mackey 498, 550. The right-wrong test was reaffirmed in United States v. Lee, 1886, 15 D.C. 489, 496, 4 Mackey 489, 496.

14. 1929, 59 App.D.C. 144, 36 F.2d 548, 70 A.L.R. 654.

15. Glueck, *Mental Disorder and the Criminal Law*, 138–39 (1925), citing *Rex v. Arnold*, 16 How.St.Tr. 695, 764 (1724).

16. Id. at 142–52, citing Earl Ferrer's case, 19 How.St.Tr. 886 (1760). One writer has stated that these tests originated in England in the 13th or 14th century, when the law began to define insanity in terms of intellect for purposes of determining capacity to manage feudal estates. Comment, "Lunacy and Idiocy—The Old Law and Its Incubus" 18 U. of Chi.L.Rev. 361 (1951).

17. 8 Eng.Rep. 718 (1843).

18. Hall, *Principles of Criminal Law*, 480, n.6 (1947).

19. *Royal Commission on Capital Punishment 1949–1953 Report* (Cmd. 8932) 79 (1953) (hereinafter cited as *Royal Commission Report*).

20. Weihofen, *The M'Naghten Rule in Its Present-Day Setting*, Federal Probation 8 (Sept. 1953); Weihofen, *Insanity as a Defense in Criminal Law*, 15, 64–68, 109–47 (1933); Leland v. State of Oregon, 1952, 343 U.S. 790, 800, 72 S.Ct. 1002, 96 L.Ed. 1302.

"In five States the M'Naghten Rules have been in substance re-enacted by statute." *Royal Commission Report* 409; see, e.g., "Sec. 1120 of the New York State) Penal Law (McK.Consol. Laws, c.40) (which) provides that a person is not excused from liability on the grounds of insanity, idiocy or imbecility, except upon proof that at the time of the commission of the criminal act he was laboring under such a defect of reason as (1) not to know the nature and quality of the act he was doing or (2) not to know that the act was wrong." Ploscowe, "Suggested Changes in the New York Laws and Procedures Relating to the Criminally Insane and Mentally Defective Offenders," 43 J.Crim.L.Criminology & Police Sci. 312, 314 (1952).

21. 8 Eng.Rep. 718, 722 (1843). "Today, Oregon is the only state that requires the accused, on a plea of insanity, to establish that defense beyond a reasonable doubt. Some twenty states, however, place the burden on the accused to establish his insanity by a preponderance of the evidence or some similar measure of persuasion." Leland v. State of Oregon, supra, note 20, 343 U.S. at page 798, 72 S.Ct. 1002. Since Davis v. United States, 1895, 160 U.S. 469, 484, 16 S.Ct. 353, 40 L.Ed. 499, a contrary rule of procedure has been followed in the Federal courts. For example, in compliance with Davis, we held in Tatum v. United States, supra, note 8, 88 U.S.App.D.C. 386, 389, 190 F.2d 612, 615, and text, "as soon as 'some evidence of mental disorder is introduced, sanity, like any other fact, must be proved as part of the prosecution's case beyond a reasonable doubt.'"

22. Ray, *Medical Jurisprudence of Insanity*, 47 and 34 et seq. (1st ed. 1838). "That the insane mind is not entirely deprived of this power of moral discernment, but in

many subjects is perfectly rational, and displays the exercise of a sound and well balanced mind is one of those facts now so well established, that to question it would only betray the height of ignorance and presumption." Id. at 32.

23. See Zilboorg, *Legal Aspects of Psychiatry in One Hundred Years of American Psychiatry 1844–1944*, 507, 552 (1944).

24. Cardozo, *What Medicine Can Do for the Law*, 32 (1930).

25. For a detailed bibliography on insanity as a defense to crime, see 7 *The Record of the Association of the Bar of the City of New York*, 158–62 (1952). And see, e.g., Alexander, *The Criminal, the Judge and the Public*, 70 et seq. (1931); Cardozo, *What Medicine Can Do for the Law*, 28 et seq. (1930); Cleckley, *The Mask of Sanity* 491 et seq. (2d ed.1950); Deutsch, *The Mentally Ill in America*, 389–417 (2d ed.1949); Glueck, *Mental Disorder and the Criminal Law* (1925), *Crime and Justice* 96 et seq. (1936); Guttmacher and Weihofen, *Psychiatry and the Law*, 218, 403–23 (1952); Hall, *Principles of Criminal Law*, 477–538 (1947); Menninger, *The Human Mind*, 450 (1937); Hall and Menninger, "Psychiatry and the Law—A Dual Review," 38 Iowa L.Rev. 687 (1953); Overholser, *The Psychiatrist and the Law*, 41–43 (1953); Overholser and Richmond, *Handbook of Psychiatry*, 208–15 (1947); Ploscowe, "Suggested Changes in the New York Laws and Procedures Relating to the Criminally Insane and Mentally Defective Offenders," 43 J.Crim.L., Criminology and Police Sc. 312, 314 (1952); Ray, *Medical Jurisprudence of Insanity* (1st ed.1838) (4th ed.1860); Reik, "The Doe Ray Correspondence: A Pioneer Collaboration in the Jurisprudence of Mental Disease," 63 Yale L.J. 183 (1953); Weihofen, *Insanity as a Defense in Criminal Law* (1933), *The M'Naghten Rule in Its Present Day Setting*, Federal Probation 8 (Sept. 1953); Zilboorg, *Mind, Medicine and Man*, 246–97 (1943), *Legal Aspects of Psychiatry, American Psychiatry* 1844–1944, 507 (1944).

26. *Royal Commission Report*, 73–129.

27. The Committee on Forensic Psychiatry (whose report is hereinafter cited as *Gap Report*) was composed of Drs. Philip Q. Roche, Frank S. Curran, Lawrence Z. Freedman, and Manfred S. Guttmacher. They were assisted in their deliberations by leading psychiatrists, jurists, law professors, and legal practitioners.

28. *Royal Commission Report*, 80.

29. Glueck, *Psychiatry and the Criminal Law*, 12; *Mental Hygiene*, 575, 580 (1928), as quoted in Deutsch, *The Mentally Ill in America*, 396 (2d ed. 1949); and see, e.g., Menninger, *The Human Mind*, 450 (1937); Guttmacher and Weihofen, *Psychiatry and the Law*, 403–8 (1952).

30. *Holloway v. United States*, 1945, 80 U.S.App.D.C. 3, 5, 148 F.2d 665, 667, certiorari denied, 1948, 334 U.S. 852, 68 S.Ct. 1507, 92 L.Ed. 1774.

More recently, the Royal Commission, after an exhaustive survey of legal, medical and lay opinion in many Western countries, including England and the United States, made a similar finding. It reported:

> The gravamen of the charge against the M'Naghten Rules is that they are not in harmony with modern medical science, which, as we have seen, is reluctant to divide the mind into separate compartments—the intellect, the emotions and the will—but looks at it as a whole and considers that insanity distorts and impairs the action of the mind as a whole. *Royal Commission Report* 113. The Commission lends vivid support to this conclusion by pointing out that "It would be impossible to apply modern methods of care and treat-

ment in mental hospitals, and at the same time to maintain order and discipline, if the great majority of the patients, even among the grossly insane, did not know what is forbidden by the rules and that, if they break them, they are liable to forfeit some privilege. Examination of a number of individual cases in which a verdict of guilty but insane (the nearest English equivalent of our acquittal by reason of insanity) was returned, and rightly returned, has convinced us that there are few indeed where the accused can truly be said not to have known that his act was wrong." Id. at 103.

31. See Guttmacher and Weihofen, *Psychiatry and the Law,* 421, 422 (1952). The M'Naghten rules "constitute not only an arbitrary restriction on vital medical data, but also impose an improper onus of decision upon the expert witness. The Rules are unanswerable in that they have no consensus with established psychiatric criteria of symptomatic description save for the case of disturbed consciousness or of idiocy." From statement by Dr. Philip Q. Roche, quoted id. at 407. See also United States ex rel. Smith v. Baldi, 3 Cir., 1951, 192 F.2d 540, 567 (dissenting opinion).

32. In a very recent case, the Supreme Court of New Mexico recognized the inadequacy of the right-wrong test, and adopted what it called an "extension of the M'Naghten Rules." Rules. "Under this extension, lack of knowledge of right and wrong is not essential for acquittal 'if, by reason of disease of the mind, defendant has been deprived of or lost the power of his will.'" State v. White, N.M., 270 P.2d 727, 730.

33. Deutsch, *The Mentally Ill in America*, 400 (2d ed.1949); Keedy, "Irrestible Impulse as a Defense in Criminal Law," 100 U. of Pa.L.rev. 956, 992 (1952).

34. Professor John Whitehorn of the Johns Hopkins Medical School, who recently prepared an informal memorandum on this subject for a Commission on Legal Psychiatry appointed by the Governor of Maryland, has said: "Psychiatrists are challenged to set forth a crystal-clear statement of what constitutes insanity. It is impossible to express this adequately in words, alone, since such diagnostic judgments involve clinical skill and experience which cannot wholly be verbalized. The medical profession would be baffled if asked to write into the legal code universally valid criteria for the diagnosis of the many types of psychotic illness which may seriously disturb a person's responsibility, and even if this were attempted, the diagnostic criteria would have to be rewritten from time to time, with the progress of psychiatric knowledge." Quoted in Guttmacher and Weihofen, *Psychiatry and the Law*, 419–20 (1952).

35. "The legal profession were invading the province of medicine, and attempting to install old exploded medical theories in the place of facts established in the progress of scientific knowledge." State v. Pike, 1870, 49 N.H. 399, 438.

36. *Royal Commission Report* 114. And see State v. Jones, 1871, 50 N.H. 369, 392–93.

37. Keedy, *Irresistible Impulse as a Defense in Criminal Law*, 100, U. of Pa.L.Rev. 956, 992–93 (1952).

38. See, e.g., Taylor v. United States, 1895, 7 App.D.C. 27, 41–44, where we rejected "emotional insanity" as a defense, citing with approval the following from the trial court's instruction to the jury: "Whatever may be the cry of scientific experts, the law does not recognize, but condemns the doctrine of emotional insanity—that a man may be sane up until a moment before he commits a crime, insane while he does it, and sane again soon afterwards. Such a doctrine would be dangerous in the

extreme. The law does not recognize it; and a jury cannot without violating their oaths." This position was emphatically reaffirmed in Snell v. United States, 1900, 16 App.D.C. 501, 524.

39. 1929, 59 App.D.C. 144, 146, 36 F.2d 548, 550, 70 A.L.R. 654.

40. 59 App.D.C. at page 145, 36 F.2d at page 549.

41. 59 App.D.C. at page 145, 36 F.2d at page 549.

42. Impulse, as defined by *Webster's New International Dictionary* (2d ed. 1950), is:

1. Act of impelling, or driving onward with sudden force; impulsion, esp., force so communicated as to produce motion suddenly, or immediately.
2. An incitement of the mind or spirit, esp. in the form of an abrupt and vivid suggestion, prompting some unpremeditated action or leading to unforeseen knowledge or insight; a spontaneous inclination.
3. motion produced by a sudden or momentary force.

43. *Royal Commission Report,* 110; for additional comment on the irresistible impulse test, see Glueck, *Crime and Justice,* 101–3 (1936); Guttmacher and Weihofen, *Psychiatry and the Law,* 410–12 (1952); Hall, *General Principles of Criminal Law* 505–26 (1947); Keedy, *Irresistible Impulse as a Defense in Criminal Law,* 100, U. of Pa.L.Rev. 956 (1952); Wertham, *The Show of Violence,* 14 (1949).

The New Mexico Supreme Court in recently adopting a broader criminal insanity rule, note 32, supra, observed: "Insanity takes the form of the personality of the individual and, if his tendency is toward depression, his wrongful act may come at the conclusion of a period of complete lethargy, thoroughly devoid of excitement."

44. "As we recently said, 'Former common law should not be followed where changes in conditions have made it obsolete. We have never hesitated to exercise the usual judicial function of revising and enlarging the common law.'" *Linkins v. Protestant Episcopal Cathedral Foundation,* 1950, 87 U.S.App.D.C. 351, 355, 187 F.2d 357, 361, 28 A.L.R.2d 521. Cf. Funk v. United States, 1933, 290 U.S. 371, 381–382, 54 S.Ct. 212, 78 L.Ed. 369.

45. Congress, like most state legislatures, has never undertaken to define insanity in this connection, although it recognizes the fact that an accused may be acquitted by reason of insanity. See D.C. Code Sec. 14–301 (1951). And as this court made clear in *Hill v. United States,* Congress has left no doubt that "common-law procedure, in all matters relating to crime still continues in force here in all cases except where special provision is made by statute to the exclusion of the common-law procedure." 22 App.D.C. 395, 401 (1903), and statutes cited therein; Linkins v. Protestant Episcopal Cathedral Foundation, 87 U.S.App.D.C. at pages 354–55, 187 F.2d at pages 360–61; and see Fisher v. United States, 1946, 328 U.S. 463, 66 S.Ct. 1318, 90 L.Ed. 1382.

46. See Great Northern R. v. Sunburst Oil & Refining Co., 1932, 287 U.S. 358, 53 S.Ct. 145, 77 L.Ed. 360; National Labor Relations Board v. Guy F. Atkinson Co., 9 Cir., 1952, 195 F.2d 141, 148; Concurring opinion of Judge Frank in Aero Spark Plug Co. v. B. G. Corporation, 2 Cir., 1942, 130 F.2d 290, 298, and note 24; Waring v. Colpoys, 1941, 74 App.D.C. 303, 122 F.2d 642, 645, 136 A.L.R. 1025; Moore and Oglebay, "The Supreme Court, Stare Decisis and Law of the Case," 21 Texas L.Rev. 514, 535 (1943); Carpenter, "Court Decisions and the Common Law," 17 Col.L.Rev. 593, 606–07 (1917). But see von Moschzisker, "Stare Decisis in Courts of Last Resort," 37

Harv.L.Rev. 409, 426 (1924). Our approach is similar to that of the Supreme Court of California in People v. Maughs, 1906, 149 Cal.253, 86 P. 187, 191, where the court prospectively invalidated a previously accepted instruction, saying: "We think the time has come to say that in all future cases which shall arise, and where, after this warning, this instruction shall be given, this court will hold the giving of it to be so prejudicial to the rights of a defendant, secured to him by our Constitution and laws, as to call for the reversal of any judgment which may be rendered against him."

47. State v. Pike, 1870, 49 N.H. 399.

48. Cf. State v. Jones, 1871, 50 N.H. 369, 398.

49. "There is no a priori reason why every person suffering from any form of mental abnormality or disease, or from any particular kind of mental disease, should be treated by the law as not answerable for any criminal offence which he may commit, and be exempted from conviction and punishment. Mental abnormalities vary infinitely in their nature and intensity and in their effects on the character and conduct of those who suffer from them. Where a person suffering from a mental abnormality commits a crime, there must always be some likelihood that the abnormality has played some part in the causation of the crime; and, generally speaking, the graver the abnormality the more probable it must be that there is a causal connection between them. But the closeness of this connection will be shown by the facts brought in evidence in individual cases and cannot be decided on the basis of any general medical principle." *Royal Commission Report* 99.

50. The court may always, of course, if it deems it advisable for the assistance of the jury, point out particular areas of agreement and conflict in the expert testimony in each case, just as it ordinarily does in summing up any other testimony.

51. State v. Jones, 1871, 50 N.H. 369, 398.

52. 1945, 80 U.S.App.D.C. 3, 5, 148 F.2d 665, 667.

53. *State v. White*, see n. 32, supra.

54. 80 U.S.App.D.C. at page 5, 148 F.2d at page 667.

55. 80 U.S.App.D.C. at pages 4–5, 148 F.2d at pages 666–67.

56. See text, supra, 214 F.2d 870–72.

57. An accused person who is acquitted by reason of insanity is presumed to be insane, Orencia v. Overholser, 1947, 82 U.S.App.D.C. 285, 163 F.2d 763; Barry v. White, 1933, 62 App.D.C. 69, 64 F.2d 707, and may be committed for an indefinite period to a "hospital for the insane." D.C. Code Sec. 24–301 (1951).

We think that even where there has been a specific finding that the accused was competent to stand trial and to assist in his own defense, the court would be well advised to invoke this Code provision so that the accused may be confined as long as "the public safety and (his) welfare" require. Barry v. White, 62 App.D.C. at page 71, 64 F.2d at page 709.

Bibliography

Allnutt, Stephen, Anthony Samuels, and Colman O'Driscoll. "The Insanity Defence: From Wild Beasts to M'Naghten." *Australus Psychiatry*. 2007, 292–98.

Aristotle. *Nichomachean Ethics*. Translated by R. W. Browne. London: George Bell and Sons, 1889.

———. *On Rhetoric*. Translated by George Kennedy. New York: Oxford University Press, 2006.

Associated Press. "Hinckley Acquittal Brings Moves to Change Insanity Defense." *New York Times*, June 24, 1982.

Bartee, Wayne C., and Alice Fleetwood Bartee. *Litigating Morality: American Legal Thought and Its English Roots*. New York: Praeger, 1992.

Baumeister, Alan A., Mike F. Hawkins, Joni Lee Pow, and Alex S. Cohen, "Prevalence and Incidence of Severe Mental Illness in the United States: An Historical Overview." *Harvard Review of Psychology* 2012, 247–58.

Bonnie, Richard J. "The moral basis of the insanity defense." *American Bar Association Journal* 69, no. 2 (1983): 194–97.

Bonnie, Richard J., John C. Jeffries Jr., and Peter W. Low, *A Case Study in the Insanity Defense: The Trial of John Hinckley, Jr.* New York: Thomson/Foundation Press, 1986.

Bonzol, Judith. "The Medical Diagnosis of Demonic Possession in an Early Modern English Community." *Parergon* 26, no. 1 (2009): 115–40.

Borthwick, Annie, Chris Holman, David Kennard, Mark McFetridge, Karen Messruther, and Jenny Wilkes. "The Relevance of Moral Treatment to Contemporary Mental Health Care." *Journal of Mental Health* 10, no. 4 (2001): 427–39.

Burns, Patrick. "If All Criminal Acts Were Judged Insane." *New York Times*, August 11, 1981.

Cardozo, Benjamin. *What Medicine Can Do for Law*. New York: Harper & Brothers, 1930.

Collins, Kimberly, Gabe Hinkebein, and Staci Schorgl. "The John Hinckley Trial: Key Figures." Famous Trials. http://law2.umkc.edu/faculty/projects/ftrials/hinckley/hinckleykeyfigures.htm.

Crowley, Sharon. *Toward a Civil Discourse: Rhetoric and Fundamentalism.* University of Pittsburgh Press, 2006.

Daftari-Kapur, Tarika, Jennifer L. Groscup, Maureen O'Connor, Frank Coffaro, and Michelle Galietta. "Measuring Knowledge of the Insanity Defense: Scale Construction and Validation." *Behavioral Sciences and the Law* 29, 40–63.

Deacon, Brett J. "The Biomedical Model of Mental Disorder: A Critical Analysis of its Validity, Utility, and Effects on Psychotherapy Research." *Clinical Psychology Review* 33 (2013): 846–61.

Drew, Katherine Fisher, trans. *The Lombard Laws.* Philadelphia: University of Pennsylvania Press, 2010.

Eagleman, David. "The Brain on Trial." *Atlantic* (June/July 2011), https://www.theatlantic.com/magazine/archive/2011/07/the-brain-on-trial/308520/.

Erickson, Patricia E., and Steven K. Erickson. *Crime, Punishment, and Mental Illness: Law and the Behavioral Sciences in Conflict.* New Brunswick, NJ: Rutgers University Press, 2008.

Fallon, James. *The Psychopath Inside.* London: Penguin Books, 2013.

Finkel, Norman J. "The Insanity Defense Reform Act of 1984: Much Ado About Nothing." *Behavioral Sciences and the Law* 7(3): 403–19.

Forcén, Carlos Espí, and Fernando Espí Forcén. "Demonic Possession and Mental Illness: Discussion of Selected Cases in Late Medieval Hagiographical Literature." *Early Science in Medicine* 19 (2014): 258–79.

Foster, Jodie. "Why Me?" *Esquire* (December 1982).

Foucault, Michel. *Discipline and Punish: The Birth of the Prison.* Translated by Alan Sheridan. New York: Random House, 1977.

———. *History of Madness.* Edited by Jean Khalfa. Translated by Jonathan Murphy. New York: Routledge, 2013.

———. *Madness and Civilization: A History of Insanity in the Age of Reason.* Translated by Richard Howard. New York: Random House, 1965.

Goldstein, Abraham. *The Insanity Defense.* New Haven: Yale University Press, 1967.

Gunn, Joshua. "Refiguring Fantasy: Imagination and Its Decline in U.S. Rhetorical Studies." *Quarterly Journal of Speech* 89, no. 1 (2003): 41–59.

Hans, Valerie P. "An Analysis of Public Attitudes Toward the Insanity Defense." *Criminology* 24, no. 2 (1986): 393–414.

Horwitz, Allan V. and Gerald N. Grob. "The Checkered History of American Psychiatric Epidemiology," *Milbank Quarterly* 89, no. 4 (2011), 628–657.

Kirk, Stuart A., and Herb Kutchins. *The Selling of the DSM: The Rhetoric of Science in Psychiatry.* New Brunswick: Transaction, 1992.

Kristeva, Julia. *Powers of Horror: Essays on Abjection.* New York: Columbia University Press, 1982.

Lakoff, George. *Moral Politics: How Liberals and Conservatives Think.* University of Chicago Press, 1996.

Lopéz, Ian Haney. *White by Law: The Legal Construction of Race.* New York: New York University Press, 1996.

Louden, Jennifer Eno, and Jennifer L. Skeem. "Constructing Insanity: Jurors' Prototypes, Attitudes, and Legal Decision-Making." *Behavioral Sciences and the Law* 25 (2007): 449–70.

Maeder, Thomas. *Crime and Madness: The Origins and Evolution of the Insanity Defense*. New York: Harper Collins, 1985.

Maxmen, Gerald. *The New Psychiatrists*. New York: New American Library, 1985.

Memon, Rafiq. "Legal Theory and Case Law Defining the Insanity Defence in English and Welsh Law." *The Journal of Forensic Psychiatry and Psychology* 17(2): 230–52.

Millon, Theodore. *Masters of the Mind: Exploring the Story of Mental Illness from Ancient Times to the New Millennium*. Hoboken, NJ: Wiley, 2004.

Molière, Jean-Baptiste. *L'Amour Medicin*. Paris: Nouveaux Classiques Larousse, 1975, p. 53; quoted in Edward Shorter: *A History of Psychiatry*: New York, Wiley, 1997, p. 20.

Moran, Richard. *Knowing Right from Wrong: The Insanity Defense of Daniel McNaughtan*. New York: The Free Press, 1981.

Mortensen, C. David. *Violence and Communication: Public Reactions to an Attempted Presidential Assassination*. Lanham, MD: University Press of America, 1987.

Ogloff, James R. P. "A Comparison of Insanity Defense Standards on Juror Decision Making." *Law and Human Behavior* 15, no. 5 (1991): 509.

O'Malley, Suzanne. *"Are You There Alone?": The Unspeakable Crimes of Andrea Yates*. New York: Simon and Schuster, 2004.

Otto, Thomas. "St. Elizabeths Hospital: A History." Washington, DC: US General Services Administration, National Capital Region, 2013. http://www.stelizabeths-development.com/docs/Full_History_of_St_Elizabeths.pdf.

Pasewark, Richard A., and M. Pasewark. "The Insanity Plea: Much Ado About Little." *Psychiatric Patient Rights and Patient Advocacy: Issues and Evidence* (1982): 101–28.

Perlin, Michael L. *The Hidden Prejudice: Mental Disability on Trial*. Washington, DC: American Psychological Association, 2000.

———. "Unpacking the Myths: The Symbolism Mythology of Insanity Defense Jurisprudence." *Case Western Reserve Law Review* 40 (1989): 599.

Plato. *Laws*. Mineola, NY: Courier, 2013.

Porter, Roy. *Madness: A Brief History*. Oxford University Press, 2003.

Ray, Isaac. *Treatise on the Medical Jurisprudence of Insanity*. 5th ed. Boston: Little Brown, 1871.

Reidbord, Steven. "A Brief History of Psychiatry: Biology and Psychology Wrestle for the Upper Hand." Psychology Today.com. https://www.psychologytoday.com/blog/sacramento-street-psychiatry/201410/brief-history-psychiatry.

Richman, Joe. "'Identical Strangers' Explore Nature Vs. Nurture." Radio Diaries. NPR, October 25, 2007. https://www.npr.org/2007/10/25/15629096/identical-strangers-explore-nature-vs-nurture.

Roberts, Caton F., Stephen L. Golding, and Frank D. Fincham. "Implicit theories of criminal responsibility: Decision making and the insanity defense." *Law and Human Behavior* 11, no. 3 (1987): 207.

Roberts, Steven V. "High US Officials Express Outrage, Asking for New Laws on Insanity Plea." *New York Times*, June 23, 1982.

Robinson, Daniel N. *Wild Beasts and Idle Humours: The Insanity Defense from Antiquity to the Present*. Cambridge: Harvard University Press, 1996.

Rose, Charlie. "Jodie Foster, Reluctant Star: Actress Reflects On Early Celebrity." *60 Minutes II*. CBS-TV, December 7, 1999.

Rountree, Clarke. *Judging the Supreme Court: Constructions of Motives in "Bush v. Gore."* East Lansing: Michigan State University Press, 2007.

Sapochnik, Miguel, dir. *Game of Thrones*. Season 5, episode 8, "Hardhome." Aired May 31, 2015, on HBO.

Schrader, Paul. *Taxi Driver*. Directed by Martin Scorsese. Los Angeles: Columbia Pictures, 1976.

Silver, Eric, Carmen Cirincione, and Henry J. Steadman. "Demythologizing inaccurate perceptions of the insanity defense." *Law and Human Behavior* 18, no. 1 (1994): 63–70.

Shorter, Edward. *A History of Psychiatry: From the Era of the Asylum to the Age of Prozac*. New York: John Wiley and Sons, 1997.

Tartakovsky, Margarit. "How the DSM Developed: What You Might Not Know." PsychCentral.com. http://psychcentral.com/blog/archives/2011/07/02/how-the-dsm-developed-what-you-might-not-know/.

Taylor, Stuart. "Insanity Law Seen as Hurting Society." *New York Times*, July 1, 1982.

Torrey, E. Fuller. *American Psychosis: How the Federal Government Destroyed the Mental Illness Treatment System*. New York: Oxford University Press, 2013.

Whitaker, Robert. *Anatomy of an Epidemic: Magic Bullets, Psychiatric Drugs, and the Astonishing Rise of Mental Illness in America*. Portland, OR: Broadway Books, 2015.

———. *Mad in America: Bad Science, Bad Medicine, and the Enduring Mistreatment of the Mentally Ill*. New York: Basic Books, 2010.

Young, Iris Marion. *Justice and the Politics of Difference*. Princeton, NJ: Princeton University Press, 1990.

Index